SMART STARTUPS

SMART STARTUPS

What Every Entrepreneur Needs to Know

—Advice from 18 Harvard Business School Founders

CATALINA DANIELS AND JAMES H. SHERMAN

HARPER BUSINESS
An Imprint of HarperCollins*Publishers*

SMART STARTUPS. Copyright © 2023 by Catalina Daniels and James H. Sherman. All rights reserved. Printed in the United States of America. No part of this book may be used or reproduced in any manner whatsoever without written permission except in the case of brief quotations embodied in critical articles and reviews. For information, address HarperCollins Publishers, 195 Broadway, New York, NY 10007.

HarperCollins books may be purchased for educational, business, or sales promotional use. For information, please email the Special Markets Department at SPsales@harpercollins.com.

FIRST EDITION

Designed by Bonni Leon-Berman

Library of Congress Cataloging-in-Publication Data has been applied for.

ISBN 978-0-06-331631-7

23 24 25 26 27 LBC 5 4 3 2 1

From Jim:
I want to thank and dedicate this book to my
parents—Susan and Edward.
They let me be who I wanted to be, somehow figured out how to
foster my motivation, and allowed me to find my passions in life.

From Catalina:
To my family for always supporting me,
to Chantal for always challenging me, and
to the entrepreneurs I work with, for always inspiring me.

"Entrepreneurship is the pursuit of opportunity beyond resources controlled."

    —Howard Stevenson, professor emeritus, Harvard Business School

"I'm convinced that about half of what separates the successful entrepreneurs from the nonsuccessful ones is pure perseverance."

    —Steve Jobs

CONTENTS

INTRODUCTION

I don't think there's a better training ground for being in a startup than being in a startup.

JUSTIN JOFFE, HENRY THE DENTIST

"What if we write a book about what entrepreneurs don't learn at Harvard Business School but *wish* they did?"

We were on the phone when Jim asked this question. At first, it sounded like a crazy idea. We had never written a book or even thought about writing one.

We first met at Harvard Business School as young students in 1989. Although we were not in the same section, we had many common friends and attended the same parties. After graduation in 1991, our paths separated but we kept in loose contact over the years.

In early 2016, when Catalina's family moved to New York City, we reconnected. Jim was a member of the Harvard Club in New York and invited Catalina for lunch. We instantly hit it off as if not a day had passed since school. We realized that we had a lot in common beyond Harvard: we had both been consultants and entrepreneurs, and had a passion for working with and investing in younger entrepreneurs.

As a result, three weeks after her move, Catalina joined Jim to attend her first angel investor meeting in New York. Jim was a member of two prominent angel groups, the Harvard Business School Alumni Angels of Greater New York, and Gaingels.

Every month, members of each group would come together and listen to six or so pitches of carefully curated startups. The purpose was to find the right startups to invest in. The dream was to invest in the next Facebook, Dropbox, or Airbnb. New York was particularly well suited for the launch of new ventures that leveraged the city's traditional market strengths in retail, finance, fashion, media/advertising, the arts, and more.

It was fascinating to listen to the pitches and meet the young entrepreneurs. The development of technology had literally empowered a new generation to launch ventures at low cost. And the pace of innovation kept on increasing. The angel investing scene was thrilling and it was clear that New York City was growing to become what it is today: one of the largest and fastest-growing startup ecosystems in the world.

In that first year back together reviewing new companies, we saw about three hundred startups thanks to the angel meetings and other events. We jointly invested in three of them. We met with the entrepreneurs and sometimes their clients, asked about their traction, business model, plans, and more. When we decided to invest, it was because we saw a unique combination of a strong idea with a solid team.

But, even then, we knew that many things could go wrong and that our investments were risky. We knew that angel investing—investing personal funds in the very early stage of a startup—means investing at the riskiest point in a venture's development, because so little of the company's business model has been proven out.

We also knew how the entrepreneur's road ahead would be full of ups and downs, and that success would depend on both sheer luck and how their team would adapt and react to new circumstances.

The statistics are known: 70 percent of startups who have raised a seed investment from angel investors still fail. They fail for multiple reasons, but in the end they fail most often because they don't establish sufficient market traction and can't raise the next round of funds to keep going. Fewer than 10 percent of seeded startups scale to $10M+ in profitable revenue or experience successful exits with solid returns for investors and founders.

So when Jim floated the idea of a book targeting entrepreneurs to help more of them succeed, we gave it serious thought. In the end, both of us had been entrepreneurs and had rich corporate careers. We could leverage our own experiences and knowledge. But, just as important, we had access to a unique network: Harvard Business School alumni. We could complement our own experiences with the experience of other HBS entrepreneurs. Quickly the idea emerged to interview about twenty Harvard Business School entrepreneurs.

The thinking was simple: if HBS entrepreneurs would open up about what they learned "the hard way" or what they wished they knew before starting, their wisdom would be interesting and relevant to younger and less experienced entrepreneurs.

The interviews turned out to be fascinating. Similar messages kept on popping up. Not in the exact same way, but with the same conclusion. Other messages were all over the place, destroying preconceived notions about entrepreneurship.

This book summarizes these pearls of wisdom. The chapters ahead provide a hefty amount of firsthand advice as well as inspiring stories from those who have "done it."

We've organized the material around the typical phases of a company's development—from the business ideation phase, to forming a founding team and launching with few resources; from the struggles of growth and financing to the ultimate exit. We've included generous quotes—more than four hundred—throughout the book to bring to life the key lessons, especially the unconventional wisdom—the kind of advice these entrepreneurs wished they had known beforehand and that wasn't taught at HBS.

Smart Startups is for those of you dreaming of becoming the next entrepreneurial success story. We hope you find inspiration in the entrepreneurs we've interviewed. Lastly, we hope this book will give you courage, arming you with pearls of wisdom for your entrepreneurial journey.

...

THE ENTREPRENEURS AND THEIR COMPANIES

HBS is the passport that opens the doors to so many things. It gives you the freedom of travel in the entrepreneurial world. But there's no Lonely Planet guidebook. You're just out there.

ANNA AUERBACH, WERK

We interviewed eighteen Harvard Business School entrepreneurs representing twenty companies to understand their journey and the lessons they learned along the way. We wanted to capture what they wished they had known before they started—the "unconventional wisdom" they didn't learn in school.

So, why would Harvard Business School founders have something interesting to say? And why not turn to self-made entrepreneurs who did not attend a business school (or dropped out of school)?

Although HBS's reputation is more about leadership than entrepreneurship, in recent years it has developed an amazing track record for breeding world-class entrepreneurs.

According to the school and its Rock Center for Entrepreneurship, approximately 50 percent of HBS graduates become entrepreneurs within fifteen years of finishing school. Half of this number start two or more businesses.

Many Harvard Business School alumni have also grown their start-ups into unicorns, private companies worth more than $1B. In fact, of the top MBA programs, HBS alumni lead with the largest number of unicorns. Some recent ones include Blue Apron, Rent the Runway, Peloton, Cloudflare, Red Ventures, and Oscar Health. We have been fortunate to interview some founders of these companies in the process of writing this book.

In short, one can agree that entrepreneurs coming out of HBS have benefited from a top education, which prepared them well for their entrepreneurial journey—or as well prepared as anyone can be. But an education is no substitute for experience. So what wisdom did they learn the hard way?

Indeed, our interviews focused on what they learned on the job, beyond the knowledge they had acquired during their education or in previous jobs. We wanted to hear their tips and tricks you can't learn in school, and the things they hadn't anticipated despite their knowledge. We wanted to focus especially on the *unconventional* wisdom that's either overlooked in school or hard to teach.

We listened to a diverse group of interviewees, representing a mix of age, race, gender, culture, and economic backgrounds. Some firms raised hundreds of millions in financing, others more modest amounts, and a few none at all. Some firms had single founders, others several cofounders. On the whole, the selected firms represent an array of business model innovations—in B2C, B2B, marketplaces, and B2B2C—across many industries.

In total, the twenty companies have raised $1.7B at time of writing. Three companies had reached unicorn status with a value of more than $1B. Two companies IPO'd and eleven were acquired. None truly failed, in the sense of going bankrupt. All have essential wisdom to impart.

Ahead, we give a short summary of each entrepreneur and the company or companies they've founded. The book was written in such a way that you do not need to know each one of the companies and their field of operation, but the summaries are here to provide context if needed.

Gil Addo and Carlos Reines, RubiconMD

Gil and Carlos, who both graduated from HBS, founded RubiconMD in 2013. RubiconMD is a web-based service that enables primary care doctors to easily connect with top medical specialists, quickly discuss patient cases, and determine if an in-office patient visit with a specialist is required. The service leads to better care and reduces costs by minimizing unnecessary visits to specialists. The company is headquartered in New York, raised $38M, and was acquired by Oak Street Health for $130M in 2021.

Anna Auerbach, Werk

Anna and her cofounder, Annie Dean, founded Werk in 2016. Werk initially started as a job marketplace and later pivoted to an enterprise SaaS platform helping companies to improve their flexibility performance through data. Werk helps companies understand their flexibility baseline and gaps, the needed investments to close those gaps, and the impact of flexibility on their business metrics. Werk is headquartered in New York, raised $3.9M, and was acquired by the Mom Project in 2020.

Jake Cusack, CrossBoundary

Jake founded CrossBoundary together with Matt Tilleard in 2011. The company started as a private advisory firm for investors such as equity funds, family offices, and multinational companies that are looking to invest in developing markets. CrossBoundary later set up its own investment funds to invest directly in energy projects in developing markets. CrossBoundary raised $100M and has seventeen offices across the globe.

Jenny Fleiss, Rent the Runway

Jenny launched Rent the Runway in 2009 with her cofounder, Jenn Hyman, who was also her classmate at Harvard Business School. Rent the Runway is an e-commerce website that allows women to rent designer apparel and accessories. It is transforming the way modern women get dressed through the concept of renting over buying clothing and supporting sustainability. Rent the Runway is based in New York, raised $541M, reached unicorn status in 2020, and went public in 2021.

Anthemos Georgiades, Zumper

Anthemos founded Zumper with three junior cofounders—of which one was a friend and two he met via serendipity. Zumper makes renting an apartment as easy as booking a hotel. It is now the largest privately held apartment rental platform, with over 80 million annual users. Zumper is based in San Francisco and has raised over $180M to date.

Greg Geronemus, smarTours

Greg acquired smarTours in 2013 with his friend David Rosner, whom he had met at Harvard Business School. SmarTours is a leading provider of direct-to-consumer, affordable travel experiences to exotic global destinations. The company offers travelers curated, prepackaged itineraries to over forty destinations across the globe. SmarTours is headquartered in New York and was sold to Summit Park, a private equity firm, in 2017.

Morgan Hermand-Waiche, Adore Me

Morgan founded Adore Me in 2011. Morgan is a French national who attended HBS with a goal to start a company in the U.S. Adore Me is a disruptive lingerie e-commerce startup. Adore Me customers can shop online and in person at the Adore Me showroom located in New York and in select retail stores. Adore Me is headquartered in New York, has raised $58M, and was sold in 2022 to Victoria's Secret for $400M.

Josh Hix, Plated

Josh met his cofounder Nick Taranto early on at Harvard Business School and decided to launch Plated a couple of years later in 2012. Plated was a subscription business that delivered fresh ingredients and chef-designed recipes at home. Plated was based in New York and raised $56M. Plated exited when it was acquired by Albertsons in 2017 for $200M, plus an earn-out of $100M.

Justin Joffe, Henry the Dentist

Justin founded Henry the Dentist in 2017. Henry the Dentist is a mobile dental practice that brings dental services to employees at their company's location. By offering greater convenience for office workers, the company ensures that more people can access dental care without needing to travel to a brick-and-mortar dental office. Henry the Dentist is based in New Jersey and raised $10M. It was acquired in 2021 by Onsite Dental.

Beri Meric, Ivy
Beri founded Ivy in 2011 with his cofounder, Philipp Triebel, after becoming friends while attending Harvard Business School. Ivy is a membership-based community for passionate individuals with interests in entrepreneurship, the arts, social impact, public policy, and wellness. Ivy has more than 20,000 members across seven U.S. cities and has hosted more than one thousand in-person and online gatherings with foremost thought leaders, cultural institutions, venues, and brands in 2017. Ivy is based in New York and raised $9M.

David Parker, Yumble Kids
David founded Yumble Kids in 2016 with his wife, Joanna, and an operational cofounder who had grown the U.S. operations of HelloFresh. Yumble is a weekly subscription that delivers healthy, delicious, and fully cooked meals specifically designed for kids. The company aims to make mealtime stress-free for parents and super fun for kids. Yumble Kids is headquartered in New York and has raised $12.5M to date.

Eric Price, SkyMD
Eric founded SkyMD in 2014 with his mother, a dermatologist, and a technical cofounder. SkyMD is enabling patients to access quality care from their dermatologist anytime, anywhere, via a mobile phone app. SkyMD is headquartered in New York. SkyMD raised $800K and was acquired in 2017 by one of its customers, RegimenMD.

Matt Salzberg, Blue Apron
Matt founded Blue Apron in 2012 with a cofounder and was later joined by a third cofounder. Blue Apron is a weekly subscription ser-

vice that delivers everything you need to make fresh meals, including ingredients in specific proportions, along with printed recipe cards. Blue Apron is headquartered in New York, raised $200M, reached unicorn status in 2015 with a valuation of more than $2B, and IPO'd in 2017.

Anthony Soohoo, Dot & Bo

Anthony launched Dot & Bo in 2011 together with two cofounders. Dot & Bo is an e-commerce site that organizes well-curated collections of furniture and decor items for the modern home. Based in San Francisco, Dot & Bo raised $18.5M and was sold in 2017 to OpenSky.

Steven Szaronos, Bespoke Post

Steven founded Bespoke Post with Rishi Prabhu in 2011. Bespoke Post offers a monthly subscription to themed boxes full of "goods for guys," plus a full e-commerce shop of uniquely cool stand-alone products. Bespoke Post raised $49M and is headquartered in New York.

Bespoke Post is the only non-HBS company. It was the first company we interviewed because Jim is an investor.

Alexandra Wilkis Wilson, Gilt Groupe

Alexandra became one of Gilt's cofounders after being recruited by Kevin Ryan, a serial entrepreneur who had observed the success of a similar business in France. Alexandra signed on with her good friend and HBS classmate Alexis Maybank. Gilt Groupe is a flash-sale e-commerce site for high-end designer clothing, home decor, and unique activities in select cities and destinations. Gilt Groupe has its headquarters in New York City. It raised $286M, reached unicorn status in 2011, then was subsequently sold in 2016 to Hudson's Bay for approximately $250M.

...

THE AUTHORS AND THEIR COMPANIES

We are the authors of this book, but also graduated from Harvard Business School and have been entrepreneurs, and therefore decided to interview each other like we interviewed all other entrepreneurs. We have included quotes wherever relevant.

Because we're also bringing our own insight to this book, we thought including our own backgrounds would be helpful for context.

Catalina Daniels, Sweetwell

Catalina joined Sweetwell in 2007, after quitting McKinsey & Company as a partner. Catalina's mentor at McKinsey had invested in the company and convinced her to co-invest and become CEO. Sweetwell developed a one-to-one sugar replacer with 60 percent fewer calories. The company focused on B2B sales while covering B2C with licensing agreements. Sweetwell is currently headquartered in Costa Rica and has raised about $5M.

Jim Sherman, WestEnd New Media; ShermansTravel Media; Hamptons Lane

Jim launched three companies. After stints as a Bain & Company consultant, marketer with Time Inc., and general manager for Martha Stewart Living online, in 1997 he launched WestEnd New Media, which provided internet strategy advice and project management services; in 2002 ShermansTravel Media, which offers online travel deals and advice; and in 2012, with a junior cofounder, Hamptons Lane, which offers monthly subscription themed boxes with artisan ingredients and unique cooking tools. All companies were headquartered in New York. Jim raised $25M with ShermansTravel Media, sold most of his stake to private equity in 2007, then reacquired the firm in 2022. He raised $1.5M with Hamptons Lane, which was acquired by Try the World in 2017.

In the pages that follow, you'll hear from these founders. Why just eighteen? Well, it could have been several dozen—or even more—but by highlighting these eighteen founders, we believe we have been able to capture the big themes and commonalities that all entrepreneurs should reflect upon and be equipped for when they start their journey.

We could have gone on and on—there are so many more stories to be told—but, as every entrepreneur knows, each story is unique and paved with its own challenges and opportunities. At some point, as an entrepreneur, you have to get started and be prepared to create your own story on the job.

One of the key takeaways from our interviews and this book is that one can learn to "start smarter" but the challenges and the learning will never stop. If aspiring entrepreneurs learn one thing from this book, it's that.

PREAMBLE:
BORN TO CREATE

No lemonade stand? No shame. You don't
need to be born an entrepreneur.

Part of weeding out people who are meant to be entrepreneurs is finding people who find and create the opportunities themselves. I think letting people find it for themselves is part of what's indicative of someone being an entrepreneurial person.

JENNY FLEISS, RENT THE RUNWAY

Knowing you are meant to be an entrepreneur is a journey unto itself. For "born" entrepreneurs, who have always been entrepreneurial—raised in entrepreneurial families, started their first businesses at a young age, had multiple ventures by the time we interviewed them—it may be a more direct journey. For those who aren't "born" entrepreneurs, who never had a lemonade stand, and who even chose to be in corporate jobs—it's a journey of discovery.

When we started interviewing entrepreneurs in 2018, we began each of our discussions by asking the entrepreneurs, "When and why did you start your business?" We expected every interviewee to answer, "I always wanted to be an entrepreneur" or "I chose it for the money" (which nobody said). Instead, all of them replied that they wanted to *create* something and that they wanted the *freedom* to do so.

Not all of them were "born" entrepreneurs, as you might expect. We met people coming from very different backgrounds, some had started a business at age eight, while others had corporate careers and made the jump to entrepreneurship later in life.

I went to college in Oxford and then Cambridge for a master's. I worked for the Boston Consulting Group for my first three years. I did a brief stint in British politics and then I went to HBS to figure out what I wanted to do for the rest of my life.

ANTHEMOS GEORGIADES, ZUMPER

I have always started companies, ever since I was a kid.

ANTHONY SOOHOO, DOT & BO

Despite their different backgrounds, we found that our entrepreneurs shared three qualities: a passion to create that propelled them forward, resilience, and an ability to understand the right time to make the jump.

PASSION IS YOUR FUEL

It is important to know what gets you up in the morning and makes you excited. I've never been happier than doing what I do right now. I fucking love what I do.

JUSTIN JOFFE, HENRY THE DENTIST

Many entrepreneurs knew from a young age that they wanted to have control over their lives—a sense of freedom—and, for most, that they wanted to have an impact on the world. They wanted to create. They wanted to innovate. The entrepreneurs felt an urge to chart their own destinies, create something from nothing, and ultimately leave a lasting impact on the world around them.

None of the entrepreneurs told us they started their business for money. Money is an important factor and motivator, but it was not about money in the first place. If money were the only factor, they might have chosen to simply go into a well-paid job that was of lesser risk. Instead, it was about pursuing something bigger and having the freedom to do so.

I started the company because I feel in my blood, in my veins, I like to create value. I like to see people through the fruit of my work getting value out of it. The monetary part is a sideline consideration.

MORGAN HERMAND-WAICHE, ADORE ME

We both wanted to do something that had a social impact, had a large impact; we had a shared passion in the health and wellness space. Both of us were very serious athletes, and both had shared experience in wrestling with how to eat relatively healthy.

JOSH HIX, PLATED

I moved to the U.S. as a refugee when I was six years old. We came with absolutely nothing and started out literally getting charity and scraps. I actually, very acutely, even as a young person, felt like we had this second chance and this ability to start a new life here. So, I've always been passionate about creating opportunities for others. That has taken different forms over time. I started at McKinsey. Moved to nonprofit. Was in nonprofit after HBS. And later, I cofounded Werk.

ANNA AUERBACH, WERK

Whether born an entrepreneur or not, the first thing you need is passion to create. Being entrepreneurial will require a lot of energy and if you do not have the passion, there is a high likelihood that you will run out of fuel.

...

RESILIENCE IS KEY

There's a resilience that you learn as a parent that applies very much to entrepreneurship. You have incredibly hard days as a parent, but you don't stop being a parent. Your child goes through all sorts of phases. And you don't just give up. You have very hard days and you have wonderful days and you have to keep going. There's no other choice.

ANNA AUERBACH, WERK

Once you decide to go for it, you will need a huge dose of resilience. A startup comes with loads of ups and downs. In entrepreneurship, you never stop or get a break—you just have to power forward. The journey is often lonely and characterized by unpredictability and financial stress, especially in the beginning. To exacerbate things, you will undoubtedly make mistakes. You can only survive and thrive if you are resilient.

Everyone we spoke to agreed that without resilience, there is no chance of success. It is needed to deal with all events, especially those you don't control, and to power through a seemingly endless cycle of learning on the job, making mistakes, falling, and standing back up. Over and over again.

A big part of your journey as an entrepreneur is dealing with events as they unfold. While there are elements you may control in a new business, which prove challenging on their own, there are a ton of other things you cannot control, and these are what most leaders find to be the most stressful and challenging.

At some point, most successful entrepreneurs accept that there will always be issues, challenges, or facts you cannot change. The best you can do is to manage through them. Whatever happens, you need to keep going and find a solution.

With parenthood you realize that your kid's personality is their personality. If they have learning challenges or disabilities or health things, no matter how hard you work, you cannot change those things. There's a huge lesson in there for entrepreneurship. Sometimes there are market fundamentals. We might be heading into a recession. There might be a competitor you didn't foresee coming. You as a human cannot change those factors, those macroeconomic forces. But you can operate within them.

ANNA AUERBACH, WERK

As Morgan puts it below, being an entrepreneur requires motivation and grit. Those two key ingredients form the backbone of resilience, allowing you to overcome challenges, stresses, and failures. It is from these that success is born.

I never really accepted a scenario in which I would ultimately fail. But it doesn't mean that there were not tons of failures along the way. Even the very beginning of the company was a terrible failure. It didn't work out from the start. It's your motivation and grit to overcome those failures that ultimately make it a success.

MORGAN HERMAND-WAICHE, ADORE ME

FIND THE RIGHT TIME TO JUMP

Knowing when to jump into entrepreneurship is one of the most critical questions we hear from potential founders and one of the hardest to answer. That's because it so often depends on personal circumstances and preferences. Entrepreneurship equals risk. And an entrepreneur is somebody who understands the risks and still goes for it.

Appetite for risk is a highly personal matter. The born entrepreneurs are typically the ones who start with the biggest appetite. The ones who came to entrepreneurship later in life needed to assess *when* and *how* to make the jump so that they would feel comfortable with the risks.

Your family background matters—if you come from a family of

entrepreneurs, you may have risk-taking in your DNA and are likely to seek out freedom and creativity.

But other factors will matter, too. Age and status, for example; if you are young, not married, have no kids . . . you might be more willing to take risks. Money typically matters, although not always in the same way for everybody; some need a financial safety net to feel free, others don't.

I come from a very poor family. When I say poor, I mean poor in the sense where my mom wouldn't buy the TV magazine costing one euro because it was too expensive. To me, that trade-off was even more vivid because I had high-paying jobs, security versus entrepreneurship. But similarly, in a very paradoxical way, I met kids who became close friends over time, coming from families where the financial power is almost infinite. Imagine billions of a parent's fortune. And yet, these kids were afraid to start a business, but for different reasons—not financially, but for reputational risks. Everybody has their own story.

MORGAN HERMAND-WAICHE, *ADORE ME*

You need to find the balance that works for you, taking the multitude of parameters into consideration, including family responsibilities, financial debts or liabilities, and future goals. Understanding for yourself what you feel comfortable with, and then building the confidence and safety net to face that risk, are critical.

Three Elements to Boost Confidence

Whatever risk profile you have, the key is to understand what you feel comfortable with and how to build confidence to get you to that point. When you reach that point, you can make the jump with confidence.

The entrepreneurs were able to articulate what risk felt like for them and how they had dealt with it. In some cases, we were impressed to hear how they had proactively worked at making sure they felt comfortable with the risk.

The recurring themes in our interviews evolved around three elements to weigh when considering the right time to jump.

1. Money—Do I have enough of it to chase my passion? And/or if I run out of money, do I have a fallback option?
2. Network and skills—Do I have the skills and do I know enough people to pull this off the ground?
3. Life—Is it the right time for me personally?

Justin from Henry the Dentist went to business school because he knew that he wanted to create a company and wanted the HBS degree as a safety net in case he failed. He also wanted to have enough money set aside and felt confident—thanks to his experience in previous ventures—that he had the needed skills to be successful.

I went to HBS to be an entrepreneur and also have a safety net of security, says the insecure overachiever. We all want that safety net.

I put away some runway [cash]. I got a lot of operating confidence. I also knew that I had a couple of secret weapons of people that I'd worked with before who could design the vision for Henry the Dentist.

JUSTIN JOFFE, HENRY THE DENTIST

Matt from Blue Apron developed critical skills while working as a venture capitalist and in private equity, but also built an impressive network of useful contacts. Some of his contacts would end up becoming investors and one of them helped him make the jump.

Throughout the course of my time at Bessemer, the venture capital firm, I spent a lot of time looking at areas of opportunity that I thought were good industries to start companies in. I had built a relationship with an EIR *[entrepreneur in residence] there who gave me a lot of advice. I was talking about all of my aspirations to start a brand, have impact in the world, and how I really wanted to be an entrepreneur. He was eventually the one who gave me the confidence and said, "Look, you should just leave venture capital and start your own company at this point, and I'll be your first investor. I'll give you $25,000."*

MATT SALZBERG, BLUE APRON

John Cusack of CrossBoundary saved up enough money to cover his needs for nearly a half year, and, like Justin, also saw his HBS degree as his safety net. He figured that if it didn't work out, he could still switch to a more traditional path in management consulting.

I had four or five months' worth of savings built up. I thought we could give this a shot and if it doesn't work out, I'll join something more conventional.

JAKE CUSACK, CROSSBOUNDARY

Alexandra Wilkis Wilson assessed her personal situation and preferences when the opportunity to join the founding team of Gilt came up. Timing was right for her, as she was just married with no financial obligations, and she had started to feel bored in her job.

Maybe the security of being married, but not having children, made me feel like I had some freedom.

ALEXANDRA WILKIS WILSON, GILT

Greg Geronemus followed a different approach when he and his cofounder decided to set up a search fund with the purpose of acquiring a company instead of founding one. He felt this was a lower-risk strategy—buy an existing company that he felt he could operate better and grow significantly. For many, this can be the right approach to make the jump.

Entrepreneurship through acquisition opens up the opportunity for a lot more people to pursue entrepreneurship because there are a lot of people, myself included, for whom a startup from scratch is just not in the cards from a risk/return perspective or a personality perspective.

GREG GERONEMUS, SMARTOURS

Eric Price from SkyMD found a different kind of safety net. He chose to keep his job while developing the minimum viable product (MVP) to get a better feel for possible success.

I had this agreement with the CEO [of Fab.com] that he would allow me to actually build an MVP while I was still working there. That was part of what made it possible for me to feel comfortable doing it, because obviously there's always a risk that you start something and you don't get that product/market fit. This was a way for me to, without a ton of risk, at least get an initial product out there.

ERIC PRICE, SKYMD

This might work for some people. But beware that if you don't go all in, you might not *give it all* to truly make it work.

Dave and Joanna Parker at Yumble Kids exemplify the all-in approach. As a married couple, they became cofounders of Yumble Kids and literally had to make it work. There was no other option. As parents of young children, and as young professionals, they could not afford to lose it all. When asked how it felt to have all their eggs in one basket, Dave's reaction was clear:

We have to make this work! From an investor standpoint they should love that, right?

DAVE PARKER, YUMBLE KIDS

PART I

The Foundation

More Than a "Good Idea"

When you do a startup you need a great idea and an even greater team. You will only be successful if you get that foundation right.

CATALINA DANIELS, SWEETWELL

1

THERE IS NO "AHA" MOMENT

> There is no random "lightbulb" moment. Landing a good idea often requires a deliberate, lengthy ideation process.

I don't believe a coconut falls out of the tree, hits you on the head, and you have an "Aha." No. You have to figure it out.

JUSTIN JOFFE, HENRY THE DENTIST

A startup starts with an idea. How many entrepreneurs come to that idea may surprise you. For the Harvard Business School grads-turned-founders we interviewed, there was no "lightbulb moment." Not a single entrepreneur told us they woke up one day with such a vision.

On the contrary, we were surprised to hear that all embarked on a true *ideation process*. They came upon their idea through a process of reflection and deep thinking that spanned weeks, months, or even years. They thoughtfully considered ideas over time, took in pieces of information as they gathered them, vetted the ideas, and ultimately shaped them until deciding whether the idea was something worth pursuing.

I don't particularly believe in the lightning bolt moment. Those moments are created by deep thought and reflection and looking at the problems, examining them, looking for solutions, looking at emerging technologies.

If anybody told you that they had a linear innovation process, you should likely throw them out of the room.

JOSH HIX, PLATED

Through the course of our interviews, we have identified two types of ideation—deliberate and organic. In the case of deliberate, the entrepreneur has no specific idea to start with and instead embarks on a deliberate process to find an idea. The entrepreneur considers multiple ideas and each is evaluated for its attractiveness. Many founders in this group gave themselves a timeline within which to evaluate each idea and ultimately land the right one.

In the case of organic ideation, the method followed by a slight majority of the founders, the entrepreneur doesn't evaluate multiple ideas. Rather, the entrepreneur develops an idea organically based on his or her life experiences or those of family and friends, and deepens and builds it over time.

Even those who have run through a systematic, deliberate ideation process—where one might think that it is more linear—talk about how nonlinear the progression actually is for landing an idea.

DELIBERATE IDEATION

About half of the entrepreneurs started with nothing. They had no idea whatsoever as to what venture might be right for them. They followed a methodical process to land the right idea.

We were surprised by the number of entrepreneurs who embarked on this systematic approach. Perhaps this is due to the fact that many used their time while at HBS to drill down in their search for opportunities. Or it may be due to the fact that these graduates are highly analytical types.

Whatever the reason, the fact is that many companies began by following a rigorous assessment process of multiple ideas.

For example, Josh and his cofounder Nick from Plated embarked on a months-long process, up to sixty hours per week, to systematically examine ideas. They ultimately settled on one that relates well to their personal lives and interests in healthy eating. But they came upon the idea only after months of rigorous vetting before landing on the notion of pre-portioned, fresh ingredients and meal recipes delivered to the home on a weekly subscription.

The idea was the product of a very deliberate design process. I don't think that there's a right or wrong answer.

We spent the first six months of 2012 looking at a number of different ideas. Looking for real problems that we could solve. Being cognizant that when you have a hammer, everything's a nail.

We spent twelve [man] months doing this full-time. Forty, fifty, sixty-plus hours a week. It was all we were thinking about. A pretty tremendous amount of time.

JOSH HIX, PLATED

While Josh and Nick conducted their deliberate process during school and focused on problems that interested them and that they thought they could help solve, Justin of Henry the Dentist had already graduated, had worked for a few years, and ran his deliberate process after taking time off traveling.

He came up with the idea for a mobile dental clinic that delivers services conveniently to the office worker, making it faster and far more convenient for regular checkups. However, he had examined about thirty different ideas—not necessarily related to his personal interests—before narrowing things down to dentistry. He gave himself a deadline, and his process included "shallow dives" into evaluating the business model and overall attractiveness of an idea.

I took a very rigid approach in evaluating ideas. First, I came up with my own criteria. What am I looking for in an idea?

I'd taken about thirty ideas, narrowed it down to five, then three, over the course of a few months. I did some shallow dives. I looked at business model transportability. Where does an idea make sense somewhere else that could make sense here?

JUSTIN JOFFE, HENRY THE DENTIST

The concept of "shallow dives"—a quick evaluation of business ideas—wasn't unique to Justin (in chapter 3, we will return to this concept of vetting ideas). In fact, all the entrepreneurs we interviewed who ran a deliberate process engaged in such dives to evaluate multiple ideas.

Similarly, Morgan of Adore Me ended up choosing a field far from any personal fit. He chose it after assessing more than one hundred other ideas, which he quickly narrowed down to fifty. But then, in a totally random fashion, when chatting with his girlfriend about possible venture ideas, she challenged him with one idea of her own—women's lingerie—based on her experience with expensive, low-quality undergarments.

I had a list of, literally, one hundred ideas or opportunities. I started to rank them based on the size of the opportunity and how much do I think my skill set can be applied to this? I spent a lot of time diving into ideas.

One day, I was looking at shoes, and my girlfriend told me, "You should look at lingerie. It really sucks." I said, "Why does it suck?" And she said, "Because Victoria's Secret is expensive, and they only do crap." Well, I looked into lingerie and that's what I ended up choosing. The outcome was not out of any lightbulb going off.

MORGAN HERMAND-WAICHE, ADORE ME

Finally, some took their inspiration by examining industry macro trends around them. For example, in the case of Blue Apron, Matt Salzberg attacked the deliberate process differently than others. He examined not fifty to one hundred ideas but rather a handful of big macro industry trends. From that starting point, he then focused on coming up with his new idea.

In the mid 2000s, he observed the rapid growth occurring across e-commerce categories. He also noted that the grocery category hadn't yet taken off. He believed that one day it would. He saw an opportunity to disrupt the grocery industry by changing the way people buy their ingredients and prepare meals at home.

In addition, he reflected on how much he himself would like a service that would deliver ingredients and recipes to the home, thereby making cooking a lot easier.

We [Matt and Ilia Papas, a cofounder] narrowed in on this idea of delivering recipes and ingredients to people as something we just wish we had in our lives.

MATT SALZBERG, BLUE APRON

Nearly all the founders who engaged in a deliberate process invested months in landing their idea. But it can also go faster if you are under pressure.

The founders of Bespoke Post entered the New York–based Entrepreneurs Roundtable Accelerator (ERA) with a concept but decided to drop the idea toward the end of the four-month program as they could not convince themselves anymore of the opportunity (more about that later).

As the ERA demo day was fast approaching, they were under intense pressure to develop a new idea. With their mentors and the founders of ERA, they went through a deliberate short process of ideation. They had to land an idea in one week. They zeroed in on what they felt could be a good opportunity—a market gap in men's e-commerce.

While many e-commerce categories were booming online, there was hardly any focus on men, much to their surprise. So Steve and Rishi came up with the idea for better curation of a variety of men's products and more convenient delivery to the home on a monthly subscription.

We literally had six days before demo day, and we had nothing. Once we removed the shackles of Nabfly, the QR code reader [which had not worked] . . . it was kind of rejuvenating because we could start talking about, "What do we think we're good at? What are interesting problems that we've had?" It was a little reinvigorating.

STEVE SZARONOS, BESPOKE POST

In sum, the deliberate process shows how some entrepreneurs systematically approached the challenge of ideation. They had no firm idea to start with, and deliberately engaged in a process to find an idea, often taking time off to do so. Some focused only on ideas close to their areas of personal interest, some looked broadly around in their spouse's or friend's lives and at business models that could be improved upon, and some examined macro trends in order to distill ideas.

In no case did anyone just wake up with an "aha moment." It was hard work, it took time, nothing came easily, and it was iterative with shallow dives until they found the best place to go deep.

...

ORGANIC IDEATION

A slight majority of HBS entrepreneurs got going with an organic idea, either based on their own experiences or that of family or a close friend. But it was just one idea that started small and developed over time.

This one idea—as opposed to multiple ideas, as was the case for those engaged in a deliberate process—matures over time and is *peeled back like an onion* to confirm its validity by evaluating the core features of the business model, and to ultimately determine if it is an attractive opportunity.

Unlike the systematic, deliberate ideation approach, an organic ideation process is likely to take place over a relatively long period of time, in most cases taking longer than the deliberate process.

In the organic case, the founder is connecting the dots from their past or current life or work experiences, talking to friends and industry experts—which often leads to pivotal moments of enlightenment—and then perfecting the idea based on the learnings.

As with the deliberate process, there is no lightbulb moment. If anything, the analogy would be more like a dim light growing brighter over time. The founders are intentionally looking for a business idea to emerge from their own lives. Being open to this possibility is the first step to making it a reality.

For example, Beri of Ivy credits his experience at Brown and Harvard with finding his new business idea. Coming from Turkey to study in the U.S., he was deeply affected by the educational enrichment and community or social development opportunities from school. Over several years, he realized there should be a way to continue that experience post–college or graduate school. He believed many people were like him, wanting to carry on with such enrichment throughout life. He started connecting the dots.

My idea for Ivy was "let's make college experience lifelong and global."
When I reflected on what was so special about HBS, a lot of it was the
dinners, the trips, and the social stuff that created these amazing relation-
ships.

We said, "Okay, we want to create a lifelong learning community with col-
legiate values." What we want to do is curate an amazing group of rising
leaders across different industries and get them involved with great learning
in a liberal arts way.

BERI MERIC, IVY

Anthemos, founder of Zumper, also developed his business idea
over several years based on personal experience. He had moved seven
times since college, and, after that seventh time, decided to launch
Zumper.

The pain point that he endured wasn't in trying to find an apartment
but in closing on a lease. While there were several major websites he
could use to search apartment listings, those sites did not "close the
loop" by completing a seamless close and signed lease. There had to
be a better way to streamline the entire process—connect the search
piece for an apartment with the transaction to rent (signing a lease).

By 2010, I'd probably moved apartments seven times since college—in
Cambridge, London, New York, and then in Boston. I felt that technology
failed me where every tech company was trying to build a search platform
for apartment rentals. But it was a real pain point when you talked to rent-
ers, or through my own experience, with what comes after search.

After you search, you then have to schedule apartment visits, apply on
paper, and wait seven to eight days to hear back.

I was like, why is there no better solution for residential, one-year leases?
That was the biggest consumer decision for me in my twenties. And it was
also the single biggest economic decision I made in my twenties.

ANTHEMOS GEORGIADES, ZUMPER

With organic ideation, the idea is something the entrepreneur weighs for many months and sometimes years. This was similar for Gil of RubiconMD, a platform virtually connecting primary care clinicians to board-certified specialists. He experienced a few pivotal moments before coming to the idea in which he connected the dots.

First, he observed health care challenges that his grandmother experienced in the Caribbean when she tried to get specialty care for her medical issues. She needed to come to the U.S., which was far from convenient, and it was costly. Second, later at HBS, when he took a student trip to India, he took note of a low cost health care delivery model there where specialists helped patients remotely, and he believed this approach could be applied to the U.S. market. Third, he had the experience, after HBS, of working for a health care consulting firm where he observed how insurance firms paid for consulting research. He learned that "research" or "specialist advice" could be reimbursed this way.

The idea evolved over several years from the mix of his family, school, and work experiences. With the onion-layering analogy, he slowly began to peel back the layers as he qualified his idea in stages.

In 2010, in my second year of HBS, I went to India as part of a health care trek. There we looked at a bunch of health care delivery models. They have a simple model where they use community centers as hubs. You can go there and get clean water. You can also get the medical care you need. They also get specialist expertise just Skyped in. So, I started iterating on that model.

It was at some point while I was in health care consulting [at Putnam Associates, after HBS] that it all came together. I started working on the business model through my second year in consulting.

GIL ADDO, RUBICONMD

Another HBS entrepreneur who developed his business idea organically after an HBS experience was Jake of CrossBoundary.

Jake has one of the more unique backgrounds of the HBS entrepreneurs. He came to HBS from the U.S. military and had direct experience working in conflict zones—Afghanistan and Iraq—that triggered his idea. It was there that he took note of the value that comes from crafting public-private solutions to needs in developing markets.

He hadn't known it at the time, but he stumbled into what would become the growing field of "impact investing"—encouraging private investment in projects and countries where the measure of success is not just a return on invested capital but also the positive societal impact.

After his first year at HBS, he began a summer research project in the field of impact investing in former conflict zones, then gave talks on the topics about which he was passionate, all of which eventually led him to create his consulting firm. His organic ideation process was one of flow, where one experience flowed into the next, until the idea was obvious.

Out of that initial summer research, these little consulting projects started springing up. Agencies of the U.S. government or private investors would ask us for a perspective on investing in Afghanistan and Iraq. The Department of Defense was trying to bring more investment into Afghanistan for the reason that if you manage to provide more jobs and economic growth, that would contribute to stability. So, the business gradually grew from there.

JAKE CUSACK, CROSSBOUNDARY

As was the case in the deliberate process, ideas can emerge from different sources. We met entrepreneurs who found inspiration from an idea that grew from a pain point that they experienced or saw others experience. Some other founders came upon an idea that percolated up from observing industry trends—trends that they observed from their work.

For example, Anthony's venture, Dot & Bo—one of the first furniture and home decor e-commerce sites—observed a trend while working at CBS Interactive and Yahoo. He observed that viewers wanted to buy products they saw on the network's TV shows. He grew to believe that the future for online content would include users wanting to not just consume online media, but to click to buy products featured within the content. In other words, he saw the merging of media content and e-commerce. His ideation process arrived at what Dot & Bo would become: online "idea books" of room designs—to inspire people with the content, but where one could also click to buy items in the collections.

Also under the realm of observing an industry trend is SkyMD. Eric and his mom, a dermatologist, came upon their idea based on his mom's professional experience. One day, she happened to tell Eric that she had been observing in her practice how patients were increasingly sending pictures of their skin condition by email to her, using their iPhone camera. The new iPhone had excellent camera capabilities and patients used the phone to email her questions rather than to come into the office. She talked to Eric about this growing trend. She thought that there could be a good business idea from this new behavior she had observed.

So together they reflected on the idea over the course of several months and came up with SkyMD—an app to make it faster and easier to get dermatology advice.

She [my mom] actually came up with an idea that I thought was compelling. As a dermatologist [in Miami], she felt that it would be much easier to treat people online rather than bringing them into the office. I remember even as a child we had talked about some of these situations where she would get texts and calls from friends being like, "What is this?"

One day we were talking about what we could do to make this easier, and she was like, "Well, I get all these texts all the time. What if it could be more of a business where I could make money off of this?" I said, "Well, let's build a product that would support that." It was very organic.

ERIC PRICE, SKYMD

Whether you run an organic or deliberate process, don't expect that the idea should come easily. It might come from personal or professional experiences; it might come from someone else's (family or friend) personal or professional experiences; it could come from examining trends (technology, demographic, or other). You don't wake up one day with an idea. Even when you come to an idea organically, it takes time to flourish and connect the dots. It is a process. And it's hard if you want to get it right.

2

THE IDEATION TRIANGLE

> A large market is not the same as a large opportunity,
> relevant skills matter more than industry experience,
> and passion drives all.

The lingerie e-commerce business sounded like the best fit in terms of the triangle of opportunity, skill set, and enjoyment/fulfillment. If you miss a piece of the triangle it's going to collapse—because if you don't enjoy it, you will never be able to put all the effort you need to get the thing out. If the opportunity is not there, you'll never be able to do anything. And if you don't have the skill sets, it's difficult.

MORGAN HERMAND-WAICHE, ADORE ME

What makes a good idea? Three factors came up again and again independently in our founder interviews: a large market opportunity, relevant founder skills, and a huge amount of passion for the opportunity.

...

LARGE OPPORTUNITY

A good idea starts with the potential for a large opportunity, which sounds logical. But let us clarify that a large opportunity should not be confused with a large market. An opportunity arises from *solving a problem* or *addressing a need* in a market, not just identifying a sizable market. Ideally, you want to solve a big problem in a large market.

Justin, who went through a deliberate process to identify his idea for his mobile dental clinics, explains how early on he assessed that there was a large opportunity to capture.

I started getting into the dental industry like I'd looked at a bunch of other industries before. What I found is that it's a $125B category. It's a massive industry. Everyone has teeth. Everyone needs dental services. Fifty percent of Americans had dental insurance. Of those who have dental insurance, 80–90 percent get it through a company. And of those who have dental insurance, 40 percent of people have not gone to a dentist in over a year! And I was one of those people.

JUSTIN JOFFE, HENRY THE DENTIST

Justin identified that many people who were covered by corporate insurance did not see a dentist. By changing the service delivery model and bringing the dental clinic to the employers, he created benefits for employees, employers, and insurance companies. That was the foundation of his successful venture.

This is a win/win/win model. I don't charge the company anything. I go to the HR benefit manager and I say, "There is no cost to you. We take your existing insurance. We don't charge your employees. Forty percent of your people don't use your current benefit and those who do, most likely take a half day of PTO [paid time off] to get the dental benefits. Whereas with us, we come downstairs, right outside your building, and we're free to you."

The employee's perspective is a no-brainer. They either don't want to use the service, which is fine. Or they want to use it because they're unsatisfied with their current ones. If they come to us, they're back at their desk forty-five minutes later; we bill the insurance; zero out of pocket. Great benefit!

From the insurance company perspective, it helps to increase their premiums over the course of time because they show utilization by the customers. That helps their business model. They get to be the hero!

Justin Joffe, Henry the Dentist

Matt from Blue Apron went through a similar process. In his deliberate search for an idea, he was looking at large industries that could be disrupted by the internet. The internet had already proven a means to transform other retail verticals, so he reasoned that grocery would be next. His wager was that consumers would flock to his subscription service of pre-portioned ingredients as they got comfortable ordering everything online. He realized, though, that this would require a behavioral change that he needed to overcome to be successful.

I narrowed in quickly on food and grocery, as a macro industry, because it is gigantic. But at the time, online penetration of this category was basically nothing. There were a lot of reasons for that. Food is perishable and complicated. Logistics are hard.

But just like every other big retail category that's ever existed, e-commerce is going to take a big share of this category. So how can we build a brand and a product experience that will capitalize on this?

At the time, perishable food was basically zero in online purchases. Amazon Fresh was nothing of a business. Instacart didn't exist. Most people go to the grocery store in person. They touch it. They feel it. They put it in their cart.

It's incredibly inefficient; an incredibly bad shopping experience. But that's just the way it's been done.

So that's the behavior change that we had to overcome with an online grocery delivery service. The quality had to be amazing. The value had to be there, too. And we had to get people to trust us to select their vegetables for them, basically, which was the big behavior change.

MATT SALZBERG, BLUE APRON

Solve a Pain Point

We cannot emphasize enough how important it is to define an opportunity not by the market size itself but by what *value* you will bring to that market.

As investors we see many entrepreneurs fail to do this. They refer to a huge market but are not clear on what problem they will solve or what implicit or explicit need they address in their target market. An opportunity is a combination of both.

The more you address an implicit need (i.e., a need that people are not aware of), the more difficult it is to know ahead of time if your idea will be successful. But even for explicit needs (i.e., those that people are aware of), you won't know for sure until you start selling. So, how can you get a better sense of your idea before investing more time and money?

What surely helps when you get started is solving a pain point that you have encountered yourself. It gives you the conviction that you are on to something, although you might not be sure about the size of the opportunity.

Go through your day and look at all your friction points. Go through your business life, and also look at all your friction points there.

JENNY FLEISS, RENT THE RUNWAY

Dave and Joanna came upon the idea for Yumble Kids to solve a major pain point in their own lives. Joanna felt a lot of stress preparing healthy meals for her children every week. She was certain that other moms felt the same way and that there was an explicit need here.

"My friends and I are so annoying," Joanna said. *"All we do all day is complain about how stressful putting healthy dinners are on the table. That's all we talk about. Coming up with ideas. Then grocery shopping for it. Then cooking and cleaning. I don't have a job and it's consuming my whole day. I have friends who aren't even home to serve their kids dinner and this is what they're stressing over."*

DAVE PARKER, YUMBLE KIDS

Because Dave and Joanna were solving a problem they encountered themselves, they were convinced that the opportunity would be huge. Indeed, other parents would have the same problem and would love Yumble Kids. Because it was a new offering, they could not precisely size up the opportunity, but they felt it would be large enough for them to pursue.

We are producing healthy kids' meals that kids actually want to eat. What's the size of that direct-to-consumer market now? Virtually zero. What is it going to be five years from now? I think $2B. It's going to grow fast. I don't really care if it's $1B or $10B, it's going to be big enough to be able to make it. Right?

DAVE PARKER, YUMBLE KIDS

Anna, the founder of Werk, recalls how a personal need drove her to believe there was a large opportunity for her business. After moving to Las Vegas with her husband and newborn son, she tried to get a job but realized how limited the opportunities were there. She knew there was clear demand from professionals for remote work (as jobs were not available in Las Vegas) and set out to organize the supply for those jobs in a marketplace.

One of the things I observed very quickly: Vegas is a city that doesn't have a broad industry distribution. It's gaming and support services for gaming. Mining in the more rural areas. But if you didn't work in those areas and you ended up in the city, you couldn't find a job. Then, through my son's day care, I ended up meeting other women. And it was women that had these amazing careers in other cities and had moved to Vegas for their spouse's career.

It seemed crazy to me there were all these women that were sitting on the sidelines because the location where they ended up just did not have the right jobs for them. Or they needed flexibility because somebody else was working in a 24/7 job.

Yet we fundamentally do not have an employment system that adapts to that. That was the spark that lit the fire to launch this.

Initially, the idea was actually that people are either dropping out of the workforce or sitting at their desks about to quit because they can't find a way to make it work. What's missing in this marketplace of work is there are people searching for flexible jobs, remote jobs, and there should be a supply of that. There's definitely demand. Where is the supply?

So we started as a job board. People created profiles. They applied to jobs through us.

ANNA AUERBACH, WERK

We will come back to Anna's story (and the pivot she later made). But initially, it was her strong belief that a problem existed in not connecting remote work job seekers with opportunities. There was a big need and no direct solution.

In the case of Rent the Runway, Jenn (Jenny's cofounder) observed the pain point of her sister, Becky, who needed a dress for a special occasion but couldn't afford it. Meanwhile, the designer suppliers were increasingly concerned about the growth of flash sales sites and fast fashion, which were undermining their business. So, Rent the Runway was meant to serve and solve problems on both sides, by renting—rather than selling—designer dresses and accessories.

Jenny and Jenn believed the potential was huge, as they would be trying to crack a new, younger, Millennial demographic and make the world of luxury fashion more affordable for them. The founders were intent on growing the existing market of young buyers of luxury fashion.

She [Jenn] came up with the initial identification of the problem and the need. It was her sister, Becky, who was purchasing a $2,000 [designer] dress for a wedding, despite the fact that Becky had plenty of other dresses in her closet and didn't have the money to spend on the designer dress. They were wearing them once and throwing them away or it'd sit in their closet.

Meanwhile, from a macroeconomic perspective, the designer industry is facing a lot of issues because there are flash sales happening online and their brands are being deteriorated in the face of fast fashion by Zara, H&M, and Forever 21, who are starting to knock off their products. So, from both sides of the table, there was a need for innovation.

We were able to say, "Okay, there is a need that exists. There are consumers that want to buy these [designer] products but who cannot afford these prices." So we insert ourselves as a way to both let the designers preserve the full retail price, but give people a taste of the product at a lower price point by renting.

JENNY FLEISS, RENT THE RUNWAY

In the case of SkyMD, Eric conducted industry research to assess the size of the dermatology market and to assess what portion of office visits could instead be replaced by use of his app.

We did market research. One of the numbers that was compelling was that there were about 100 million dermatology visits in the U.S. annually. And that 75 percent could be done online based on clinical studies that we had found. Market size didn't feel like a challenge for us.

ERIC PRICE, SKYMD

However, while the market size seemed to be large, Eric didn't adequately vet whether busy city dermatologists would encourage their patients to download the app. Eric assumed that they would, given the utility of the app. But this turned out not to be the case. His mom's contacts with dermatologists did not represent the true willingness of derms to push patients to use the app. Dermatologists were not willing to change their behavior.

The top of the ideation triangle is "large opportunity," and for that you need to be sure that the market is large enough *and* that your solution in that market is truly compelling.

Finally, "large" is a relative notion. What is a large business for someone may not be large enough for someone else. You need to give thought as to whether the business potential is large enough for you. And, importantly, after taking risk into account, what do you believe is the risk-adjusted potential?

I was not focused only on seeking a billion-dollar business. Those are incredibly risky, and you lose control of the venture. I would rather shoot for an opportunity with solid medium upside and lower risk. There are a lot more exits in the $100M to $250M range.

JIM SHERMAN, SHERMANSTRAVEL MEDIA

Do You Need to Reinvent the Wheel?

I firmly believe there are very few, if any, new ideas. And most things have been attempted before. We were not inventing cold fusion.

JOSH HIX, PLATED

Most "innovation" does not introduce entirely new products. In fact, a large majority of innovation improves on an existing product or service. Entirely new innovation is rare.

For the HBS firms, while a few introduced new and improved products or services, the vast majority fall into the category of new business models. They did *not* believe that you must invent something brand-new to be successful. As a matter of fact, most focused on leveraging technologies to disrupt existing industries with better business models. The HBS entrepreneurs were not inventing tech so much as rethinking its use—how existing products or services could be better designed, delivered to solve a problem, enhanced for convenience, or produced and marketed for lower cost. Most of the time, they were targeting existing markets. They are mostly what we call "tech-enabled" business ventures.

Common to all of them is that they were driven by the desire to solve a need.

For example, in the case of SkyMD, Eric targeted an existing market—dermatologists and their patients. He was not inventing dermatology but he and his cofounder, his mom, believed that the advent of the smartphone's new camera capabilities made it possible to get an accurate diagnosis via online and use of their app. The business potential seemed huge.

In talking to my mother and some other dermatologists, they said that pretty much everything they would see on a daily basis could be solved through images. Part of our user research also confirmed that.

ERIC PRICE, SKYMD

Matt recounts Blue Apron's core appeal and the fact that they were not inventing any new technology and instead upended the business model for buying grocery ingredients, all the while making it a lot more convenient for the consumer. They were not changing the fact that consumers like to eat.

One of the things that gave me a lot of confidence is that people cook and eat already, right? We weren't inventing Twitter, where it was, like, this is a brand-new product.

We were trying to help people cook at home better, easier, and more affordably. I knew that if we could do that, we'd have a big market for it.

MATT SALZBERG, BLUE APRON

RubiconMD also crafted an attractive business model for medical professionals and insurance firms. With their enabling a faster, easier connection between primary care physicians and specialists and ultimately saving insurance companies money, the founders did not disintermediate medical specialists in health care. They made the process of gathering their advice more efficient by using online communications tools. In other words, they made an existing behavior easier and more convenient.

This isn't a magic algorithm that's going to predict a rare form of cancer. No, this is something that we can execute on.

GIL ADDO, RUBICONMD

A lot of the HBS businesses have value-adds that are convenience-focused, leveraging existing technology to make a product or service more convenient and sometimes cheaper. Many expanded an existing market and fostered behavior changes.

With the one non-HBS-founded firm, Bespoke Post, the founders, Steve and Rishi (who graduated from the Kellogg School of Management at Northwestern University) also tapped into the internet to deliver on convenience—in their case a service that targets men. The need was not an explicit one, but once men tried their monthly service, they liked the regular curation of cool products conveniently delivered to the home.

At the time, nobody was doing much in men's e-commerce. We thought, everybody's doing all these interesting things in commerce for women, so there's a hole in the men's space. And that'd be cool, if we actually sold physical products, then I could make a meaningful contribution to that.

STEVE SZARONOS, BESPOKE POST

In another example of bringing convenience to an old, traditional industry, Justin of Henry the Dentist didn't change dentistry, but he made the service a lot more convenient for office workers to get their checkups with his mobile clinics. The service delivery model is what makes for a different and appealing business model improvement.

Henry is taking an existing industry and an existing service, not asking people to change their behavior. People want dental services. . . .

What I'm doing, I'm literally bringing the dental clinic to your office. It's high-end. Well branded. You're back to your desk forty-five minutes later. Insurance pays. It's free for you.

People have an awesome experience. You come in there; the fun music is playing. You get Bose noise-canceling headphones. You're watching Netflix or HBO. You've got a massage chair. It's great.

JUSTIN JOFFE, HENRY THE DENTIST

In some cases, you do not even need to change the business model or invent a new product; you just want to execute better than others do. As an example, Adore Me improves product quality in an already established product category—in their case, lingerie.

It's not about revolutionizing the world. There are hundreds of thousands of companies created in the U.S. every year. Maybe 0.1 percent of them are innovations. The rest don't need an idea, they just need to do things better. That is how the world evolves.

The ones we talk about all the time: Facebook, Google, Apple . . . You name it. Truth is, the real innovation in most companies that are successful comes from how you do things, not from what you do, which is the easy part.

It is about executing better. We sell bras. That's very basic. But the way we do things, if you compare Adore Me to Victoria's Secret, is 100 percent different. This is the unconventional side I would love to talk about. Because we spend our life challenging the way things are done. We have an unconventional way of looking at everything: how we do shootings, how we sort the products, pretty much everything we do.

MORGAN HERMAND-WAICHE, ADORE ME

Lastly, Gilt found inspiration (some would say copied) in a European business, the flash sale e-commerce site Vente-Privee (now Veepee). The founders imported the business model, but they made crucial adjustments for the U.S. market. Those changes—which may seem small—did make a huge difference between success and failure.

We did a lot of things differently in the U.S. Now it's hard to appreciate so much of the innovation that we did back then because a lot of things have become normal today. Even in the way we photographed all of our inventory, we made the decision to shoot on models, which a lot of the full-price luxury department stores didn't do at the time. They would shoot on mannequins or flat inventory. We were like, no, we want to make this look beautiful. It made for a very different experience than the off-price industry of companies like Loehmann's, TJ Maxx, and Filene's Basement. I've certainly shopped at all of them. But they don't feel like an elevated experience. We wanted ours to be special and elevated and beautiful and exciting.

ALEXANDRA WILKIS WILSON, GILT

RELEVANT SKILLS (NOT TO BE CONFUSED WITH INDUSTRY EXPERTISE)

I had to find a business that I understood, that I could execute on, and that I truly enjoyed.

JUSTIN JOFFE, HENRY THE DENTIST

The second leg of the ideation triangle is relevant skills for your business venture. What is absolutely critical—and what founders talked about at the stage of idea exploration—are two skills: the skill to *understand your customer* and the *critical skills to run your business*. The latter will vary depending on the nature of your business.

Skills should not be confused with industry expertise. As we will see later, industry expertise can even play against you if you are coming up with new business models and want to disrupt the status quo.

As a founder (or founding team), you don't need to have all skills in-house by definition. You can in some circumstances hire people with the needed skills.

Ensuring that you have all the relevant skills needed for the business is not only crucial for crafting the optimal launch and scale-up team, it will also impact how investors view the founder's fit for the opportunity (see our chapters on fundraising). Investors want to know why your venture fits with your skill set. Having "founder fit" is as important as achieving product/market fit.

One of the most basic yet critical skills is to understand your customer. And what better way to do that than to be your own customer. It certainly helps to more naturally understand the customer mindset and empathize with the customer. Many of the HBS founders were *the ideal target customer* for their business and were well positioned to understand what the customer wants.

For example, Dave and his wife, Joanna, ultimately came upon the idea for Yumble Kids to solve a major pain point in their own lives. Joanna felt a lot of stress preparing healthy meals for her children every week. She was certain that other moms felt the same way and felt there was an explicit need there.

In 2015, we had a five-year-old, a three-year-old, and a one-year-old. You don't necessarily want them eating frozen processed chicken nuggets and pizza and mac and cheese every single night. We were trying to solve our own pain at that point.

DAVE PARKER, YUMBLE KIDS

In the case of Gilt, both Alexandra and Alex were their own target customers. Alexandra would often seek deep discounts on fashion clothing at retail outlets. Even her friends would ask her to buy things because she was so on top of the sample sales.

People would be texting, "If you see something in my size, whatever it is, pick it up for me." That was always on our mind. We understood that consumer mindset.

ALEXANDRA WILKIS WILSON, GILT

Although it can help to *be* your customer, many founders went after ideas far from their own profiles. The key in this case is to have enough *empathy* to understand your customer. As an example, Morgan's profile puts him the furthest away from his customers: women's lingerie buyers.

I think you don't need to be your customer, you need to understand your customer. Sometimes customers don't understand their own selves. You just need very strong empathy and emotional intelligence, which is something that I really try to equip myself with a lot every day.

MORGAN HERMAND-WAICHE, ADORE ME

In addition to having empathy skills for your customer, you should have the *relevant skills* for building your business over time. The more tech- or science-focused the venture is then the more you (or a co-founder) need to have technology or science skills. If the venture is a media business, then you should have skills related to creating an editorial product and to selling advertising and subscriptions, depending on the business model.

Jim recalls how he possessed the relevant skills to launch ShermansTravel, an early website that curates travel deals from advertisers.

As a passionate traveler myself, I felt that I intimately knew how travelers would use the internet to research travel. I also had a media background, having worked in publishing and online media before. And one of the crucial skills to launch the business would be selling ad sponsorships. I felt that I could be good at that. I didn't like selling widgets but I liked selling an audience.

JIM SHERMAN, SHERMANSTRAVEL MEDIA

While it is critical to know which skills are key, it is okay if you—as a founder—do not have these skills, especially if they are functional. Indeed, if you are a good leader and manager, you will be able to surround yourself with people who complement your own set of skills.

As an example, neither Matt of Blue Apron nor Morgan of Adore Me was their target customer, and neither had what one might expect to be key skills for their ventures.

Matt was not a chef. He was not a food enthusiast. He didn't have an operations background. But he had excellent skills in strategy and fundraising. And he knew that to be successful, the business would require a tremendous amount of capital to fund it to a large enough scale to become profitable.

I didn't know anything about how to manage people, or how to run a perishable supply chain. That was the stuff I had to learn. But the financing, the governance, the strategy—those were what I had learned beforehand.

MATT SALZBERG, BLUE APRON

As we will see later, Matt carefully complemented his founding team by attracting people with the right functional skills.

Meanwhile, Morgan of Adore Me launched in a market in which he had no background. He didn't know anything about designing, manufacturing, and selling women's lingerie. But he articulates how his analytical and people skills would serve him to pull it off.

I had no prior background in lingerie or e-commerce. My only experience was two years as a general consultant at McKinsey. And prior to that, I had a degree in computer science and physics. I had never done anything working in fashion, retail, [or] lingerie. I didn't know shit about shit.

We [as founders] can define our skill set later because, as I said, I didn't know anything about lingerie or e-commerce. And clearly, in my world, knowledge is not part of the skill set. Skill set is different. It is a combination of characteristics such as analytical skills, people skills, motivation. This whole thing would be a skill set, but not prior knowledge of an industry.

MORGAN HERMAND-WAICHE, ADORE ME

Industry Expertise Can Play Against You

I think when you come from outside of an industry, you're a little bit naïve and you're not as jaded, which can be helpful. It means you're able to think more creatively and think outside the box. It means you're often able to approach people like Diane von Furstenberg, whom you otherwise might be intimidated by, because you know about her and her important background. You go after bigger dreams with a new perspective. So, net to net, I don't know that this concept [Rent the Runway] would come from someone who worked in the fashion industry for years.

JENNY FLEISS, RENT THE RUNWAY

Not coming from an industry allows you to rethink it—to have a fresh logical look. To be (more) creative. And to get a chance at disrupting it.

Jenn and Jenny from Rent the Runway strongly believed that women would like to rent fashion clothing, particularly for special events. They knew that the participation of fashion brands would be crucial for their business concept but they did not know if those brands would be willing to do so. The concept of renting clothes was entirely new.

They reached out early on to Diane von Furstenberg, the famous fashion designer, for feedback. Diane's initial response was not enthusiastic and she discouraged them. She believed fashion brands would be reluctant to make their clothes available via such a channel and doubted that women would wish to rent clothing.

Other industry experts that they approached also had doubts. Fortunately for the founders, they did not rely only on these opinions. They persevered. They kept to the concept and by 2021 Rent the Runway had raised $450M, had more than 100,000 subscribers and went public.

In almost all cases, the founders who had no industry expertise were more willing to ask "Why not?" They were open to new ideas in industries where insiders were likely to see the obstacles to something new. Being an outsider allows for innovative thinking.

Alexandra sums it up succinctly as she reflects on Gilt and her outsider status.

People in the industry might not have attempted this.

ALEXANDRA WILKIS WILSON, GILT

Anthemos of Zumper and Anthony of Dot & Bo also reflect on how coming from within an industry can often be a disadvantage.

Sometimes I think it may be an advantage [to come from outside the industry]. If you don't come from the industry, you are more likely to try and disrupt things.

I think if you come from the industry and you then try to redesign, it's much harder because there is always a reason why things shouldn't change. Whereas I think that if you are from the outside, where you come in fresh, you can redesign it. You have less experience, but your endgame vision is probably more innovative because of that reason.

ANTHEMOS GEORGIADES, ZUMPER

If you want to innovate in any space, my belief is that you need to not know anything about the business. Innovation comes from a lack of resources. With forced constraints, as well as the fact that you have a new view on a market, that's how people innovate.

ANTHONY SOOHOO, DOT & BO

An important point to keep in mind is that if you need industry expertise, you can always attract it with advisors, key hires, or even (junior) cofounders. For example, Justin from Henry the Dentist was entering the dental industry. Yet he is not a dentist. So, while going through the stage of assessing his idea, he reached out to an industry insider who could help validate his business concept and also design the mobile clinic. Justin also needed someone with a dentist's license to be able to operate. He found this with Jeff, whom he brought on as an early partner.

Jeff [dentist and industry expert] was my last filter [to validate the idea]. But I needed Jeff because I'm also not a dentist. The only part of the dental business I don't know is dentistry! I had Jeff. It was important for credibility and the team, but also legally I'm not allowed to own a dental practice.

JUSTIN JOFFE, HENRY THE DENTIST

PASSION FOR THE OPPORTUNITY

Passion shouldn't be underestimated. If you are Amazon or Apple, people will listen—they will answer calls. As a startup, you have to use your personal energy and persuasion to get people to listen. I recall how hard it was to recruit key talent in the early stages of the business. That requires founder's passion. Striking business deals with big brands also requires passion. Not to mention fundraising. And sales: for sure, no one can sell to a customer better than a founder who should radiate passion and determination.

JIM SHERMAN, SHERMANSTRAVEL MEDIA

Rounding out the last leg of the ideation triangle is passion. You must pair a large opportunity and relevant skills with your passion for the opportunity.

Sure, passion is your fuel, necessary to get through the rough patches during all phases of a business. But passion is also what enables you to recruit a team, convince investors to back you, and attract customers to your offering.

There is no chance that any of the HBS businesses could have been successful without founder passion for their nascent ventures. One has to be truly passionate about the idea and the product to be successful.

Some of the entrepreneurs we talked to compared their passion for their current ventures with previous ones. For example, Justin reflects on the venture that he had before Henry the Dentist. It was a collection of hair salons that did *not* get him excited at all.

I wasn't passionate about the thing that we did. I didn't care about hair blowouts and manicurists and laser hair removal.

JUSTIN JOFFE, HENRY THE DENTIST

But today, his passion for what he is doing for patients is entirely different, in that it is "all heart" to him. He enjoys it.

Three and a half years in, it was a grind. But, my view was, it's all heart. It doesn't matter what you do, whether you're a startup or an operator, whether you work in a big company or you work at McKinsey or Google, it's all heart.

JUSTIN JOFFE, HENRY THE DENTIST

Passion is especially important when you're bringing to the market a new solution that solves needs that people are *not even aware of.* When the needs are implicit and even more so require significant behavior change, the more *passion* you will need to propel it forward, to convince yourself and others of its value.

An interesting question is, *What should you be passionate about?* Is it the industry, the product, the impact you are trying to achieve, monetary reward, independence in your life, or the challenge of climbing a mountain?

Ideally you want to be passionate about it all. But what we heard from HBS founders is that the end result and the impact are probably the true driver of passion.

As we talked about earlier, many HBS founders created their ventures to have an impact on society and do good. In that sense, having an impact on people's lives fuels their founder's passion.

Josh from Plated felt that fostering healthy eating is not just good business, it's also good for society. That was a big part of why the founders felt so passionate about their venture.

Food is clearly a huge component of health and wellness, weight management being probably the most obvious. Most folks would agree that eating more fresh food, and in the right portions, is a good thing for all of us.

JOSH HIX, PLATED

3

THE VALUE OF SHALLOW DIVES

> A great idea is only as great
> as its business model.

The business model admittedly came later because we said we're going to put this in a couple of practices and get feedback and start to think about how we monetize. We didn't think as much about the economics of it up front. We thought about it, but we didn't develop a business model until later. That was a mistake.

ERIC PRICE, SKYMD

Whether your idea came about organically or through a deliberate ideation process, by the time you set your mind to it, you undoubtedly believe that it is worth pursuing. You believe the opportunity is large, that you have relevant skills, and that your passion will enable you to succeed. But the ultimate test for your idea will come from the customers: *Will they like it? Will they buy it?* and, even more importantly, *Can I make money from it?*

While you won't know for sure until you have a beta version to sell, there are a few things you want to check before further investing (whether time or money) in your idea. Shallow dives allow you to quickly evaluate an idea and gain visibility into its potential. Shallow dives should at the minimum include the following:

- Am I really solving a meaningful problem (or satisfying a need)?
- Am I riding a wave?
- What are the building blocks of the business model? Can I pull it off?
- Can the (unit) economics fly?

At this stage, you are not looking for detailed analyses and all the answers, but you want to convince yourself that the idea is worth pursuing and investing in (time and some money).

ARE YOU SOLVING A MEANINGFUL PROBLEM?

Traditional research (any relevant industry data) can provide useful information on the size of the opportunity. Total addressable market (TAM) and serviceable addressable market (SAM) are common concepts used to estimate market size and your business potential. But they won't tell you if your idea is a good one. To vet your idea's attractiveness, it behooves you to check that the problem you are solving has tremendous appeal by speaking to lots of people. You should be "sniffing out" the opportunity by talking with potential customers, industry experts, partners, and anyone else you can think of.

Many entrepreneurs don't spend enough time talking to others about their idea. This is a crucial step because too often founders believe in their idea, but it doesn't match with the reality after they get going.

Be aware that when you talk to a lot of people, you will find it much easier to qualify *out* an idea than qualifying one in.

With Henry the Dentist, Justin strove to qualify his idea before he had any prototype to show, before he spent any money on building his mobile clinic. He was not shy in asking anyone that he could.

I don't believe in this idea of keeping your idea secret because someone's going to steal it. They're not. And if they do, it's all about execution anyways. I believe in talking about it. Go to parties and talk about it and get the reactions. Find the experts in the space and ask them. I asked them all. I went on YPO's [Young Presidents' Organization] network and I found the CEO of Heartland Dental, who runs the biggest potential competitor to me, and I just asked him.

I don't think you actually should listen to the specific advice of any one person. You should look generally at pattern recognition, where people fall on the bell curve. You're always going to have a certain percentage of people that said, "Dumb idea. I don't like it. Stupid. Don't do it." There are going to be the other extreme people that say, "Oh my God, I love it. That's amazing. Best thing since sliced bread," and they're overenthusiastic. And you have to most likely quiet those extremes.

You can probably qualify out more ideas than you can qualify in. To qualify in, you're not going to probably know until you start. I think we qualified out a lot.

The consumer question of "Would you use this service?" was ultimately the question that I asked of every single business idea that I was thinking about. "Would you buy it? Would you use it if I did this? If I build it, will you come?"

JUSTIN JOFFE, HENRY THE DENTIST

In seeking pattern recognition, as Justin mentions, be aware that not all people who answer your questions are of equal value. We're sure you value the opinion of certain friends over others, but as we will see in the Feedback chapter, they are often biased.

When I was considering doing Sweetwell, I talked to many people who were close to me. I pitched the product and got tremendous feedback and encouragement, which convinced me to go for it. If I reflect back, most of that feedback was too enthusiastic and not taking into account the difficulties of pulling it off. The feedback from true experts and customers, which came later, was much more nuanced.

CATALINA DANIELS, SWEETWELL

In the example of Plated, Josh confirms the importance of talking directly with consumers, avoiding friends-and-family bias. In his case, their vetting actually took place by running some early tests with a rudimentary website.

I definitely believe there's a difference between qualitative and quantitative research. We weren't trying to build an enormous cohort of statistically significant data and all these things to prove to ourselves there's some level of product/market fit. There's a qualitative, more conviction-oriented thing that you develop in the early days. These are not friends and family. We trial with them first, but they're obviously sort of biased. We had enough people, strangers, spending $60, $70, $80 with us. They were trusting us to deliver the food. Cook it, eat it, and do it again.

JOSH HIX, PLATED

Talking directly to your target customers is also a means to avoid bias by industry experts. The founders of Bespoke Post believed that there was a market opportunity to better serve men, particularly the Millennial guy, with a monthly box of cool, attractive products curated along a theme. However, when they approached a number of e-commerce experts, many didn't believe men would buy much online aside from technology products and games. Bespoke Post launched anyway, following their beliefs and passion, and today exceeds 300,000 subscribers to its monthly box. Steve confirms the importance of talking to enough people and making sure that you don't rely on the feedback of just one person.

No one person should influence how you feel about something more than a few percentage points. However, if you talk to enough people and they move you 10 percent, if you get thirty people to tell you this isn't a great idea, then maybe you should start reevaluating what it is you're doing.

STEVE SZARONOS, BESPOKE POST

When asking people for feedback, whether it be experts, customers, or others, beware that on average they will feel most comfortable telling you that your idea is "okay." That is why (as we will see in chapter 6) you should expect to get *really* positive feedback.

Most people, when you interview them, tell you to your face that your idea is good. And especially when you talk to customers, unless your idea is completely bat shit crazy, they will say things like, "Oh, that's cool. If that existed, I'd look at that. I'd buy that." They're not going to tell you to your face, "Hey, you're a complete idiot."

Of course, no sweat off their back to let you put in all the hard work to build some product that they could have an option to evaluate as a customer later.

MATT SALZBERG, BLUE APRON

ARE YOU RIDING A WAVE?

The central question for a lot of new companies, especially technology-centric companies, is "Why now? What has changed in the world that makes this possible now?" Which is a way of answering the question of why past attempts have failed.

JOSH HIX, PLATED

Most entrepreneurs we interviewed became successful not only because of their idea, but because they launched it at the right time. They were lucky or, in some cases, had the vision to anticipate changes that would create the right circumstances for growth. Luck or smart anticipation? Most would say there is a mix of both.

It's typically easier to succeed in a fast-growing market—or what we call "riding a wave"—than one in decline or one that's flat. Of course, there are cases of companies being successful in a stagnant or even declining market if they offer a disruptive proposition that solves a problem; in such a case, one can do well.

But with our cohort of HBS entrepreneurs, most benefited from the positive effect of a rising tide. They had an inkling of what was coming based on observing trends or emerging technologies. They may have taken a step back to reflect on what trends were emerging, how the world was changing, and how this could create opportunities— opportunities stemming from new needs of people and of companies. But few imagined the full force of these rising tides. Jim recalls the boom of Internet 1.0 in the late 1990s, when he launched WestEnd New Media, his internet strategy consultancy.

With the advent of the internet, it was clear to me that businesses were going to pour money into the launch of new web ventures. They needed advice and few people understood the web at the time. Did I really know the extent of this new wave driven by the internet revolution? No. But I knew it would be big, and I wanted a piece of it.

JIM SHERMAN, WESTEND NEW MEDIA

As you think about your business ideas, a key question that you need to ask is "Why now?" What market factors are taking place that can support a fledgling new business?

These might include changes in user or customer behavior that are often driven by new technologies and new platforms, the emergence of

new marketing channels, the growth of a new demographic, or changing macroeconomic conditions.

The rise of the internet led to the launch of many new businesses,
including, by the mid-2000s, an explosion of e-commerce ventures.
Anthony's Dot & Bo benefited from this growth along with the trend of
merging online content with commerce.

*I noticed a majority of people were calling in to CBS trying to buy products
from their favorite TV shows. They wanted to buy the couch on* How I Met
Your Mother. *They wanted to buy the driftwood on* Survivor. *It was odd and
fascinating that people were shopping while they were being entertained.*

*Initially, I had three insights. The main concept was that media was go-
ing to be consumed in a different way because of mobile. It left an opening
for new entrants to enter the space. Number two, the majority of the media
models at the time were ad driven. If you look at ads, eventually they're
trying to sell you something. If that was the case, what if you just collapsed
that and made a site where everything you considered an ad was actually
content?*

*The third insight was that e-commerce is probably a better business model
than an advertising-based media model. My goal going in was to build a
media company that monetized with an e-commerce business model.*

ANTHONY SOOHOO, DOT & BO

Similarly, the meal kit companies bet on changing consumer behavior. Matt explained how he viewed that consumers would eventually
buy groceries online. While they hadn't been buying much in the way
of groceries up to that point, consumers were in fact buying everything
else online. He believed the grocery category would ultimately be disrupted. The meal kit firms, such as his, benefited from that eventual
shift in consumer behavior, and the consumer's increasing willingness
to buy fresh ingredients online.

Both Plated and Blue Apron also benefited from another trend—

the rapid rise of Facebook as a huge new marketing channel. Facebook opened up a landscape of opportunity for businesses that could thrive by leveraging its revolutionary ad-targeting capabilities.

In its early days, Facebook allowed brands to post messages that surfaced for *free* on the news feeds of those people who "liked" the companies. While the free promotion did not last very long (since Facebook eventually wanted brands to pay for such promotion), there were many startups that took advantage of this powerful new marketing capability.

For us, the "why now" was a number of things—social media probably the biggest of which. Facebook was relatively new at the time. They were two or three years public, early in their life cycle.

Acquiring customers on Facebook was easy and cheap. You could do it with a budget of $10 a day and hypertarget people. And that was a new thing in the world in 2012. That's gone now.

As one data point: When we got started, remembering back to that era, everyone wanted you to like their page. The reason they wanted you to do that was you could reach close to 100 percent with an organic [free] post. I could go on to the Facebook Plated business page and post a piece of content, which was really just an ad, and 80 percent of our audience would actually see it. If we had 100,000 followers, I could reach 80,000 people a day for free.

JOSH HIX, PLATED

Rising tides occur not just from emerging new marketing channels, changes in customer preferences (sometimes driven by demographics shifts) and new technologies (think of AI, cloud computing, robotics, and many other technologies that are driving new business ventures). For example, the rise of the smartphone and apps enabled a whole series of new businesses—from Uber to Seamless—that appeal to customer convenience. That was Anthemos's experience with Zumper.

At the time I went to HBS, the biggest trend which made me quite bullish that now is the right time, was going to be mobile. iOS and Android apps were becoming quite common. The iPhone 3 had just come out. I thought that was a really interesting time to execute the idea because we could actually empower renters and open houses from their phones to search and then transact for an apartment rental.

ANTHEMOS GEORGIADES, ZUMPER

The challenge is that waves are very hard to predict—none harder than a macroeconomic shock.

In 2008, the recession that followed from the unexpected financial meltdown was an uncontrollable crisis that helped Gilt. Luxury fashion clothing brands, suffering from slow sales at department stores, suddenly decided they needed to work with Gilt to move volume.

The world started to implode in 2008. For us, it was actually lucky in the sense that brands that originally had been in a position to be picky and choosy and say no, they were all in these cash crunches. Department stores were returning all the inventory to them. We literally kept the lights on for them. I can think of ten brands that wouldn't have made it past that time if we hadn't shown up and said, "Sure, we'll buy $100,000 worth of inventory."

The recession was great because then we got access to the best of the best inventory.

ALEXANDRA WILKIS WILSON, GILT

In business school, it's classic training to focus on industries that are high growth. However, if an industry is already experiencing high growth, you might be late to the table to benefit from that growth.

As soon as you observe the rising tide, you're too late. The people who were on the rising tide, they're on the rising tide two years earlier. That strategy of identifying the rising tide and participating in it: I quickly learned I was too late by that point. The places that I was looking were places that the world had already identified as the rising tide. If Profit *magazine,* Fast Company, *and* CB Insights *and* Crunchbase *were already pooling trends, well, then I'm too late to the party. That was my "aha."*

JUSTIN JOFFE, HENRY THE DENTIST

Timing—the *why now* question—is one of the critical factors in the success or failure of your venture—growth of the sector you are active in and/or the advent of technologies that facilitate new business models. The more you are a visionary and can anticipate the right trends and rising tides, the more successful you will be. But frankly, for most, it will be sheer luck. In all cases, it is healthy to think about timing and how it influences your idea's attractiveness.

WHAT ARE THE BUILDING BLOCKS OF THE BUSINESS MODEL AND CAN YOU PULL IT OFF?

Are we crazy? Can we actually make it work? Do the physics of it work? Can we ship fresh food in the mail, and have it show up fresh? And have people do this? And will they enjoy it enough to want to buy it again?

JOSH HIX, PLATED

An idea needs to turn into a product and a product needs to turn into a business. And there is a big difference between an idea and a business. You can have what seems to be a great idea, but if badly executed or saddled with the wrong model, it will not turn into a great business.

In the ideation stage, you want to make sure that you define the "arms and legs" of your idea. The business model encompasses all elements needed to bring your idea to life: the product, pricing, marketing, operations, distribution, technology, partners, competition, and more.

In Plated's case, Josh explained that they realized early on that shipping fresh food by mail—every week with new recipes—is not a trivial matter. It's intense. They needed to convince themselves that they could pull it off operationally.

At this stage, you don't want detailed answers—business models evolve over time to reflect a changing environment—but you should be kicking the tires to know enough about its profitability, what's crucial for your operational focus, and who your ideal first customers are. In addition, you want to feel that you are up for the challenge and will be able to succeed.

You also want to be on the alert for any red flags—are there land mines? Can you efficiently acquire customers with your go-to-market strategy? What operational inputs do you need to get going? If you need a warehouse, fulfillment center, or co-packer, can you find the right partner? What critical talent are you missing on the team? How intense is the competition? What's the financing needed to get going? And over the life of the business?

In RubiconMD's early days, Gil sought out an industry health care expert to help him evaluate if his idea was good. In particular, he knew that he needed to vet the assumption that insurance would pay for his service. This would be a critical hurdle. While patients are the end user of medical care, it's the insurance firms that are the main payers. There was not going to be a large opportunity without insurance paying for his venture's service. Would they cover this?

So, to get that critical input, he managed to meet with Bob Lufrano, the former chairman of Blue Cross and Blue Shield of Florida. Bob's advice was crucial in understanding that insurance firms would likely agree to reimburse if Gil could show real savings or return on investment (ROI) from the doctors using the service.

To check the business model assumptions, you want to focus on the aspects that truly matter and will make a difference.

For all entrepreneurs with no exception, this includes the question of *How will you market your product?* We have met many entrepreneurs who focus on their product and the operations but neglect marketing.

They assume that everyone will just love their product or service because it is great. This is a dangerous assumption.

You need to have a sense of how you will acquire and retain customers and what their lifetime value may be. Entrepreneurs often don't spend sufficient time thinking about the marketing model. Surely your potential investors, employees, and partners will want to know more about this—especially if the product's need is less than explicit.

With the HBS companies, Gilt and Rent the Runway built virality into the business. Gilt's focus on incredible designer savings led women to spread the word, while their "invitation-only" model helped to make their offering even more special. Rent the Runway encouraged users to share pictures on Instagram of their elegant clothing worn for special occasions.

We never wanted it to be snooty in terms of our tone. It was about getting consumers excited about something, getting them to feel special in being part of this by invitation only community—a members-only community where members told lots of others about it.

ALEXANDRA WILKIS WILSON, GILT

Consumer businesses can require a lot of money to build their customer base, hence any financier is going to be sensitive to your marketing economics.

With B2B ventures, similarly, there are crucial sales and marketing economics. An enterprise-focused product or service will likely involve the hiring of an expensive direct sales team. You need to give thought as to what it will take to get and convert prospects into customers—the cost of sales and how long it will take.

Beyond the sales and marketing side, you want to have an idea of your other *key operational hurdles*. And what these will cost. This was critical in the case of Plated, as Josh described above.

For CrossBoundary, the main operational challenge was hiring the right talent. Finding talent was crucial to delivering on their consulting services. Without the talent, they could not sell engagements. Plus, they had to time the hiring of costly talent to revenue coming in from projects.

You also want to assess your *competitive environment*. That includes direct competitors if you are entering an existing market, like Adore Me, as well as indirect competitors if you are offering a substitute that is different but would take business away from existing players (for example, the meal kit firms).

The good news is that existing players may present de-risking for you. They have validated the market opportunity, and what looks like a viable business model already exists. On the other hand, muscling in your venture may be challenging unless it is adequately differentiated.

For Anthemos's Zumper, there were already several other competing sites offering the search piece for apartment rentals. They validated that a large user base existed. Yet Zumper banked on the idea of combining search with a closed transaction, enabling a better user experience.

In terms of the competitive landscape, there were a lot of people playing in search already: Zillow or Apartments.com. But no one was playing with the transaction, closing the deal.

ANTHEMOS GEORGIADES, ZUMPER

The flip side of all this is, what if you find no competitors—is that a red flag? In the case of Yumble Kids, Dave thought that there had to be competitors. He was astonished that there were none.

I said to Joanna, "I bet you if we googled it for five minutes, we'd find a hundred VC-backed companies that are three years ahead of us." Well, we googled it for more than five minutes and didn't find anything.

It was shocking. I said, "Red flag. Maybe no one wants this. Maybe this is just a problem that you and your friends have. Let's test it."

DAVE PARKER, YUMBLE KIDS

There is no one answer when it comes to competition. Your success will depend on what you offer and how unique it is in addressing a need, even if there is existing direct competition.

Every business has several core competencies that ultimately can become competitive advantages. At this stage, focus on these building blocks, sniff out what it will take to stack them, and assess if you are up to the challenge.

WILL THE (UNIT) ECONOMICS FLY?

I spent most of my time, before we did our first deliveries, validating the unit economics of what I thought the business could ultimately achieve and what the operating model of the business could be.

Part of the key was getting good unit economics at an affordable price point for the consumer. We want to figure out how to disrupt the supply chain and how to get fresher food to people at better prices.

MATT SALZBERG, BLUE APRON

As Matt explains, you should get a sense for your financials and margins. You might be able to turn your idea into a business, but it won't succeed if you lose money and have no prospect of turning your losses into profits.

Here again, you don't need to dive into complex spreadsheets, but you need to have a sense of what the operating economics of the business will look like. This does not mean detailed financial planning but rather directional (unit) economics. This includes understanding your gross margins—at launch and what they will likely be at scale. The tighter the gross margins, the harder it is to cover your sales, marketing, and other expenses. This impacts your financing needs.

You also need to assess any capital expenses or product development costs that you will incur to launch your business. These are part of the economic equation that influences how much money you need to raise—and when.

We realize that there are many companies that are not focused on profits, such as private company unicorns and even companies who IPO'd (think of Uber). A number of ventures cite user growth, but without any monetization strategy. That being said, such ventures that are unconcerned with ongoing losses are particularly risky. If financing dries up, you will run into trouble (for a disastrous case in point, see WeWork).

I don't believe in all-or-nothing. I believe in playing a calculated, safe play, and making sure that you're better tomorrow than you were yesterday. This "build an unprofitable pool of customers and one day you turn on the tap to make them profitable," I just don't think makes sense.

JUSTIN JOFFE, HENRY THE DENTIST

The unit economics is not just an issue of how profitable the venture can be at scale. It impacts the need for financing over the life of the business. We see lots of businesses that forecast improvements in gross margin with greater scale, but then fail to achieve them. The worse the unit economics and timing of cash flow *are*, the more intense the need for financing will be.

With the HBS firms, on one end of the spectrum are businesses such as CrossBoundary and WestEnd New Media. Both of these companies required no external financing. They produced positive margins and cash flow quickly from consulting services, and the founders chose to match the hiring of staff (their principal costs) with projects in their respective work pipelines.

On the other end of the spectrum are a number of ventures such as Gilt Group, Rent the Runway, and Blue Apron, who took in hundreds of millions of dollars each in funding to fuel their rapid growth and achieve profitability at scale.

Vetting your idea's economics means you will better understand the ballpark financing needs of your venture.

In sum, once you have landed your idea, make sure you check a couple of things before investing too much money and time. You want to make sure that you are not the only one thinking that it is a good idea addressing a large need, that you have thought about timing and about the business model and unit economics. You need to assess these factors only at a high level but sufficiently to feel confident that you are not dreaming.

4

THE FOUNDING TEAM THAT'S RIGHT FOR YOU

> There is no one answer to the team. It's okay to
> go solo or team up with your spouse, best friend,
> or whoever is more right for you.

As an entrepreneur, your team is everything. You can have the idea, but you're not doing everything from building the tool to sales and marketing to customer service. You're ultimately enabling the success of your team to deliver on your vision.

ANNA AUERBACH, WERK

There is a myth that the perfect founding team is either two or three people—a CEO, CTO, and perhaps a CMO. Our interviewees burst that bubble.

With the HBS cohort, we saw everything. Single founders and founding teams with more than four. Married couples. Best friends. Mom and son. Cofounders recruited by headhunters. The founding team comes in all shapes and sizes. It all can work. What's critical is finding the right solution *for you*.

It is not surprising that investors invest in teams. They know that ideas evolve, that so much is unpredictable, that pivots will be necessary, and that the venture stands or falls with the team. VC professionals, especially seed and other early-stage investors, regularly explain that the team is their number one factor for evaluation when deciding whether to invest. Whatever your team ends up being, it is the foundation of it all. The team *is* the startup.

We heard from most founders that having the mythical twosome (CEO and CTO) or threesome (CEO, CTO, CXO) would *not* have been the right setup for them. They did not feel they needed it and were more comfortable alone or with one other cofounder.

Building your founding team is, without a doubt, one of the most important decisions you will make in your venture.

DO YOU EVEN NEED A COFOUNDER?

Are you the kind of person who prefers to share the ups and downs with somebody else? A partner with whom to bounce ideas and who provides motivation and support? Are you willing to be diluted early on with a cofounder? Or are you concerned about making fast decisions—and smart decisions—alone?

Morgan of Adore Me was a bit unlike most of the other entrepreneurs with whom we met in his forthrightness to prefer making decisions quickly himself—although he goes on to explain he was "not alone."

Being alone has many advantages in the early phase. Advantage number one, in a period where flexibility is probably one of your best assets—you do not need to vet any decision with someone else that might slow down the process of adapting along the way.

Number two, in terms of motivation, when you have 100 percent of the company and not 50 (or a lesser split), it makes a big difference to motivate you in the long term. At the end of the day, if you have not much left over in the company, how do you motivate yourself to stay there for the long run? Maybe that's also why the biggest companies are solo founders, because they're still incentivized, even when the company is bigger, to do something.

No, I am not alone. When you start a company, in your social network of family, friends, colleagues at school or work, whatever it is, tons of people are excited to support you. You have friends that are strong in finance, friends strong in tech. And they'll all help you.

But do you need a cofounder? No. What a cofounder brings for most people: emotional support, that maybe they feel they're going to get comfort in their own decision-making. It requires some level of confidence to say, "I'll do it," on your own, versus if you're two people to say, "We'll do it," maybe it's easier to make the jump.

MORGAN HERMAND-WAICHE, ADORE ME

Morgan hits on the key assets of a partner—sharing the work, critical business advice in decision-making, and emotional support. But for him, he personally did not feel he needed any of this. He could hire others for work that was needed to get done and he felt he could gather advice and emotional support from other places.

In another example, Justin from Henry the Dentist wanted to build the business entirely his way and make quick decisions. He felt that he did not need a cofounder, but only a passive junior partner. So Justin brought in Matt, a dentist, who had the needed dental industry expertise. Justin felt he didn't lack any emotional support or energy to build the business primarily on his own.

I wanted to have the freedom to make decisions and I wanted to move fast. I didn't want to create processes. I wanted to work from my apartment or We-

Work when I wanted and how I wanted. I'm incredibly self-driven and moti-
vated. I didn't need a partner to share the motivation or drive the workload.
I had a dentist who was a small, passive dental partner. But I didn't need
a technical cofounder. I wasn't missing a skill set. I didn't need someone in
the trenches to keep me motivated or share those scary moments. I've been
through the scary moments enough. I cried in the corner of my office enough
times. I don't need somebody to console me for that. I was starting my own
company to build it my way. I didn't want a cofounder.

JUSTIN JOFFE, HENRY THE DENTIST

However, for other founders, having a partner was crucial in making tough strategic decisions. The close cofounder relationship between Steve and Rishi of Bespoke Post helped them enormously as they pivoted from their initial business idea to their current venture. Steve believes that having Rishi as his partner helped to validate his instinct to abandon their initial business idea (a QR-code-based app), which was not taking off, and to instead pivot to an entirely new direction with their new men's e-commerce venture.

I can't tell you what it would have been like if I was solo. Once one of us
voiced concern, we very quickly got to a point where [we said], "We need to
move off of this." And that probably made it easier. When you're questioning
that and the person that you really trust and you think is smart is also saying
[it], it is validating.

STEVE SZARONOS, BESPOKE POST

So, the bottom line is, what kind of founder are you? Do you want to share the journey with somebody for motivation, emotional support, and better decision-making? And are you willing to part with equity in terms of company ownership? Or do you prefer to do it alone?

...

WHO IS THE RIGHT COFOUNDER FOR YOU?

If you decide that you need a cofounder, it will be critical to create the right founding dynamic and to find a balance of two key factors: shared values and vision, and supplemental skills and experience.

Shared Values and Vision

While we had different skills, we have very, very strong shared vision and values. When people ask, I'd say that's 90 percent of the success of RubiconMD—that we have very shared vision and values and have been able to stay together through a lot of different things along this five-year timeline.

GIL ADDO, RUBICONMD

It's absolutely paramount to have a cofounder with whom you agree on the basics of how to run the business and what the longer-term goal is. If you are not aligned, then you will get into trouble, fast.

Obviously, cofounders can disagree on specific topics, and discussion should help them find a better solution. But when the going gets tough, cofounders need to be able to agree on shared values and vision.

Josh from Plated explains this well. He and his cofounder, Nick, had met during the first days of business school. They came from very different backgrounds and were very different people. HBS brought them together. They had a common passion for health and wellness and wanted to jointly go after it—but could it work long-term?

We [Nick and I] both wanted to do something that had a large social impact, and we had a shared passion in the health and wellness space.

But we also spent a lot of time discussing what our own personal financial *goals were, because that impacts how you finance the business, how you build the capital structure, the valuations you're willing to accept, and what happens if you're so fortunate that somebody shows up in the early days and offers you $50M for the business. It's life-changing generational wealth, but it's not a billion-dollar world-changing business.*

The biggest thing that kills startups is founder conflict. If you're on different pages about what happens when that acquirer shows up and offers you $50M twelve months into the business, it will likely kill your business.

JOSH HIX, PLATED

Conflict can easily emerge throughout the startup and scale-up, especially when things aren't going well. When the business is under duress, founders run a particularly high risk of conflict. As we will see in chapter 17, shared values and vision with your cofounder(s) additionally forms the basis of your startup culture. At the same time, being aligned helps avoid fatal conflict.

Supplemental Skills and Experience

Another important aspect is experience in building a startup and skills to supplement your own. First-time founders with limited management experience can especially benefit from creating a complementary founding team.

I had never run a company. I had never, in fact, even worked at a company other than as an investor. And I was entirely business product marketing oriented and didn't have technical experience. It was important for me to get a cofounder—even if it wasn't a 50/50 one. I was looking for someone who could be the CTO of the business because I was a nontechnical, business-oriented, product-oriented person.

MATT SALZBERG, BLUE APRON

Tech is often a critical part of the success. But success can also depend on skills related to other areas like supply chain, operations, or some specific industry expertise. The key is that ideally you want the founding team to cover the critical skills to make your startup a success.

Matt ended up recruiting Ilia Papas (who had been his cofounder at his previous venture), to become a technical cofounder—a crucial complementary role to Matt's business skills.

Matt also realized he needed someone who knew something about the food industry and recipe development—someone who could craft all the recipes, figure out the right ingredients, and plan the fantastic meals that Blue Apron promised its customers.

I recruited a third cofounder because I thought I needed additional expertise on the team that we didn't have between me and Ilia. Matt Wadiak was a friend of my wife's from many years ago. He had run a catering business that my wife's mom used in her job as the New York State film commissioner. He became our key guy to craft the recipes and plan out the meals.

MATT SALZBERG, BLUE APRON

Matt acted methodically and logically in crafting his launch team with two cofounders. He had strategy and fundraising skills, and he came up with the idea. But he recruited two others to complement himself and fill in for the other skills needed for the meal kit venture.

Meanwhile, in another case, Dot & Bo's founder, Anthony Soohoo, had significant experience both at the corporate level (with Yahoo) and in a startup, having launched and sold a prior business of his. So he had been around the block, and he was familiar with the emerging trends of content and commerce that would underpin Dot & Bo's approach to selling products. Yet he wanted to complement the team's skills with design and tech, which he saw as critical for the venture.

I recruited a designer and an engineer that worked with me prior to my last startup. I brought them in as [junior] cofounders into the company.

ANTHONY SOOHOO, DOT & BO

When you get a cofounder to complement your skills, the key is to agree on who does what—how to split responsibilities. In addition, be careful to ensure that your cofounder will continue to provide the value you expect *over time.* This avoids the chance of resentment that can build when a cofounder with equity isn't pulling his or her weight.

Carlos of RubiconMD recounts how he and Gil had different skill sets despite having similar backgrounds in engineering and business. They divided up the business's responsibilities, recognizing their different skill sets and strengths.

We have, technically, a very similar background. We're both biomedical engineers by training and did MBAs at Harvard. But we see the world differently. We have different skill sets. But we have very complementary skill sets, and it became apparent immediately.

He figured out this platform connecting general doctors to specialists. And I found [medical] specialists through my network. We took different approaches to sales and different approaches to building.

The split in responsibilities happened somewhat organically. He focuses more on product engineering and operations. I focus more on sales, business development, and fundraising. It ended up happening organically. But we both have the ability to step in and can do the other's role.

CARLOS REINES, RUBICONMD

Another consideration is the issue of outsourcing a key function versus finding a cofounder or hiring staff. It depends on how core the skill or expertise is to your venture. If technology is absolutely core, you want to make sure that you get a cofounder on board who is motivated to stay by their shares and ownership of the company.

Anthemos with Zumper hired two engineers from Google as junior cofounders for their apartment rental search and transaction site. For them, the build of a robust search site meant that they needed "founder talent" in engineering. Gilt also had a couple of key software engineers as founders of their team. Eric of SkyMD had a junior founding partner, located in India, to aid in his dermatology mobile app development.

On the other hand, several venture founders initially outsourced the technical development of their e-commerce ventures since it was not viewed as core to their business.

WHERE TO FIND THE RIGHT COFOUNDER?

We met at a Hacking Medicine event at MIT in March. I was pitching to try to get developers to help on coding the platform. Started working on it through the weekend. Kept in touch. I reached out, told him, "Look, we form a pretty great team." We worked together for three, four months before we incorporated. Got a very good sense for our style and how we work well together.

GIL ADDO, RUBICONMD

Many HBS founders had actually known each other well before they became cofounders. Some were family and many were best friends— a departure from conventional wisdom that says, "Don't go into business with family or friends." For those who had met more recently, serendipity played a key role.

Long-standing (Close) Relationships

We had, and still have—which is important to say because sometimes founders split—a great relationship. We're still super close. We really knew each other well. We knew each other's personality strengths and weaknesses, as well as somewhat professionally, too. We hadn't worked before in a company together, but she convinced me, "Do this with me. I wouldn't want to do it with anyone else."

ALEXANDRA WILKIS WILSON, GILT

A plurality of the founders got to know each other well, initially as friends, and then became business partners. This is a great way to find another person with whom to launch a business. You can develop a rapport, determine if your personalities are a good match for one another, perhaps work on some school projects together, and gather a sense of what each of you excels at.

Jenn and Jenny of Rent the Runway met on the first day of class at HBS since they were in the same section. Similarly, Greg of smarTours met his cofounder, David, in his first-year section at HBS. Beri of Ivy knew his cofounder, Philipp, when they lived in London before they both headed off to start their MBA at HBS.

In a somewhat similar fashion, Josh met Nick at a summer analytics camp at HBS. While they realized they had very different backgrounds, those differences did not keep them from starting a venture. They saw the differences as helpful, complementary, and ultimately the basis for a good friendship and partnership.

We had the shared experience of HBS, but outside of that very, very different life experiences. My background is technical: electrical engineering undergrad, a lot of software engineering in that curriculum. Built a software business afterward, that was my in-between college and HBS experience. Nick was a liberal arts major and went off to Indonesia on a Fulbright grant to build a microfinance group. He spent the better part of two years living in very remote Indonesia. No running water, no power. Handing out small loans to farmers and the like. Very, very different experience than mine.

JOSH HIX, PLATED

Of these cofounders, all formed equal equity (or approximately equal) partnerships. From the start, they viewed themselves as equal participants in the entrepreneurial journey upon which they chose to depart.

Besides friends, we were surprised by the HBS family teams that seem to have worked it out. We saw how Dave launched Yumble Kids with his wife, Joanna. When asked if it played against them to be married, especially when fundraising, it was interesting to hear that, although it was tough in the beginning, it later turned into their advantage.

A lot of VCs would run away from a married couple; that's like rule number one. In the first round, that was a liability.

Now they're pitching it to us as an asset, in part probably because they've seen the way that we work together and the fact that we didn't crumble.

DAVE PARKER, YUMBLE KIDS

Further in the realm of family, Eric of SkyMD launched his dermatology app in partnership with his mom, who is a dermatologist in Miami. Eric has deep expertise in product strategy and development, and his mom understood the needs of dermatologists and their patients. She knew the industry and Eric knew digital product management.

Working with family can be a blessing, but here again you should make sure that you can work together professionally and that there is a professional reason to start the venture jointly.

(Forced) Serendipity

When I look back on it, there's no clear path for me to either of them [my cofounders]. But you take so many meetings, you meet so many people, you have to force serendipity. It doesn't just happen. You have to force it and be aggressive. That was true with those two guys and how I brought them on board.

ANTHEMOS GEORGIADES, ZUMPER

The role of serendipity should not be discounted in determining whether or not cofounders come together and establish a relationship.

Jake of CrossBoundary had the good fortune of meeting his future cofounders, Matt Tilleard and Erik Malmstrom, while in his joint degree program at the Harvard Kennedy School of Government and HBS. These other guys not only had a passion for government like Jake, but they also had shared interests in economic development, having also worked in Afghanistan.

He and his friends began to work together by putting on a social enterprise conference panel specifically about private sector development projects in postconflict zones.

When I started the joint degree program, I met two other students: Erik Malmstrom, who had been an Army Ranger in Afghanistan and was also in the joint degree program, and Matt Tilleard, who had been at BCG [Boston Consulting Group], but then also worked in Afghanistan at an NGO. We shared this interest in doing private sector development in conflict zones. And so in our first year of school, we put on a panel at the HBS Social Enterprise Conference on private sector development in conflict zones.

JAKE CUSACK, CROSSBOUNDARY

Jake then further developed his rapport with Erik as they both ventured off to Afghanistan during their first year summer to explore the private sector landscape there.

We published our research in a couple different papers on entrepreneurship, Afghanistan, and private sector development in Afghanistan. That research

attracted some attention and led to speaking engagements and other op-
portunities. Just because there wasn't a lot of work in this space, we rela-
tively easily began to build a bit of reputation and expertise in this very niche
space of investment and development in conflict zones.

JAKE CUSACK, CROSSBOUNDARY

The process was step by step, as Jake and his two co-students built both a foundation of expertise and became comfortable with their working relationship. They came together at graduation to form Cross-Boundary.

Forced serendipity is more likely to happen just by pushing oneself to "get out there." Relentless networking increases the likelihood of getting connected to appropriate people. Wherever you go, never stop talking about your venture.

Dave of Yumble Kids recounts how at a Sabbath lunch one day, he was talking about his nascent venture offering freshly prepared meals for kids and his need for a great head of operations. This led to someone at the lunch commenting that they knew someone from meal kit company HelloFresh and that maybe he would be interested. He was interested, and he soon joined Dave as a junior cofounder. That was luck—but not entirely luck. Dave put himself, his venture, and the business's needs out there.

In another example, when Anthemos was focused on launching Zumper, he lacked any real estate industry expertise. He believed in his idea, but he didn't have experience in dealing with brokers, understanding various legal issues, and more. He recalls networking in San Francisco, which led to his finding the right industry-experienced person and technical lead to join his fledgling business.

When I moved to California the first time that summer, I scanned the HBS
alumni network for anyone working in real estate in the Bay Area. I emailed
them and about 10 percent of the people replied to me. One of those was a

woman called Naomi Glass. She was an alum who is now a top real estate broker in the Bay Area. She met with me very generously to help me with the idea.

In one of the meetings she brought her son, Taylor, who is the same age as me and had gone to Cal and worked for her up in Berkeley for ten years. He and I really hit it off. So we started the company together.

Of the first ten hires we made, he [Taylor Glass-Moore] was the only person with a background in real estate. Crazy when you think about it.

It was one of those things where you just have to force serendipity.

ANTHEMOS GEORGIADES, ZUMPER

ATTRACT A COFOUNDER OR HIRE ONE?

Finally, you have the people that can help based on the fact that you hire their services. You're a business guy and you don't know anything about tech. Okay, do you need a cofounder for tech? Of course not; you can hire a great web development agency for as low as $15,000 or less. My first bill that I had to pay for web service was maybe $1,700 for a month worth of work and it was great. A cofounder wouldn't have necessarily done more than that.

MORGAN HERMAND-WAICHE, ADORE ME

If you decide you won't go it alone, you should not forget that you have the option of not taking on a cofounder but onboarding the person by hiring them, either on the team or at arm's length (think of outsourcing). This assumes that you have the financial flexibility to pay them and, we would argue, that the role is not of capital importance for the company. Indeed, if you are looking to fill a role that is crucial for the future of the company, you want to make sure to incentivize the person with equity participation.

When thinking about hiring or attracting a cofounder, as always, there are a spectrum of options.

Going out and hiring the resources that you need, without any equity involved, is one approach. Morgan of Adore Me hired a small tech firm in Romania at low cost to build his site and tech, instead of granting founder shares to anyone early on.

However, if you have no or limited financial resources and cannot afford the salary, you may need to get a cofounder even though you would rather hire this person. The amount of equity for that person will of course depend on how valuable you believe he or she is and the stage of the company's development. The earlier the stage, the greater the equity you will need to award.

In the case of Blue Apron, Matt opted for several cofounders, awarding them a smaller part of equity than his but also paying them a salary, which was key to attracting them. Matt admits that his first cofounder would not have joined if he had not been able to offer him a salary.

Presumably, the point of having a cofounder (or multiple cofounders or junior cofounders) is that you believe you will have much more success (and reduced risk) as a team than you would by trying to launch and scale the business yourself. By having equity-incentivized partners, the company should have a strongly motivated team that's willing to work hard.

But there is no doubt that taking on a cofounder is the biggest dilution hit you will more than likely ever take. With a 50/50 cofounder and then following this with a financing round that triggers dilution of 15 to 20 percent more, you can quickly see how fast your ownership stake gets diluted. You lose control of the firm after your first equity financing round.

The biggest dilution event you'll ever encounter is getting a cofounder.
MATT SALZBERG, BLUE APRON

As you think about dilution as an issue, you should reflect upon how large the business opportunity is. That's because owning 10 percent of a $1B pie or 50 percent of a $100M pie is better than owning 100 percent of a $1M pie. Clearly, dilution is much less an issue if the opportunity is sufficiently large.

You should also take into account how you plan to build out the top team, as you might award some of your new hires stock options. This is important because in any case, postlaunch, you will end up rounding out the founders' skills with key hires based on the business needs.

I hired one guy for the director of business development. Mainly I hired him to manage the channel at Delta Dental [insurance] and all the HR and client leads—that was my first major hire. I also brought on my fiancée, who worked at Drybar for seven years, scaling up Drybar. We both are brand marketing. She was behind the scenes with me in all this stuff. She joined full-time in January of this year. She runs brand and marketing. She also helps with hiring and operations as well. The three of us are a team. We go to war together.

JUSTIN JOFFE, HENRY THE DENTIST

The founders of Bespoke Post illustrate early on where they needed to build out the team, as a complement to their own skill sets.

You've got to take into account what the founders' skill sets are and then augment from that. We were both businesspeople. Rishi has a really good design sense. We definitely needed a designer. And we needed a developer. Those were the first two hires.

STEVE SZARONOS, BESPOKE POST

You can incentivize these early hires with stock options. Even if you have financial flexibility to hire whomever you want, you should prefer that many of your people—especially the early-stage hires—have founder's shares or options since both are excellent motivators.

As a founder, you need to balance multiple interests—you want to own a chunk of equity; cofounders will have equity; your investors will have equity; and you need to plan on key future hires getting equity. So, you need to think about where you want to end up. Then work your way backward and figure out what amount of equity you wish to give away to the founding team and to additional staff. There likely will be an option pool created, often 15 percent of the company stock, for key hires. And you want as many people as possible to be motivated with an ownership stake so that everyone is superexcited by what you're building.

JIM SHERMAN, SHERMANSTRAVEL MEDIA

It is a challenge to decide who should be on your launch team. One or two may be cofounders. Others may be critical hires and they receive equity but not cofounder status. You need to decide which functions are most crucial. For the HBS founders, several admit that they did not give technology enough focus early on. They weren't technology-focused ventures so it didn't seem core to their value proposition. Yet it became clear in time that the founders needed to course-correct.

We're both engineers by training, but we were never coders or deep into technology. And I think we took the technology for granted. We just thought, you know, it's a simple platform. We prioritized other areas of the business: sales, BD [business development], the customer portion of it was always more important at the beginning.

And we didn't give it the respect it deserved. The early people who were building for us were not great developers. There's a huge delta between a good developer and not so good developer. And we just kind of treated it a little bit too much like a commodity. Great developers will tell you that the technical piece is table stakes but you've still got to do it well.

GIL ADDO, RUBICON MD

Beyond technology, it is also crucial to improve the teams with key hires in industry—people who can educate you about their particular expertise. For Gilt, this meant hiring in merchandising folks who understood how to buy products—how many items, how many sizes, what works for what season, etc. Alexandra already had some facility for doing this, but she was far from an expert.

I hired people who had been properly trained out of the department stores. I was managing people who I could learn from.

ALEXANDRA WILKIS WILSON, GILT

Building and rounding out teams is a process and an art in finding those with the right skills, the industry experience (if you need it), and cultural fit for your nascent venture. You need to decide which roles need to be filled for launch and then what roles need to be filled after launch. In addition, you need to decide who is a cofounder or hired with options (or outsourced), and find a balance between motivating them and your own dilution.

PART II

Starting Out

The Ignition on a Shoestring

One of the big lessons I learned from the last two ventures: Just because you have money, don't spend it. Spend it as if you don't have it. You will be shocked at how cheap I am.

JUSTIN JOFFE, HENRY THE DENTIST

5

VALIDATE DEMAND
AS CHEAP AS YOU CAN

> To get started, you just need the cheapest,
> simplest version that customers want.

We were forced to launch very quickly. We had to build the site, source the product, and get people to sign up in forty-five days. We weren't paying ourselves. The only expenses were the products. We just wanted to sell one hundred boxes the first month. That's all we were focused on. We weren't worried about other metrics. We just wanted one hundred people to sign up. We got eighty-six people to sign up.

Steve Szaronos, Bespoke Post

The moment your idea becomes a startup, your first objective should be to prove that the product or service can generate demand from customers. Once you have proven demand, you can start building out and investing in the rest of your business model.

The interesting question is, *how buttoned up does the product need to be* in the ignition phase? If your goal is to prove product/market fit, you should focus on developing the product or service that allows you to prove the fit. And nothing more. This sounds obvious but we see so many entrepreneurs investing way beyond what is needed.

Typically entrepreneurs talk about a minimum viable product (MVP). This is the minimum version of a product to test with customers and get feedback. It has minimum features and will not cost as much as a full-blown product, but, if designed well, it will help you understand if customers like it. If they do not, it will help you figure out what needs to change and whether you need to pivot.

In our discussions, we were impressed that whenever possible, HBS entrepreneurs took the MVP concept to the extreme, literally creating the *illusion* of a product with close to no investment. Besides being creative and cheap with their MVP, HBS entrepreneurs also won early *free visibility*, getting their product out there for free.

Being cheap forced them to be creative and focused on what truly mattered, as they needed to find ways to *make it work*. When you have money, you can spend it on people, stuff, tests, and more to try things out. When you *don't* have money, you need to find a way. And you need to find the right way—including the most efficient way—as you might only have one shot, one way to go. That in turn will force you to be creative. It is often under such pressure that you get the best, core ideas that give your business an edge.

In sum, do not make the mistake of going full-blown and investing heavily early on. Start small, go step by step, and make sure to keep on getting regular feedback so as to adapt and optimize. In particular, focus on getting your name out there and building your reputation early on without spending big dollars. Even if you have the money, take it easy to start with, be creative, and make sure you get it fully right before going full-blown.

...

FOCUS ON THE "FRONT END"

The first big question was: Is this something that truly benefits patient care? It made sense as a concept. But are doctors going to get real value from doing this? That was the first thing, because if doctors don't get the value, then who pays and who doesn't, that doesn't really matter.

GIL ADDO, RUBICONMD

The HBS entrepreneurs we interviewed started with a focus on the "front end"—that is, the product or what customers perceived to be the product—and were not distracted by the "back end," that is, logistics, complex operations, etc. They developed the front end in a creative, simple way to compensate for the lack of money.

The advantages of this approach are twofold. First, you get customer reactions with minimum investment. Mistakes are common in the beginning, so it is wise not to invest too quickly until you have acquired points of validation. And if the MVP is well designed, you will get invaluable input for further product development and for your business model.

Second, it allows you to prove there is demand. This validation makes a world of difference in anything you do next, including raising funds and building out operations. The more you can prove fit and traction, the better off you will be.

In the case of RubiconMD, the founders wanted to connect primary care providers with specialists so that patients would get a good diagnosis faster. The first thing the cofounders needed to prove was that they could get primary care providers and specialists to use their platform and that it would result in true, added value. Such proof was critical to confirm key aspects of their business model and convince insurance companies, who were paying for the service. To validate demand, they tested in the field.

We were able to run the small test with a few primary care docs and one specialist. What we've found is that 80 percent of the time, they [the specialists] can make some change that improves the downstream care plan. But half the time you never actually need to go see the specialist. You would have gone, but, because of our platform, it gets resolved online and avoids an in-office visit.

There is a dual advantage for the insurance companies. They pay less for the online consult than for an in-office visit to a specialist, and they have fewer consults as well. There are fewer unnecessary visits to specialists.

GIL ADDO, RUBICONMD

These early findings turned out to be critical for the future of RubiconMD. With a very basic product, RubiconMD confirmed that half of the visits the primary care providers would have scheduled with specialists were *not* needed. And they truly confirmed the business case, including for insurance companies.

When we talked to the founders of RubiconMD, they were five years in and they had done multiple studies to measure the benefits of their platform. It was remarkable to hear that the very initial results were still valid: half of referrals are avoided.

The founder of Plated, Josh, had the same front-end focus. In the business of delivering ingredients on a subscription basis so that people can cook at home, they built a basic but functioning website that accepted consumer orders. They wanted to test how hard it would be to get consumers to pull out a credit card and pay.

Josh spent many hours chatting online with potential customers. The ultimate purpose was to convince themselves that there was a business, and to do this before taking on money from friends, family, or others. The feedback from the first few customers who used the prototype website was overwhelmingly positive. As a conclusion from this live test, the cofounders thought they had a good chance to make it, despite the huge hurdles ahead in setting up such a complex logistics operation.

Yumble Kids followed somewhat of a similar approach with minimal investment, to test if their idea would fly.

When David and Joanna decided to test the idea of prepared meals for kids, they posted on a Facebook mommy group. At that stage, they had not even invested in the product and had absolutely nothing but the idea. They first wanted to know how people would react and wanted to get a feeling if a group of strangers would be excited by their product concept. To them, this was the first big test.

To their surprise they got instant positive reactions with all kinds of questions. Given the positive response, Joanna picked ten interested "customers" and charged them for meals. Those became Yumble Kids' first customers.

David and Joanna had yet to invest in anything like a warehouse, kitchen, kitchen staff, logistics, etc. The operations and technology were basic to get going. Joanna cooked the meals at home, as if they would've been for her own children, and went on to hand-deliver them herself. David recalls the first deliveries:

Joanna's first delivery, she got a one-dollar tip, which was really funny. Customers didn't realize they were talking to the founder.

DAVE PARKER, YUMBLE KIDS

The key point here is that they were able to prove that there was demand by focusing on the front end and without investing much of anything. One would think that a business of prepared meals to kids would require substantial up-front investment. In their case, and given the way they set it up, they only invested once they were further along the way. For both Plated and Yumble Kids, in the beginning, they merely needed to know whether or not people valued the meals enough to order them.

...

KEEP IT SIMPLE AND CHEAP

We had initial MVP tests where we literally went to college campuses. We bought dresses with our own money or we borrowed dresses from friends. And we set up shop with racks of dresses. You could call them pop-ups. We called them MVP tests.

JENNY FLEISS, RENT THE RUNWAY

All HBS entrepreneurs showed great creativity in investing minimally in their front-end solutions to test customer demand. Whenever possible, they created the illusion of a product or service.

The founders of Rent the Runway started testing their business concept by making clothes available for rent on college campuses. Their first step was not to even sell online. Instead they visited five southern college campuses and created pop-up stores with racks of borrowed dresses and a few items they had bought with their own money. The purpose was to prove the demand for renting dresses instead of buying them. They saved money by not even building a website—there was no website or permanent storefront—and limiting the range of clothes. They were testing to see if young women would like the service, and thus creatively came up with a low-cost method of testing.

While Rent the Runway had received negative feedback from industry experts (Diane von Furstenberg was not the only one with concerns), it became clear to the founders early on that their customers loved the concept. The feedback from the campus tour was not just that women liked the service, but that they loved it.

As a matter of fact, every HBS entrepreneur who talked about their MVP explained how creative they had been and how minimal it actually was.

For example, in the case of Yumble Kids, they had a splash page and simple website, no real supply chain, and they were cooking in their own kitchen and delivering themselves. But customers didn't see the difference, believing it was all buttoned up.

In the case of RubiconMD, Gil and Carlos were able to prove that specialists and primary care providers would use and value their platform. To begin, instead of going full-blown and offering all kinds of specialties, they chose one specialty to focus on and recruited just a few specialists. Then, instead of investing and building a costly fully functioning platform, they chose to work with a Google form, which was embedded in a website. It looked like an automated website to primary care doctors but, besides the Google form, absolutely everything else was manual. Reflecting back on the process and its simplicity, Carlos comments on how simple it was.

I copied the HTML of a web form into the website, and every time somebody submitted a consult, I would get an email. And then I would forward that email to one of the four or five specialists that we had found by walking into hospitals and begging people to work with us.

I remember going back to school in September and being in class and being, like, "Crap, we just got a consult." And on my computer, doing the writing of these consults while I was in class.

CARLOS REINES, RUBICONMD

Despite the minimalist approach, RubiconMD was able to prove that primary care providers and specialists would use the product and that it created clear value.

Similar to the example of RubiconMD, Anthemos from Zumper, the real estate marketplace, explained that he invested a minimum amount of money to build an MVP in order to gather data and convince himself (and investors) that his idea was worth pursuing and investing in more.

I took $7,000 from an HBS award in the Rock Center and contracted a developer in Serbia to build the MVP that I used over the summer to test the *hypotheses. It was the best money I've ever spent in my career at Zumper because it generated that data.*

When we checked that data, I think it was only thirty-five transactions we had over the summer, a modest number, but the data was so compelling of how quickly transactions closed, and how high the NPS was of the renter experience, that even with such a tiny data set we told investors in our thesis that the next generation of platforms will be end-to-end and transactional, not lead generation.

ANTHEMOS GEORGIADES, ZUMPER

Anthemos did *not* build out the full marketplace to prove that there would be customer demand. He did *not* invest in the full software development for this real estate rental platform, nor in the marketing spend to attract both landlords and renters across multiple cities. Instead, he focused on a targeted renter test and got the data that proved he could sell it.

What If You Can't?

The nature of some businesses is such that offering a test "front end" does not work.

Sometimes building the MVP will be as expensive as building the product. We saw this situation with Henry the Dentist. Justin understood that the only way to truly test customer demand for his mobile dental clinic was to actually build it. He could not fake it. The product was the service. He had to get the design of the dental truck exactly right. To keep investment to a reasonable level, though, he focused on just one mobile clinic in one geographical area. In other words, his MVP was his first clinic in New Jersey.

Similar situations exist for medical or scientific ventures. There is not any half measure or minimal product investment. Either the science works or it doesn't. The need is a clear, explicit one, and so the entrepreneur in these situations understands that the risk is not in demand but in whether or not the scientific discovery works (for a disastrous case see: Theranos).

Sometimes you have no choice but to build the product or service. Steve Jobs was famous for stating that he understood what people wanted better than they knew themselves. Addressing implicit needs, he believed that customers would love his products once they saw and experienced them. How could they understand them until they saw them and used them?

Kickstarter, WeFunder, and similar sites exist precisely for companies to test demand for their new product ideas. No front end is needed. The site allows quick tests to determine if customers want a particular product—before the company commits resources to produce the products. In this way, it's possible to test a new product concept before the product is actually built.

Also, one can engage in direct marketing to test all sorts of products and services before actually enabling their delivery. Elon Musk took orders for his electric car before production began. Thousands signed up.

So, depending on the nature of the business, you should test the concept before jumping into production. In these situations, you want to test the business concept before committing any resources to product development.

GET EARLY FREE VISIBILITY

We got press in a million different directions that was helpful to our marketing success.

The fascination with female empowerment with Jenn and I as female entrepreneurs and having a customer who was aligned with that helped enormously. Wearing these outfits to power meetings at work and events has been another big part of our story. Press was a very cost-effective way of changing consumer behavior, because you're able to tell the full story about what you're doing.

Female founders, female businesswomen, entrepreneurs—our story reso-nated with our customer base and felt authentic to the brand we were build-ing. But we got press separate from just us as founders, such as a lot of press around fashion shows.

JENNY FLEISS, RENT THE RUNWAY

You should never underestimate how important it is to get visibility and awareness for your company and your product, especially early on. More important: find a way to get your name in the press, on social media, and anywhere else while paying as little for the coverage as possible.

Customers need to know about your product to test it and buy it. But there are other good reasons why building awareness very early on is important.

When your name is in the press or news, it means that you are in-teresting enough to talk or write about. It draws attention and creates trust. People will read or hear about you, which will create interest and maybe sales. We obviously assume that the press coverage or content is positive, but even if it is not, it might be better than no attention what-soever.

If you can get enough people to talk about you in positive terms, it can create a "buzz" that has a positive effect. Customers, partners, and investors will look at you differently if you get many mentions in social media or in the press. You are not just that small, anonymous startup anymore.

But how do you create awareness with minimal investment? The thread here again is *creativity*. The HBS entrepreneurs found ways to get on large platforms for free or without much investment.

One of the best examples is Plated, which by the time we talked to Josh had had three appearances on *Shark Tank*. The program is watched live by millions and "rewatched" by many more afterward on social media. Plated got a huge awareness boost with every one of its three appearances, which led to sales. Josh explains it is all about free PR.

It is effectively an infomercial that families and individuals sit down with the intention to watch. The response that it drives is unbelievable.

The real point: the cost basis is zero. Even if you acquire one customer, it would probably be worth it, sort of illustratively. For many businesses, they end up acquiring more customers than they can handle. The return is infinite.

JOSH HIX, PLATED

Bespoke Post followed a more traditional approach to get their name out there and reach customers. Thanks to early press coverage, they tripled their subscribers in one day.

We had an intern who was reaching out to all these blogs asking them to post about us. The editors for UrbanDaddy saw one of the blogs. The blog that originally posted about us didn't drive that much traffic. But it did drive UrbanDaddy to us.

UrbanDaddy is like a Thrillist. They did a dedicated national email on us; it was unpaid. I think we got four hundred subscribers that day. And we had two hundred by that point.

STEVE SZARONOS, BESPOKE POST

After that, the company continued to be creative about how to get their name out there and reach customers without spending marketing dollars. A big part of their strategy was based on cheap Facebook ads (when it was still cheap), but it included other initiatives like a clever partnership with a magazine: the magazine's advertiser would put an item in Bespoke Post's box and Bespoke Post would get some advertising space in the magazine.

They also managed to get in the American Airlines seatback book-let, when it was running an edition on startups. That was free again. Most of their initiatives were of that kind. It is only much later that they started to spend money on advertising.

Although the previous examples are also applicable to B2B compa-nies, B2B entrepreneurs have additional levers to pull. Werk, the B2B company in the field of HR, developed their own content to share with prospects.

We write a ton of articles. We publish our research. We release it in nug-gets. This is data that nobody else has. And that's been the most powerful thing to us as an inbound driver. We also have a bunch of technology that enables us to capture those, anything from as simple as a lead-gen[eration] form on our research on our site and on our case studies and on our bench-mark.

ANNA AUERBACH, WERK

CrossBoundary, which focuses on private sector development in conflict zones, also focused early on content (marketing) and acquired its very first client that way. Jake and his cofounder had realized there was limited information available on the topic and decided to travel to Afghanistan during their first summer at Harvard to do research about entrepreneurship. They came back with the strong conviction that there were opportunities and published their research, which led to other opportunities and their first client.

We published our research in a couple different papers on entrepreneurship, Afghanistan, and private sector development in Afghanistan. That research attracted some attention and led to speaking engagements and other op-portunities.

Out of that initial research these little consulting projects started springing up—agencies of the U.S. government or investors would ask us for a perspective on investing in Afghanistan and Iraq.

JAKE CUSACK, CROSSBOUNDARY

In the case of Catalina at Sweetwell, her main objective early on was to convince food companies to use the sugar replacer in their own products (think of cookies, bars, etc.). Discussions with the Mars of this world were long and difficult, starting with the R&D departments that needed to have absolute proof that the product was as good as sugar. This always included testing, but Catalina found a way to support her point by convincing a two-star Michelin restaurant to use Sweetwell for its dessert menu and inviting the press to cover the event.

We approached a two-star Michelin restaurant and convinced them to change their dessert menu and have half of the desserts prepared with Sweetwell. On the announcement day, we invited journalists to a press conference. They all got desserts to taste but were not told which ones were prepared with sugar and which ones were with Sweetwell. All the journalists got it wrong, not being able to identify which ones had real sugar in them. That, combined with the quality label of a two-star Michelin restaurant, helped us to get substantial positive press coverage for free. We were also able to leverage that PR way later in the development of the business.

CATALINA DANIELS, SWEETWELL

While free visibility is ideal, it is not always obvious how to get it and you might—even early on—need to invest in marketing. If (or when) you do, be as cheap as you can to understand what approach works best to get your first customers.

I bought lists and I would e-blast lists. I would do drip campaigns. I just sprayed and prayed. I bought some money on LinkedIn. I did a Squarespace site for $1,000. I designed everything pretty scrappy.

I got the business off the ground with nothing. I capped every project. I did most of the heavy lifting myself. I drafted things or edited things. I did a lot to build this for nothing. And even when it was SBA [Small Business Administration] money or investor money, every dollar went to marketing.

JUSTIN JOFFE, HENRY THE DENTIST

THE BIG VALUE OF SMALL STEPS

Everything we do, we test it out first through MVP testing. We did that first with college pop-ups to test the designer dress rental business. Then for our retail store concept, we first tried it out in our office, where were set up dressing rooms. Then we further tested the retail concept by doing an event with Henri Bendel. Before signing any monthly leases for retail, we tested the retail concept. And, later for our subscription business, we even tested it by picking a group of fifty consumers to test out the renting of more everyday apparel.

JENNY FLEISS, RENT THE RUNWAY

Sometimes, and for some businesses, it is difficult to imagine how to start small and grow in steps. But in our discussions with HBS founders, we learned that even in the case of the models for which you would think it not to be feasible, they truly started with small steps, building it out one step at a time.

Take the example of Rent the Runway. It is hard to imagine how a company whose model and success depends on high volumes and critical mass started small. In today's offering, Rent the Runway's value proposition is a wide choice of dresses, clothes, and accessories for women. If there were only a few dresses in a limited number of sizes, the company would not be as successful.

Yet they took it step by step, starting on college campuses with a few dresses they bought or borrowed and expanded the business step by step while not taking too many risks.

There are many advantages to taking small steps. First, you will spend less money. Second, you will minimize your risk since the mistakes you make will be smaller. Third, taking it step by step will allow you to ultimately test more. Last but not least, taking small steps will allow for short feedback cycles and more frequent feedback, which in the early stages is so important. Ultimately you will be in a much better position to know what the right next step is and how to adapt your strategy.

Many HBS entrepreneurs talked about how they would continue to develop their businesses with the same step-by-step approach, minimizing the investments while making sure that they would get the needed feedback for the next step.

Dave from Yumble Kids explains how, after they convinced themselves of customer demand, they moved on to "upgrade" their website to test if demand could be recurring with a subscription model. The upgrade was minimal, just enough to prove the point.

We put an email address on there. That was all there was. Next step—will anyone move to a subscription model? Because I don't see this working as a one-off thing. It was a crappy website that processed subscriptions.

DAVE PARKER, YUMBLE KIDS

Many entrepreneurs also applied the "starting small and taking it step by step" approach not only to marketing and sales, but also to other areas of their businesses.

We saw other people trying to go out at the same time and raise $50M or $100M, and they ended up flying around, doing a bunch of meetings, but

never actually raising the funds. Those were just too big of an initial target. I
think starting a little bit smaller helped.

JAKE CUSACK, CROSSBOUNDARY

CrossBoundary started as a consultancy in conflict zones but later evolved to raise funds to invest in these countries. Initially it targeted family offices (who were easier to convince upfront) with a small fund of $10M. For a fund, this is small, but the size actually allowed them to build a track record and prove their impact. As Jake notes, it is obviously important that each step fits a larger plan, a goal that you want to reach.

Adore Me, the women's lingerie company, exemplifies a different kind of step-by-step approach that can be applicable to many startups.

One of the big questions when you get going is, *When do you take the step to hire somebody and put them on the payroll?* In today's world, with an increasingly flexible workforce, we heard multiple examples of HBS entrepreneurs getting people on board as freelancers first, then hiring them at a later stage.

Morgan explains that the company remained small for a long time. In the beginning, they were a small team of eight or nine employees, all located in a New York–based office without windows, which they rented for $500 a month. When the business started to pick up, Morgan did not hire employees but worked with freelancers and external providers.

I would hire IT consultants that were based in Romania, for various reasons, but mostly because they were extremely smart and affordable. As business picked up, I started to hire two, three, four, up to the moment when I hired pretty much all ten employees of this consulting agency. And then I told the owner, "Look, this is ridiculous, we've become your biggest client, why don't you all officially become part of Adore Me?" That day we created our Bucharest-based office. And they all became part of Adore Me. And now this office is about sixty to seventy people, and that covers both IT and customer relationships.

MORGAN HERMAND-WAICHE, ADORE ME

Adore Me followed the same approach for their distribution center. In the early days, they outsourced distribution to a third-party logistics (3PL) provider. They relied on the outside party with expertise and assets to fulfill their distribution needs. But when the moment broke that they had reached a certain volume, they decided to internalize distribution and overnight grew their team by sixty people.

As we have seen in other examples, one should be careful about when to freelance or not. You do not want to outsource a core technology or a truly differentiating factor of your business model. Also, you obviously want to be critical of the quality you get. But if you can, it is a good way to take small steps.

Finally, two companies used the step-by-step approach in an out-of-the-box way: they initially launched with a different name. The reasoning was simple: it would allow them to test the offering (and make mistakes) while not damaging the "real" name. In addition—and not to be underestimated—the launch name was much cheaper.

Plated started as "Dine In Fresh," which always remained the legal name of the company.

There were at least two reasons. There was a practical reason: we had no money. We in fact had negative money. I think we cumulatively had about $300,000 in stand loans and next to nothing in savings. No money to spend on a real brand name. And even in 2012, domains were hard to come by. Dine In Fresh, it's an awful name, literal, hard to spell and pronounce, everything else. It was the best we could come up with. It was available. Eight bucks on GoDaddy and there we were.

And the more strategic reason was that we didn't want to run all of our early experiments under a brand name that we thought we might damage.

JOSH HIX, PLATED

In the case of Yumble Kids, they started with the name "Panda Plates" because David's wife, Joanna, liked the alliteration and because it was cheap and available. They ended up changing the name at a later stage because it was confusing.

"Panda Plates," too many people thought it sounded like Chinese food. We literally got the question five or more times, "Do you sell actual panda meat?" "No, we don't." So, we wanted to have "Yumble," a name that was fun. It tested very well. And the brand we have is superfun and candy colored to be able to make mealtime fun for kids.

DAVE PARKER, YUMBLE KIDS

6

GOOD FEEDBACK
IS NOT GOOD ENOUGH

> Customer feedback should blow you away. Anything
> less means you keep refining.

*It's very hard to decide whether your idea is working or not at the early
stage. And people grasp for any kind of evidence that they can to validate that what they're doing is working well. It's an art, not a science, in
terms of figuring it out.*

MATT SALZBERG, BLUE APRON

Matt summarizes the difficulty entrepreneurs face in understanding whether or not their idea is truly a good one—knowledge that is
especially important in the ignition stage, as they turn their idea into
an MVP.

Problems arise when you become so entangled with your product
that the only outcome you can see is success. After a while, it becomes
difficult to have the necessary distance to objectively assess if the
product is being received as intended. You're at risk of pushing your

product not because of its great market fit, but because you fiercely believe in it and want it to succeed.

You obviously want to be passionate and defend your idea, but you need to pick up the signs from the market. Don't let your optimism blind you. For all entrepreneurs, there comes a point when you need to answer the critical question: *Is my idea truly as good as I think it is?*

Only customers can answer that question.

The real test comes from the market: *Will customers like it? Will they buy it and/or use it? Will they repeat their purchase or use? Will they tell others about it? And will they want to pay for it?*

So, as you validate demand, how exactly do you know if you should press forward or not? And if you continue, do you keep the product as is or adapt? These are million-dollar questions and probably the toughest ones for entrepreneurs to answer.

We were surprised to hear from all the HBS entrepreneurs that the only way to know you are on to something is to get feedback that blows you away—feedback that is *overwhelmingly positive.*

When asking people, you need to discard the extremes [positive and negative] and take the 70 percent in the middle. These need to be overwhelmingly positive.

JUSTIN JOFFE, HENRY THE DENTIST

GATHER FEEDBACK FROM THE RIGHT PEOPLE

By the time you've decided to develop an MVP, a front end, some wire frames, or any other minimal way to test demand, you have already gotten feedback for your idea from friends, family, potential customers, and perhaps industry experts. But the real test is to hear from customers or users. There isn't any real substitute to customer feedback in trying to understand the likelihood of success for your venture.

Although it sounds obvious, you should make sure to gather feedback from the right people. Depending on your business model, you might indeed have multiple stakeholders, like users (who consume your product), customers (who pay for your product), and partners (who are key to get your users on board) from whom to gather feedback. It is critical that you have a clear view of the business model and relevant stakeholders from whom you want to gather feedback.

Yumble Kids got it right and figured out that they needed to satisfy both the kid who is the consumer and the parent who pays, and that they needed to appeal to both, too.

We say we have a consumer, the kid, and a customer, the parent. The kid is consuming our product and the parent has to click "buy" and continue to not skip or cancel. We have to make two people happy. That's a tough marketing challenge. It's also an opportunity.

We think the right way to do it is to have the kids choose the meals, to be able to build a fun experience for them to choose their own meals and actually make it modular so they can actually choose their own sides with the mains. That's our vision.

DAVE PARKER, YUMBLE KIDS

Another good example of how important it is to identify the right people to gather feedback from are the different approaches taken by RubiconMD and SkyMD, which both operate in the medical field.

The companies are similar, in the sense that they are medical companies with a vision to connect patients with doctors. But both companies took a different approach at gathering feedback.

RubiconMD was clear early on that insurance companies would play a key role to attract customers and so they decided to include them in their key stakeholders to gather feedback from.

This was different for SkyMD, which did not have that assumption in their early model. In addition, SkyMD gathered feedback from doctors, not from patients, and failed to understand that patients' usage would be contingent on insurance reimbursements. The app could be perfect in terms of its convenience, ease of use, etc., but if insurance companies would not cover the consult, patients would not use it.

We spent a lot more time with the doctors than [with] the patients, although we spent time with both. We knew that our customer was going to be the doctor. They were going to be the one paying us for the platform. While we did speak directly with patients, we relied a little bit on the doctors to help us understand what they thought the patients would want, because they're seeing patients all the time and they talk to them. We asked them to ask some of their patients how they would feel. A little bit of that information came second hand. And we relied on the doctors to have an intuition about whether insurance impacts the patient.

We knew that insurance didn't cover our service, but we felt that a lot of people go to dermatologists for out-of-pocket services and so that won't be an issue. But as we got deeper into the market, we realized that there were certain patient populations for which that was a deal breaker. And that we would never be able to reach a lot of people until we had insurance coverage as part of the model. We underestimated the impact of that and that was a big risk to the business because it was something we couldn't control.

ERIC PRICE, SKYMD

Unfortunately, in addition to the issue of insurance reimbursement, SkyMD made another mistake, which was from the hypothesis that doctors would not only pay for the product but also play a key role in convincing patients to use it. Because of this, they focused on how to best support the doctors in doing so.

Our initial model assumed that doctors were going to help us get patients to engage within their own practices. And we did a lot to support them. We built all these workflows in the front desk and stuff like that to get people to sign up. But it was very difficult for us to fit into their workflow in a way that we could get sign-ups. That became a lot more complicated than we expected.

ERIC PRICE, SKYMD

So, SkyMD suffered from a focus on getting feedback from dermatologists and didn't scrub the assumptions that individuals would not use the product without insurance coverage. Furthermore, they wrongly assumed that the doctors' office personnel would promote the app. All of this may sound obvious after the fact, but it is always easy to dissect a situation in retrospect.

RubiconMD took a different approach and ended up gathering feedback from three parties: the primary care providers, the specialists, and the insurance companies.

As was the case for SkyMD, their main initial focus was the doctors, both the primary care providers and specialists. They set up a pilot in a community hospital with a few primary care providers and one specialist.

The notion that primary care providers could contact specialists was not new. But primary care providers admitted that they would often not do so because they would have the feeling of bothering the specialists and asking for a favor. RubiconMD's solution was therefore perceived as a much more efficient interaction with the specialists.

The specialists, on the other hand, confirmed that they were interested in answering the requests. Despite the fact that the RubiconMD requests came on top of their normal workload, they found it interesting to use small periods of downtime to help the primary care providers, while testing their own knowledge.

It's quiz-like and it's catered to their expertise. And it's really fast. They're going to look. They're going to see a picture of this rash. They'll see this question. And then they've solved it. And then they type a quick answer on their phone. And it comes back. We make it a very easy and enjoyable interaction.

We had specialists who told us that they've forgotten that they were get-
ting paid for this. They were doing it for the intellectual exercise.

GIL ADDO, RUBICONMD

Although the founders of RubiconMD focused on piloting the products with the doctors, they understood early on that insurance companies were critical players and that they should understand how to get
them on board.

The entire time, while we were testing, I was taking the approach of talking
to the insurance companies to try to get them on board. That was how we
knew that we needed to show that there was a real ROI and that people
were using it.

At the end of every case we asked the doctors a question, "What did this
do? Did this avoid a referral? Did it approve a referral? Did it just provide
peace of mind? Or did you have no effect?" And we collected that data.

GIL ADDO, RUBICONMD

Thanks to these questions, they were able to collect the data that
allowed them to prove that with the use of RubiconMD, half of the referrals were not needed. They focused on understanding what the value
of RubiconMD had been not only for the doctors, but also for their
patients. And saving insurance companies money by reducing unnecessary specialist visits proved a clear ROI.

RubiconMD ultimately managed to onboard insurance companies
because they clearly understood what was needed based on the input
from the constituencies. Having the insurance companies on board
turned critical since primary care providers would otherwise not have
been in a position to reach out to the specialists, because patients might
have objected to it due to financial reasons.

As angel investors, we often come across entrepreneurs who haven't
done sufficient homework on whom to get feedback from, or who have

sought feedback from only a subset of customers and key constituencies, or who made risky assumptions about vital elements of the venture's market fit and business model.

Some entrepreneurs will tell you that they don't ask for feedback because they are afraid that somebody will steal their idea. This is unlikely to happen, though. As an entrepreneur you have invested time and R&D in your product and it will not be that easy for others to copy it. Seeking feedback is so beneficial it will far outweigh any risk of giving away your idea.

Others, working on a disruptive, new product, will tell you it does not make sense to ask people, including potential customers, since they will not be able to fully understand the product and its value. If you are working on such a groundbreaking product, you should follow your vision and your passion. Steve Jobs reportedly said, "Some people say give the customers what they want, but that's not my approach. Our job is to figure out what they're going to want before they do." But even in these cases, at some point later in the process you will get customer feedback and it will need to be from the right customers.

FEEDBACK THAT BLOWS YOU AWAY

That's one of the challenging parts, which is deciphering the "Oh yeah, that's good" from the "My eyes are going to bulge out of my head, I need this tomorrow" pain point.

MATT SALZBERG, BLUE APRON

There are multiple ways to gather feedback from your customers, but whatever method you choose, what matters is that the feedback needs to be pretty darn good.

The more concrete the feedback, the easier it is to understand how good or bad the opportunity is.

There is a big chance, however, that early on you will not be getting the feedback on a quantitative scale, and that is when it becomes more tricky. Every entrepreneur wants to hear something positive and will perceive the feedback that they want to hear.

So the only way to know that you are on the right track is when you get feedback that blows you away. When it is way better than you expected.

If the feedback does not blow you away (which is highly likely in the beginning), you should learn from what you hear, using it to understand what the best course of action is. In any case, the feedback will tell you what to do and help you refine (or abandon) your offering. It was surprising to us that all HBS entrepreneurs clearly emphasized that this was an area where you don't want to compromise.

They all told us, independently from one another, that the only way to know that you are on your way to success is to get extremely positive feedback. There should be no doubt about how positive it is.

Dave and Joanna from Yumble Kids believed in the concept of providing healthy meals for children, delivered to the home. They had gathered positive feedback from family and friends, but they did not know if parents with whom they had no relationship would actually like the meal service and pay for it. When they posted the offer on a Facebook mommy group, where they knew nobody, they did not know what to expect.

We didn't expect very many responses. Hours later we had to put up a waiting list because we couldn't fulfill the demand. That people were willing to pay, sight unseen, an expensive price point from no reputable brand led me to believe, "Okay, we have something interesting here."

And the next week even more people asked. "My sister just tried this." "My friend just heard about this." "When are you bringing this to LA?" "When are you bringing this to Miami?" "When are you bringing this to Boston?" "To Memphis?" Insane. Classic story, right, real traction.

What we quickly learned was that this is a huge pain point. Incredibly, people are willing to trust a complete stranger with literally no menu, no pic-

tures of the food. Could have been the sketchiest thing. People were willing to do it.

DAVE PARKER, YUMBLE KIDS

Matt had founded Petridish prior to Blue Apron. Petridish was a crowdfunding platform for science projects. The site funded some exciting projects, but by early 2012, Matt concluded, based on the feedback from different constituencies (schools, researchers, donors), that the business would be tough to grow. So Matt decided to shut it down and used the remaining capital to eventually launch Blue Apron.

The early qualitative feedback he got at Blue Apron was substantially better than with Petridish. After the first deliveries, the feedback was overwhelming. The comments he heard from early customers of Blue Apron included things he would never have predicted.

When we got our first real customer feedback, I knew the business would be successful because the feedback we got was just so night-and-day different than the feedback we were hearing from customers of Petridish, where it was like, "Oh yeah, this is great." But at Blue Apron it was like, "Oh my God, let me tell you for twenty minutes about the steak dish you helped me make. It was the best thing I've ever eaten. I think maybe if you had just done this differently with the herbs, it would have been even better." They just wouldn't want to stop talking about it. They thought it was delicious, regardless of how it turned out, because they were the ones that made it. They told all their friends and then they shared it on social media. It was this interesting co-creation thing that we had going with our customers that really fueled the growth of the business in the early days.

With Blue Apron people would write me diatribes about how this was the best thing that's ever happened to them. Essentially saying, Blue Apron's going to change their life.

MATT SALZBERG, BLUE APRON

In the B2B market space, RubiconMD's pilot proved a success with overwhelmingly positive feedback from the primary care providers.

The doctors would say: "This is amazing. I've had more communication in the last two months than I've had in the last ten years with specialists. Not only that, a lot of my patients don't get good access and I end up sending them to the Emergency Department many, many times. And I'm avoiding a lot of unnecessary Emergency Department visits."

GIL ADDO, RUBICONMD

Justin from Henry the Dentist received early positive feedback on his concept from HR managers he talked to. This gave him enough confidence to invest in the first prototype mobile clinic. But he knew that the real feedback would come from the first patients in the clinic. He knew he was on to something when patients, who weren't from vendors, said, "This was awesome. I would come again." Justin remembers that the look on their faces said it all. The patients did not just feel that their dental visit was all right, but rather, that the experience was exceptional.

You can gather feedback from customers in a number of ways. The above examples are all related to the early stages of a venture when an entrepreneur gets first verbal reactions from customers. Although anecdotal, the feedback was sufficient for entrepreneurs to know that they were on to something.

In some cases, the feedback will be numerical and hence less anecdotal. Think of the number of people who sign up on a wait list for your product or the number of people who download your app. One would naturally think that this is better because it is less anecdotal and more fact based. Although that is mostly true, it does not by definition make it always easier. Let us give you two examples.

Gilt had a very ambitious quantified goal when they first launched the product. They wanted to have 25,000 people sign up between the date of launch and their first sale, about two weeks later. They ended up having "only" 13,000 people signing up with an email and a password in those first two weeks. Alexandra explains that there was disappointment because they had not met their goal. Yet, when she shared these numbers with other peers, it was clear that this was an amazing result and clearly fantastic feedback.

On the other end of the spectrum, Zumper, the real estate marketplace, surpassed its expectations on launch day, but realized that those numbers were not sustainable thereafter.

We launched in September 2012 at TechCrunch Disrupt, a big tech conference. And we launched onstage in front of five thousand people at the audience, fifty thousand people streaming it live on TechCrunch. We had a bunch of traffic. Day one was just amazing. And we thought, wow, this is easy. We had so much attention.

And the next ninety days were like crickets. Unless your product is sticky or you have multiple launches in turn, it's hard to bring anyone back— because just the product was so early and we didn't have enough landlords using it, so we didn't have enough listings.

ANTHEMOS GEORGIADES, ZUMPER

Anthemos and his team realized that the early numbers were truly encouraging but that there was much more needed before they could be satisfied with the feedback. As always, you should be smart about how to interpret the quantitative information and make sure that enough thought is put into assessing it.

...

LISTEN, LEARN, AND ITERATE TO PRODUCT MARKET FIT

While feedback from customers and key constituencies should be your compass, you should not get discouraged if the initial feedback is not overwhelmingly positive. It is normal to iterate based on user/customer feedback as you seek to fine-tune your business offering in a bid to attract buyers.

As a matter of fact, many of the founders we talked to had calculated the risk of not getting it quite right from the beginning. Plated even started with a different name in order to save money but also to test its offering without negative impact on its brand name and with space to experiment before getting it right. Do not give up but rather draw from the feedback what you can change to better position yourself in the market.

This is exactly what happened at Zumper. Anthemos explains how his team used the information not to question the longer-term viability of their idea but to truly think how to take the business forward.

The first ninety days, all of us actively talked about how "wow, what a fall from grace from the first day of launch." And "wow, this is difficult. Should we just be focused on one side of the platform or should we continue to invest in both sides?"

I don't think we had a conversation about, "is it going to work or not." But we had a very difficult conversation about "should we actually give up on one of the two sides of our platform because it seems like it's too unfocused and nothing's working."

ANTHEMOS GEORGIADES, ZUMPER

Even in the case that you get positive feedback early on, you should "listen" to the feedback, since it will provide invaluable input as to how to refine your positioning and value proposition.

Dave and Joanna from Yumble Kids got tremendous feedback after their post on Facebook. Based on their own experience, they expected that the healthiness of the meals would be a key pillar of their offering. But Dave explains that in talking to parents, they realized that health would *not* be as important as they had expected.

Before we started, we thought health was going to be the number one concern to parents. When we actually went out and did it, health did not even register as long as you cleared the threshold. When Joanna asked the parents what the most important thing was for them, we would get answers like "My kid eats the food" or "This is really no hassle for me." When she would ask about healthiness, we would get reactions like "Oh, I saw it on your website, it looks healthy."

DAVE PARKER, YUMBLE KIDS

The feedback allowed Yumble Kids to refine its positioning. By now they see three pillars to their brand: the fun for the kids, the convenience for the parents, and the healthiness. The founders initially believed that the latter would be top of mind for the parents but it turned out to be a "bar you need to pass."

RubiconMD went through a similar experience. Their initial pilots resulted in extremely positive feedback from primary care providers and specialists. Early on it was clear that RubiconMD could facilitate the connection between doctors and that, as a result, patients would be better attended at a lower cost. But Gil and Carlos also learned a few additional things that would turn out to be critical. One of them is that they understood that email was a better way to communicate than video interaction.

What we found early on—and the reason we went away from a video interaction between the primary care docs and specialists—is that you have to make this operationally very flexible for the docs. It's about the level of engagement in responding to a quick email. That they're willing to do. They get a flexible time period. This doesn't take time in the day for specialists. The specialists do this when they have a few minutes in between their office or hospital patients.

GIL ADDO, RUBICONMD

In addition, to further expand their operating model, they learned from the feedback that not all specialists would be willing to equally participate.

We go to academic medical centers because they're salaried. They tend to have a little bit of research time. They also bring a big brand. They like to teach. This is a teaching interaction, after all. And they have a little bit more flexibility in their schedule, so they can do this in between rounds when they have a few minutes. We have people say, "I just did it while sitting on a beach on vacation." It doesn't take much. Private practice docs don't have that same type of incentive. It doesn't work quite the same.

GIL ADDO, RUBICONMD

These examples are all related to situations where the entrepreneurs got it right to start with, but learned along the way how to optimize their positioning for further development. It is fair to say that most, if not all, entrepreneurs will have to make changes before finding the right positioning.

In some cases, the feedback might be perceived as "okay to start with" but can in fact indicate a much deeper problem. That is when you should pause and have the courage to question what to do. Far worse is to keep going without making changes. Don't let your busy days and list of tasks keep your mind from focusing on what is a crucial point of evaluation for your startup. You might need to rethink your product or business model, and pivot.

In the case of SkyMD, while early feedback was "okay," it already included warning signs, which Eric and his team should have picked up.

We had doctors using the app in five practices in the country. We had qualitative feedback on the product and we could see that people were using it and getting value out of it. We didn't have amazing numbers, because the product was very simple.

We were also surprised to find out that it wasn't working in every way, especially because my mother was a dermatologist. She was like, "This is something that I would want, and so therefore I'm surprised other people are not seeing that."

ERIC PRICE, SKYMD

As we will see, SkyMD struggled to make it work later on. The early feedback should have been a warning sign and a reason to pause and reflect. Was the product truly solving the problem for the people whom Eric had in mind when he started, or not? Was there a problem with the business model assumptions?

In the most extreme situation, the feedback will tell you that—despite all of your efforts and beliefs—you are far off and it is probably better to quit (and start over again). This also happened to some of the HBS entrepreneurs.

Prior to Yumble Kids, Dave Parker had launched Vouch, an app designed to aggregate the "likes" of celebrities and then monetize the traffic from a large number of users. It was a big idea during the early days of app launches, but he ran into problems in terms of developing a truly sticky product that users would return to frequently. He came to the conclusion that the product was "wrong" and decided that it was not worth investing in more.

I wanted to take all these celebrity connections that I had [from my prior venture in influencer marketing] and allow a platform where they could share things that they like. What restaurants are they eating at, what clothing do they like, what music are they listening to right now, what movies are they fans of? Et cetera. You can see what 50 Cent's favorite movie is.

We got great traction in terms of downloads and Apple loved our design and featured us on the home page of the App Store. The problem was, the product was wrong. We did not invest enough in product management at the beginning to understand what people wanted in order to retain daily active users. So, we had a leaky boat. That taught me a lot about retention. It's not all about growth and top line. It's also about creating a product that's very sticky.

If I were doing it again today, I probably would have stuck to one vertical, instead of restaurants and movies and music, to create a beachhead that we could expand out of as opposed to going after everything all at once. It was a mistake.

DAVE PARKER, YUMBLE KIDS

Lacking a sticky product is a fairly common problem for entrepreneurs. Their expectations don't end up matching reality, and once the product launches that becomes apparent. Sometimes changes to the product itself or to the marketing of a product can lead to much greater market acceptance. But often such pivots aren't enough.

The founders of Bespoke Post went through a similar experience when they got their first market feedback for the venture they had launched before Bespoke Post. Rishi and Steve were part of the ERA accelerator program in New York, and had developed a QR-based application called Nabfly to scan for information and deals at retailers. They planned to make money from retailer advertising. It did not take off, for a number of reasons, one of which was the market feedback they got.

It wasn't working for a variety of reasons. Rishi had a computer science de-gree, but he wasn't really a computer scientist and it was very much a tech product. Neither of us are technical cofounders.

We weren't advertising people, either, and it was an advertising play. That was our business model—at least, that's what we said. We didn't have any experience in this space. We just didn't know what the hell we were doing, basically.

And we came to this realization after a few months operating, asking our-selves, "Other than me and you, how many people have you seen scan a QR code in New York?" The answer was zero.

We just didn't do any consumer research. We eventually got to a point where we just didn't believe in the idea.

Once you've admitted to yourself that you don't believe in the idea, then it's like, what's the point of continuing? For us, we were emotionally at the point where we were ready to cut our losses. We were ready to move off of this.

STEVE SZARONOS, BESPOKE POST

So, Steve and Rishi started over by launching an entirely differ-ent venture in men's e-commerce, Bespoke Post. They launched it as a monthly subscription box at a time when Facebook had emerged as an effective marketing platform for firms selling products to particular demographics. It worked.

In summary, unless you get exceptionally positive feedback, the feedback that blows you away, you should listen and iterate until you get it. In some cases, this will lead to the difficult conclusion that you were wrong and that your idea is not worth pursuing. But in most cases, you can fix things to find that oh-so-critical product/market fit. But don't be mistaken: you don't want to take the next step until this hap-pens, as you will be sent back to the drawing board at a later stage.

7

YOU ARE THE CHIEF
SALES OFFICER

As CEO, you are the chief sales officer. You are
the heartbeat of the company, its number
one sales person—and you need to tackle
the first hurdles to sales.

*Founders wear many hats, but I literally had to do what everyone in the
retail industry told me was impossible, would never happen. I had to convince the best brands around the world to sell to us, when in the beginning we had nothing.*

ALEXANDRA WILKIS WILSON, GILT

Among our HBS cohort, all founders were deeply involved, with most
taking on the role of "chief everything officer," but no responsibility
was more crucial than driving sales.

As a founder, you have the combination of vision and passion that
can get you through the sales hurdles. By "sales," we mean sales to customers but we also include selling to anyone in your company. So if you

need to close deals to get suppliers, cajole key hires to join your team, get a bank to fund a dental clinic, or get your first B2B sale, then you are the sales engine making that deal happen.

Excelling at sales means you learn the ins and outs of your business. Such knowledge is critical to be convincing and is invaluable in helping you define the next steps and, in the long term, form and manage your team.

THE FOUNDER IS THE SALES ENGINE

For the first three years of the business I went to every single event in every city. I was in three to five cities per week.

BERI MERIC, IVY

Selling to a "first" is really tough and a founder will be in the best position to radiate the passion and the persuasion needed to get customers and partners on board. Jim remembers how he took an active and critical role in getting the first customers at ShermansTravel and growing that customer base.

I called the agencies for Expedia and Travelocity. I explained the size of our travel deals newsletter and sold them on a weekly program. I personally grew the Travelocity deal from $5K to the millions. No one can sell your value and vision better than the founder, especially in the early days.

JIM SHERMAN, SHERMANSTRAVEL MEDIA

Not everybody is born a great salesperson, but the HBS entrepreneurs were all involved in early sales. They were doing it all and learned from the interactions with customers while attempting to close their first sales.

Josh from Plated did exactly that. After they built a very rough prototype web page, they put it up with a chat on the site, which was reasonably new at the time. They ran $10 a day of Facebook ads to drive small amounts of traffic to their website and he was the one who replied to every message.

The chat would proactively pop up. "Hello, how can I help you?" and I would just talk to them. Why did they click on the ad? What was appealing? What wasn't? What questions could I answer? I did this for days, weeks. We refined the messaging until finally somebody converted, actually pulled out a credit card, and ordered.

JOSH HIX, PLATED

The role of the founder is key not only when selling to customers, but also when convincing partners to get on board. In the case of Gilt, Alexandra described how difficult but important it was to get the brands on board in the early days, and how she gleaned the insight necessary to pull it off.

As an entrepreneur, in general, you're always selling yourself and selling your vision. But my functional job every day was listening and selling, and then not taking no for an answer. If a brand would say, "I'm not sure. Come back to me in six months when you have traction," I would listen. And I would listen to what their concerns were. And we would tailor our message to whoever we spoke to.

ALEXANDRA WILKIS WILSON, GILT

As a founder, you have the most drive to stick to it, especially when sales require intense perseverance.

While still a student at Harvard Business School, Carlos from RubiconMD was trying to get one of his first pilots going. Every day after class, he would walk up the street to a clinic that was about ten minutes away. He sat there and tried to talk to the medical director for days, without any results. They never kicked him out, though. Eventually, after about a month and a half of him going every day after class, he got his chance and the medical director loved the idea of the pilot.

As a founder, you have a key role to play as the sales engine. You radiate the passion needed to convince customers and partners that your project will succeed. It can take time and require resilience, but it is your job to make it happen.

Learn the Ins and Outs

If you are involved as a founder, you will know how to build it out, you will know how it works inside, the guts and operations of the product because you have been doing it yourself.

CARLOS REINES, RUBICONMD

If you are serious about building your business, you should roll up your sleeves, get involved, and learn every day about what works and what doesn't.

By doing so, you learn the nuts and bolts of the business. You are in a better position to sell and later on, when you are managing others, you have a good grasp of things and you understand the critical metrics that drive your business and its growth. If you did it all before, then you will be a better manager later.

We grew with Joanna playing customer service, customer product designer, recipe creator, head of commercialization, head of innovation, and all those things.

DAVE PARKER, YUMBLE KIDS

Catalina learned a ton when she initially had no team and was forced to do it all. This allowed her to develop a realistic plan, in terms of timing and volumes, which was critical to define what the fundraising needs were.

In the early days, I spent time in the lab to understand the product and the production process. I needed this to inform my discussions with manufacturers. I was also starting licensing discussions for the B2C side of the business and selling to B2B clients locally. The latter was an eye opener to me: I realized—contrary to early beliefs—that sales cycles would be very long.

Our product was great but I soon realized that it was much more complicated than that: the R&D departments needed to approve of the product and run their own tests and due diligence, which sometimes took months; then marketing needed to agree and packaging needed to be changed; then existing stocks needed to be sold first; then supermarkets and distributors needed to agree on shelf space, etc.

For those who know the food retail business, this would not come as a true surprise. But for me, it was all new. And being the one doing it gave me invaluable insights related to the ins and outs of the sales cycle. One of the direct implications was that I changed all initial financial forecasts to reflect the longer sales cycles and started a discussion with the board and shareholders about a new timeline and its impact on fundraising.

CATALINA DANIELS, SWEETWELL

TACKLE THE KEY HURDLES TO SALES: FIVE CASES

The ultimate objective in the ignition phase is to get sales going. It is often underestimated but every single company must overcome initial hurdles to get it off the ground.

In marketplaces, where you match supply and demand, there is always a chicken-and-egg problem: users will not join if there are no suppliers, and suppliers will not join if there are no users. So how do you overcome that hurdle and get the ball rolling?

With B2B startups, one of the key hurdles is not having references in the beginning. Corporations are risk-averse and will follow when a model is proven or when there is at least the perception thereof. There are numerous examples of managers at corporations getting in trouble for making a deal with an unknown startup. There are many fewer examples for making a deal with an established company. So, it is difficult for a small B2B startup to get their first corporate clients, even if it is for a pilot.

For B2C companies, the initial hurdle to get a first customer can be lower, but the issue becomes how to continue attracting more customers while keeping costs to acquire these customers to a minimum.

For high-tech or science-based ventures, the key hurdle simply may be convincing customers that "it works."

Every startup will have its own unique hurdles to overcome. Yet we often see entrepreneurs minimize the importance of hurdles, in the sense that they just assume that "it will sell," "people will change their behavior," or "marketing dollars will automatically convert into customers," etc. Understanding your specific key hurdles to your first sales is critical and you should spend enough time identifying the hurdles and figuring out how to tackle them.

Ahead we have selected five hurdle stories that we particularly like. Each has a different angle and focus, but they all prove that you, as a founder, have a key role to play in getting sales off the ground, which means truly understanding the hurdles and playing a key role in overcoming them.

...

THE CASE OF HENRY THE DENTIST

All my first customers were my vendors. I got my bank—they were my customer. My law firm was my customer. My accounting firm was my customer. They took me to their companies, and I serviced their employees.

JUSTIN JOFFE, HENRY THE DENTIST

Justin developed state-of-the art mobile dental trucks that travel to corporations and offer dental treatment to the corporations' employees. Unlike many of our other interviewees, Justin needed up-front capital to invest in the trucks. Like most B2B startups, he faced the issue of convincing the first customers without having any references.

In converting all of his vendors to become his first customers, his approach was remarkably pragmatic and efficient.

In addition, Justin needed to convince at least one insurance company to get on board—and preferably before he invested in the first mobile truck, since this would increase his chance of being successful. He managed to get discussions going with Delta Dental, which he had identified as a good partner. His approach was likewise unconventional.

I went to the gala of Summit Medical Group, paid $500 of my own pocket to go to a black-tie gala to sit at the table with Delta Dental. They didn't know that. I knew that. I went and made sure that I got seated at the Delta Dental table. Happened to sit next to the CMO and the VP of sales, "coincidentally," and started chatting.

"Oh, what do you do?" "No way, I'm in dentistry, too. I just started this mobile dental clinic. Yadda, yadda, yadda." Bounce forward the next two months. We signed a distribution deal. They basically represent us to their clients and introduce us as a benefit because we're in-network. We take the company's insurance. We don't charge companies. We don't charge patients. It promotes preventive care. And Delta Dental is the biggest dental insurance

carrier, with 1.8 million members in New Jersey and Connecticut alone. Fifty million members across the country.

JUSTIN JOFFE, HENRY THE DENTIST

THE CASE OF ZUMPER

Zumper is a marketplace for renters and landlords. Anthemos created it because he had moved multiple times within a few years, experiencing firsthand how difficult it was as a renter to close a deal. His vision was to create an online marketplace that not only connects renters and landlords, but allows them to close the deal online.

When he launched Zumper, the market was already competitive, with players like Zillow and Apartments.com offering well-developed search capabilities. And so Zumper faced the hurdle of building a marketplace combined with the additional hurdle of well-established competition in that space.

Anthemos decided to attract landlords by focusing on the basic search engine and not yet focusing on his unique feature to close a deal online (which competition did not offer). So the question became: How do you convince landlords to join yet another platform, which basically offers the same value as the competition but with fewer renters?

Borderline impossible. Straight chicken-and-egg. You have no users, so there is no reason for landlords to post. And you have no landlords, so there is no reason for users to come to the site. It was so difficult. The way we got around it was to build what is now a massive B2B tool for small landlords called Zumper Pro, which was a free tool for small landlords. It did two things: it allowed landlords to put their listings in all major sites, including Zumper, although in the first couple of years no landlord cared about Zumper.

And then, two, for all the leads that came in on those listings, we built a tenant screening tool for the landlords to use so they could kind of decide on who the best renter was. The whole point of that tool was just to get the listings before anyone else got them. And it worked. And the hack here was that it leveraged other platforms' demand to make it quite a compelling tool for small landlords.

ANTHEMOS GEORGIADES, ZUMPER

The free tool enabled Zumper to attract landlords who would otherwise not have been interested in joining their platform. At a later stage, when Zumper was big enough, they switched off all the third-party sites and only kept the listings on Zumper. It took them about two and a half years to get there. By then they had more than a million visits per month.

THE CASE OF GILT

Gilt, the well-known shopping website for flash sales of luxury items, faced a similar challenge as Zumper. Gilt had to persuade both suppliers and customers, which was particularly complicated because Gilt was a new concept. At the time, in 2007, luxury brands were barely selling online, and the notion of selling online at a discount was totally unheard-of. So while Gilt was positioning itself as an online channel, the brands had to see it as a way to get rid of unsold inventory.

Many of the brands at the time barely even sold online full price. Online was unfamiliar for many of them. And then online plus discount was very uncomfortable for most of them. So most of the brands, initially, when we spoke to them, never thought of Gilt as a marketing channel. It was really just to make the inventory go away.

ALEXANDRA WILKIS WILSON, GILT

Convincing the brands, especially the first ones, was a particularly difficult task. Gilt surmounted the challenge by approaching each brand in a tailor-made way, focusing on developing a true partnership based on the benefits for them. Slowly but surely, the brands came around to the new model of Gilt. As always, it was also crucial to get a first good brand to sign up, which then helped to get to the next.

The approach was very tailored to each brand, to each category. It took a lot of convincing, a lot of analysis. This is where having very, very smart, top-quality buyers going through the analysis of a perfect world, what they would want to have, was great.

Our first brand was Zac Posen. He was a darling in the fashion industry. He was cool. He used to get written about a lot in Vogue. Initially we had a very fashion-savvy audience. As we scaled, it went to a broader appeal.

We worked very closely with so many of the brands to figure out how we could get ahead of the supply chain. We would pick our inventory at the same time that all the full-price buyers would. And we would create a way to be a great partner to the brand, because we would commit to a certain amount of inventory. We wouldn't be allowed to sell it at discount until they told us, until it broke price in the department stores.

And then, if they were ever getting returns from places they sold, like the department stores were sending back inventory, we always were guaranteed a minimum of certain inventory levels, but we could also tap into more.
ALEXANDRA WILKIS WILSON, GILT

To attract customers in parallel, Gilt followed a path of creating tremendous excitement by allowing customers to join by invitation only. In addition, they used a referral program that gave an incentive for existing customers to bring new ones on board. All of this was very low cost, without marketing dollars. Alexandra recalls that she used every single contact she had to get the word out there.

*I had, at the time, nine thousand contacts in my phone. And I emailed every-
body in my phone. We didn't use social media. It was email marketing. And
then guerrilla-style marketing.*

*We opened up our membership on Halloween night, basically started No-
vember first, 2007. We spent no money on this. The mentality we had was
we wanted people to feel special that they were being invited.*

*The analogy of a hot new restaurant or even a nightclub that might have
some pretense of a long line outside of the nightclub with the red carpet and
the rope: the reality is it might be empty on the inside, but because you create that excitement around it, people just want it even more.*

*If a stranger came to the site and wanted to join, they could fill something
out and a few days later they got in. It was very much smoke and mirrors.
But it didn't matter. People still were excited by it.*

*We also would run around the city. We had interns with little cards that
we'd leave in strategic places to spread the word. And then this give/get
$25 incentive, the referral, was really compelling. All of our marketing was
paying for that $25 credit.*

ALEXANDRA WILKIS WILSON, GILT

THE CASE OF BLUE APRON

For Blue Apron, which sells subscription-based ingredients to cook
meals, the major hurdle was to get people to subscribe not knowing if
the ingredients were fresh and if they would like the model, including
the home cooking. To overcome it, they developed a creative and innovative low-cost referral program.

The program was creative in the sense that it allowed Blue Apron,
a new concept, to naturally grow customers who would otherwise not
have felt compelled to try it. The company leveraged existing relationships and developed what Matt calls a "genuine referral," since the ben-
eficiary of the referral would be the new member—which is contrary to
most programs, which give the benefit to the person who refers.

The genuine referral allowed Blue Apron not only to overcome the hurdle of convincing people of the new concept, but also to do so at low cost. At time of writing, it is still a big part of their acquisition volume.

It was a bizarre referral program. We did not let anyone refer anyone. We only allowed you to refer a friend after cooking with us for three full weeks. At that point we did not give you anything to refer your friend. Usually, in a referral program, you get something like a commission or a discount. We gave you nothing. We just said, "Hey, would you like to refer a friend? If so, we'll give your friend a free delivery." We took all the value that we would normally provide to a referrer and gave it to the person being referred. And we only let people who had been cooking with us, knew our product well, and liked our product enough that they had been cooking with us for three weeks, do that.

So the referral was a genuine referral. No one felt like it was being given to you by a person on paid-commission who's only in it for the money.

One of the marketing barriers that we had to overcome in the early days, especially at the time in 2012, when no one was buying food online, was, "Hey, if I'm going to get an online grocery delivery, how do I know it's going to be good? How do I know it's going to be fresh? How do I know it's going to be cold?" And we got over that hurdle with new customers because, one, they were hearing about it from a trusted friend who had already tried and used the product for three weeks, and two, there was no risk. You got it in the mail for free.

The referral program is an incredibly effective return on investment for us, incredibly scalable, and still to this day represents a gigantic portion of our overall acquisition volume in terms of registrants and new customers. Even at the scale we're operating at today, and we have millions of customers.

MATT SALZBERG, BLUE APRON

...

THE CASE OF SHERMANSTRAVEL MEDIA

In the case of ShermansTravel, the major hurdle was amassing a large enough audience of qualified travelers who would entice online travel advertisers. Jim believed that consumers wanted to save time in their online research of great travel deals. The online and email advertising market—especially in travel—was large and growing rapidly in the early 2000s.

By curating and handpicking travel deals from hundreds of suppliers, ShermansTravel would save the consumer time on their research. He could have spent loads of money on advertising to build up his own consumer newsletter list of email subscribers. This would have cost him millions. Instead he managed to strike a deal with the *New York Times* to test the waters. This turned out to be a crucial way for him to assess advertiser demand and get the business off the ground.

I struck a distribution deal with the Times *to "rent" their list of 500K active travelers every Wednesday, and then I would put together a published list of travel deals from ShermansTravel advertisers—cruise lines, airlines, etc.—to send to that list cobranded with the* Times. *I pitched advertisers on getting their travel deals listed as text links in front of this qualified list of travelers plus placements on our website. It was a great way to test the market to see if I could sell the online ads to travel suppliers. It took off. We were sold out every week. In one call, I sold Expedia on a weekly program. Then Travelocity, and then every other major travel booking site.*

From these early advertisers, I could then invest earnings into spending money on our own list building marketing efforts and the expansion of our website. That's how it grew after the first hurdle.

JIM SHERMAN, SHERMANSTRAVEL MEDIA

PART III

Scaling

The Struggles of (Explosive) Growth

The first year we thought we'd be lucky if we hit a million dollars. We had over $5M in orders, so we had to cancel half of it. And then the next year we ended up thinking we would do $10M and we ended up having $30M in gross orders.

ANTHONY SOOHOO, DOT & BO

8

IT'S ALL ABOUT EXECUTION

> Scaling is a grind. Execution never comes
> easy, but it teaches you the essentials
> of your competitive advantage.

Nothing's about luck. People didn't fail because of lack of luck. They failed because of lack of execution.

JUSTIN JOFFE, HENRY THE DENTIST

After your first sales, the next phase is growth. If you are doing well, you will grow fast. Congratulations—you will now enter one of the trickiest phases of your entrepreneurial journey.

Why? There are multiple reasons. To name just a few: you need to move from a minimum viable product that tested well with some customers to a real business with many, many more customers; your team must evolve from a small nucleus, often composed of friends, to an organization; your vision and passion, which were initially sufficient to propel you, must translate into traction and metrics; and on and on. If you are growing fast, it can feel like running a new company every six months.

When you sum it up, scaling requires a massive transition, where at any point one or several things can go wrong. The simple reason why so many startups fail during this phase, despite a great idea and proven product/market fit with early customers, is execution.

Before we continue, let us clarify what we mean by execution. Execution can relate to marketing, operations, technology, logistics, software, systems, etc. It's both any aspect of business building and your capacity to deliver what you promised, on time, and within certain financial limits independent from external factors.

In other words, as the HBS founders showed us, execution in many ways becomes more important than your idea or MVP. To execute well, you must get stronger, not just bigger. You must learn what you're good at. You must balance the tension with your customers between scale and intimacy. Finally, you must use the hurdles you surmount as a competitive advantage to grow fast and well.

GET ON THE GROWTH CURVE

We launched summer 2012. By 2014 we already did $80M in revenue. And then we did $300M revenue in 2015. And then $800M revenue in 2016.

MATT SALZBERG, BLUE APRON

We don't want to state the obvious, but the first thing when we talk about scaling is to get on the growth curve. Execution in this case means making growth happen day in and day out in a sustainable way. While you may have achieved product/market fit with early customers during the ignition phase, getting on the growth curve in scaling is crucial to confirm the product/market fit and demonstrate that the opportunity is in fact a large one.

What you read about in the news (and what we heard from some entrepreneurs) are the fabulous growth stories, when sales take off like a rocket to the moon. Although every entrepreneur dreams about such a scenario, reality for most startups is different. It doesn't "just" happen and it is a lot of work.

It was harder than we anticipated to get the engine going and to scale. It took us longer than we thought. The low-hanging fruit was not that tasty. And the obvious growth levers, for the most part, didn't work.

GREG GERONEMUS, SMARTOURS

For a B2C company, to scale up, you will need to choose the right channel(s) to accelerate growth. The critical question is whether the costs to build sales are sustainable. In Greg's case, what he thought was obvious, low hanging fruit was optimizing digital marketing but this didn't work. What did work was traditional direct mail marketing.

If you are fortunate, you will have a great deal of word of mouth and this will propel growth.

With Gilt, the founders relied on word of mouth from their early adopters to help drive initial traction. The strong word-of-mouth marketing also helped to propel them during their scale-up phase.

In a similar way, Matt's Blue Apron leveraged the fact that their customers loved talking with their friends about the meals they made. Due to this behavior, he created a referral program that propelled the growth of their meal kit business.

The very first week I came up with the idea for a referral program, which I thought was critical to the business because it's genuine marketing from your customers. And it doesn't cost the same kind of money that traditional paid marketing costs. The business grew exponentially through our referral program in the earliest days.

MATT SALZBERG, BLUE APRON

In the cases of both Gilt and Blue Apron, low-cost referral or word-of-mouth marketing was essential to getting the business on the growth curve.

Meanwhile, Zumper got on their growth curve by cracking Google search engine optimization (SEO) for organic traffic. They wouldn't attract real estate customers if they didn't have a large volume of potential renters browsing their listings. So they focused on figuring out the puzzle of Google search.

Others scaled up by experimenting with traditional paid marketing. As we discussed earlier, Bespoke Post used Facebook, a young marketing platform at the time, to launch and scale its venture. Without Facebook, the firm arguably could not exist. The platform was and is a growth traction channel that they used to efficiently reach and convert subscribers.

There was a point where we got our paid marketing to work. Figuring out acquisition was a scaling pain point. And that's what led to our Series A. We could show a payback period. We had a good handle on the unit economics, and we felt that we could scale the business if we had more money.

STEVE SZARONOS, BESPOKE POST

These founders and others needed to ensure that acquisition costs were low and retention high as they scaled. If costs rise or retention suffers, then you will face new challenges as your marketing investments will have diminishing returns. Finding your growth marketing or traction channels to ensure profitable, healthy growth is essential.

With B2B companies, the challenges are similar, though the tactics will differ. Getting on the growth curve means deciding who your ideal next prospects are, how to optimally price, how to generate qualified leads and how to get the ball rolling.

For example, Justin focused initially on selling one key strategic partnership, Delta Dental, on his unique service for their corporate customers. He then realized that the most efficient way to scale and onboard companies and their employees to try his mobile dental clinic would be to work through dental insurers, rather than trying to sell directly to corporate HR directors.

I went to all the carriers to try to create distribution deals. My spray-and-pray. I didn't know HR benefit managers. That isn't where my relationship networks are. I tried to get big insurance carriers—Mercer, Cigna, Dental, Aetna, MetLife—to be my marketing channel. This was all hustle—the constant, all-day, every-day hustling.

JUSTIN JOFFE, HENRY THE DENTIST

Getting on the growth curve is a huge accomplishment. While challenging to achieve product/market fit, it is even more challenging to demonstrate sustained traction with users and customers. If you succeed, you are proving that your initial success was not a false positive.

Finally, if you are not getting on the growth curve, you need to understand why. It might be related to your sales and marketing strategy or to your product. You might actually not have found the product/market fit you thought you had. Or, you have it but the market for it is not in fact a large one as you expected. If that is the case (which it often is), you will need to adapt or pivot (we will dig into these topics in the chapters ahead).

At first, you're like, "We totally have product/market fit" and you think you figured it out. But selling to a couple of accounts isn't product/market fit.

ANNA AUERBACH, WERK

...

MANAGE THE GRIND AND CHAOS

We were on fire in terms of growth. But there was chaos. There were tech challenges, infrastructure challenges. The infrastructure you put together for a startup, it's pretty much not the infrastructure as you scale. We used to say, "At some point every bit of our infrastructure is almost going to break," and so you have to repair everything and set it up for scale. Those were painful times.

ALEXANDRA WILKIS WILSON, GILT

Once growth kicks in, you need to deliver. That is when many entrepreneurs realize that their model is not yet scalable, at least not in the way they thought it would be. Many insufficiently anticipate what is required in technology, operations, supply chain, and back office to make growth happen in a sustainable way.

It can be a long, intense grind to iron out the kinks as you scale. In the case of Gilt, faced with the severe infrastructure issues Alexandra mentioned above, Gilt's head of engineering came to her with some tough news. "We need to redo a lot of our tech. Please don't sell any of the good brands for the next six months because the site will crash," he said.

That was a crazy thing to say. Inventory's seasonal. I'm not selling bathing suits in November. We had to work through that and manage that. And we didn't want to be stuck with our own excess inventory. So, we had to get really creative about solutions. That was a stressful period.

ALEXANDRA WILKIS WILSON, GILT

Matt from Blue Apron explains the grind well. Blue Apron grew its customer base fast thanks to its innovative customer loyalty program. Once the growth kicked in, they lacked some of the required systems, which impaired their execution.

On the operations front, it was a constant struggle to make the supply chain come together to ship a box every week. And so we'd have periods of time where we wouldn't ship all of our deliveries on time. We'd have to tell customers, "Sorry, you're not getting your box this week because we had an upstream supply chain issue," or, "Our labor scheduling and management in our fulfillment centers wasn't done appropriately and we didn't have the manpower to physically do all the work we had to do." There were constantly issues with trucks breaking down.

I would describe a lot of the problems as upstream supply chain planning because we had not yet developed all those systems. And we were managing the complexity without robust systems to manage labor planning in our call centers, upstream supply, purchasing, and more. A lot of it was done manually through intuition and spreadsheets.

I also wish we had invested in more robust HR systems and processes earlier on in the company's life in order to be more prepared for that huge growth in employee population.

MATT SALZBERG, BLUE APRON

As Matt explains, many of the problems could have been avoided if they had invested earlier in the right systems. But it is not always easy to anticipate and know what to invest in. The problem is that operations might seem manageable and simple in the early days, but, as you grow, the sheer volumes create the complexity. Josh from Plated explains how increasing volumes created a true challenge.

The hardest thing is the sum of the parts. It's not one thing. It's not that hard to package ingredients. It's not that hard to write a recipe. It's not that hard to acquire a customer. The challenge is the operational intensity and the cadence. And it's gotten bigger and more complex over the years.

We write a set of recipes and then do some fairly sophisticated demand forecasting to manage food waste. And then receive, and then portion, and then kit, and then ship, and then deliver, and then do the customer service for said recipes every single week. It's that cycle and the speed of it and the turnover that creates the difficulty, in my opinion. It's doing all of that and doing it over and over at Six Sigma levels of quality and accuracy. It's not one thing. Retail is detail. What is hard about what Walmart does? Buying. Stocking the shelf. Selling. It's none of those things; it's doing everything right every single day in a way that is high quality so you can drive low prices.

Josh Hix, Plated

Executing at scale is a grind. And that is not necessarily because operations are hard, but because they become hard at high volume. That is when things get missed.

So, as you grind, there are a couple of things to keep in mind.

First, take the mindset that things will take much more time than you expect. Build that in. If you have no previous experience, you will be ill-prepared and it will take even more time.

It takes time to know the answer to questions like, "This person should be with me or not," or, "I should do this partnership or not," or, "I should take this investor or not." It takes time to work through those things and think about the ramifications.

Justin Joffe, Henry the Dentist

Second, take the mindset that you will make mistakes. Rent the Runway, for whom technology was key, initially tried to outsource it, as they did not have the skill in-house. Jenny remembers that this did not work out too well.

Initially, we tried to outsource technology, and we were too trusting about a partner whom we didn't know enough about. And we went too long just trusting and letting them run and go build stuff. That's definitely one of the biggest mistakes we made.

JENNY FLEISS, RENT THE RUNWAY

For many startups, this will be a recognizable situation. If you out-source technology and you are not 100 percent aligned with your technology partner, it can lead to very tricky situations with disastrous consequences.

Very often, issues arise in areas that you have not identified as truly critical. But the mistakes can still be devastating. Jake from Cross-Boundary recalls that they were late in getting a back-office function because they were too focused on building the business. To face the problem, they hired somebody external with a good résumé who had loads of experience in larger companies. It turned out this person was not used to working in smaller environments and made many mistakes.

There were a lot of things being missed. Somebody might get onboarded and their insurance might not get started until a month late. Or we're work-ing in all these different countries and we're looking at stuff where we might not be fully tax compliant and stuff like that.

JAKE CUSACK, CROSSBOUNDARY

It is important to embrace the mindset that it will take time and that you will make mistakes so that you avoid getting stuck or demoralized because things don't work out as well or as fast as you wish. The good news is that by grinding away, you are identifying and creating the business advantages that are crucial to long-term success.

...

FIND YOUR COMPETITIVE ADVANTAGE IN EXECUTION

Every startup has a plan and a strategy to ultimately scale. However, it's one thing to have a scaling strategy, and it's another to execute and manage the grind and chaos day-to-day. For many startups, this led them to identify and develop a competitive advantage that would give them a true edge.

While certain startups may have proprietary technology or scientific IP, there are others that may find ways to develop different kinds of competitive advantages related to execution—mastering operations, reaching scale, sourcing supply, marketing skills, or developing network effects. For most HBS entrepreneurs, their competitive edge became clear as they scaled.

Jim shows how competitive advantages arise when surmounting scaling challenges.

One of the key challenges in an online media business is finding an efficient way to build a large audience. I knew that if we could crack the marketing code and find efficient marketing channels to grow our audience, then we could achieve scale and a competitive advantage.

The problem as we executed on the plan was that we would tap out one marketing channel—would hit a ceiling on efficient user acquisition—and so needed to find another. So, we built a competency in marketing, including investment in our tech and data analytics, to rapidly test and optimize. This competency allowed us to achieve scale advantages. Interestingly, when I raised money, some VCs discounted marketing as a competitive advantage. They thought it could be copied. No moat. Yet, I always believed that being a first mover and even sometimes a second mover in marketing can create a competitive edge if you succeed in rapid scaling, making it hard for others to beat.

JIM SHERMAN, SHERMANSTRAVEL MEDIA

In some cases, the execution skill that ultimately becomes a key competitive advantage is unexpected. Such was the situation with Rent the Runway. Jenn and Jenny discovered a few competitive advantages that came later in their business evolution. For example, Jenny explains how logistics—not just relationships with the designers—emerged as the *true* competitive advantage in which they needed to invest.

Designer relationships definitely continue to be a trend and something that for a long time we had to consciously work on a bunch. But our venture capital partner had a sense of how logistics would actually be the key crux for us, both as the competitive advantage and as the most capital intensive, the hardest part of the business. It's been where we've invested a ton of time and energy. And it's become the competitive advantage that's kept others from becoming a player in the space.

JENNY FLEISS, RENT THE RUNWAY

Jenny's cofounder, Jenn, comments on another advantage that came as a surprise. In an interview with Reid Hoffman on his *Masters of Scale* podcast, Jenn noted that "as technologically advanced as Rent the Runway's operations are, the most important quality-control functions come down to expressly human tasks, like . . . smelling."

There's nothing that replaces a sniff test. There's nothing that replaces a visual quality inspection of being able to zip something up and move the zipper down, seeing if the hook and eye can close, stretching the material out and seeing if there are small holes that you wouldn't have noticed via the technology. I think that this is a business where specialized labor has to exist in our warehouses.

JENN HYMAN, RENT THE RUNWAY

Rent the Runway had initially thought that they would outsource the dry cleaning, but realized later on that it was such a big part of the execution, they had to keep it in-house—so they made it a true competitive advantage.

As Rent the Runway scaled, their success became largely dependent on becoming one of the world's largest dry-cleaning operations, on managing complex logistics, and on developing a data insights practice that was unseen in the fashion industry.

Hoffman has described this approach to execution as the founder's need "to master the business behind your business," which "just might be the critical factor that lets you break out."

In the case of Bespoke Post, Steve talks about his company's multiple strengths, which they used to create a fortified moat for their business to become a leader (arguably the leader) in men's e-commerce and subscription services, with over 300K members.

We're good at three things. We're good at merchandising and curation, i.e., picking things that people like. Second is we have scale and we're good at sourcing. We can get good quality products for a really good price because we can commit to a lot of units. That's an important one. Nobody's buying as many units as we are from small brands in just a few SKUs. Third is that we've been able to market to and acquire men. Eighty-five-plus percent of the people who are actually typing in their credit cards are guys, which is very unique. Even for companies focused on men, a lot of times it's women who are actually doing the purchasing. Women do about 70 percent of all nontech purchasing anyway. Even in men's companies it's often a 50/50 split. So, we're overwhelmingly guys buying for themselves.

STEVE SZARONOS, BESPOKE POST

Today it would be hard for a competitor to compete directly with Bespoke Post because their moat is deep and wide.

The key point is to at all times take a step back and have a crystal-clear view on what part of execution can or should be your core competitive strengths. You might be surprised by some that emerge unexpectedly during the scale-up.

9

SEE THE FOREST
THROUGH THE TREES

> When scaling up, keep your hands on your business's
> metrics and your eyes on its future.

I'm trying to always think about not what the problem is this month, but where we are in a year, what are the potential problems that we'll face in a year, and what are the potential opportunities for growth.

JAKE CUSACK, CROSSBOUNDARY

As you grow and scale, one of the biggest risks you will face is to lose perspective, become overwhelmed by what is going on, and address significant problems too late. Anticipation will save you many execution-related problems. But to anticipate you need to know where to focus.

You can't get lost in day-to-day problems, so you want to know enough to allow you to anticipate which problem(s) might become a key issue. At the same time, you must always think about the future, making sure that you spot and don't miss the next big opportunity.

So, what enables you to both anticipate problems and focus on opportunities?

During our interviews two things emerged. First, metrics are critical as you scale. You want to have the right metrics to understand where you stand. Especially as CEO, you must know the metrics, which show you how to focus your time on what truly matters. Avoid getting lost in detail and instead focus on the future, the most difficult issues, and the most promising opportunities. Second, you want to run your finances in order to not run into trouble: cash is king, and profits (or the prospect for them) become paramount.

METRICS, METRICS, METRICS

I need 30 companies per mobile clinic and it's full. I know that I get 7 to 10 percent utilization in a company. If I go to a 1,000-person company, I know that 70 to 100 people are going to come to me. I know that I see 20 people a day, which means I need five days on-site. I'll book a 1,000-person office with five days at a company.

Merck is 4,000 people, it's four weeks. I go every three to four months. Basically, 30 companies of 500 or more employees fill a clinic. If I get 90 companies of 500 or more employees, I've filled my three clinics in perpetuity, and that's a $4M run rate of just the mobiles, and spinning out more than a million profit. These are really big unit economics.

JUSTIN JOFFE, HENRY THE DENTIST

Justin exemplifies what it means to know your metrics. Justin knew exactly what the key drivers of his business growth were.

As a founder, you need to be able to tell anybody at any point in time how your business is scaled and what the impact is on financials. But in our experience as angels, we see many entrepreneurs who do not know their metrics. They know some numbers, but they can't explain how the business works and where they stand. Doing so is absolutely critical because if you don't know your metrics, you are managing blindfolded.

Knowing your key metrics is something you should start doing before you are scaling.

As your business grows, the metrics will become more encompassing and should reflect your business's finances, marketing, and other operations. Specific key metrics could include the cost to acquire a customer per channel; the lead generation cost per inquiry; the cost of goods sold (COGS) percentage of revenue; operating profit percentage; website traffic data; and monthly cash burn, among many others. The trick is not to have too many of them but to always have your pulse on the few key metrics most important to your business.

Finding the right metrics takes time but it is a game changer once you have them. I would argue that—as a founder—you don't need more than ten metrics. People in the organization should have their own ten metrics, but those should be in sync with yours. They cannot be disconnected. You will know when you have the right metrics because they help you manage the business. I would use some of the metrics with my board [always the same] and with prospective investors. If you have the right metrics, they will help support these discussions.

CATALINA DANIELS, SWEETWELL

Data and metrics are also at the heart of creating a culture of experimentation. A test-and-learn culture. Without capturing the data and having the metrics, it is impossible to have this test-and-learn capability.

The founders of Rent the Runway understood that they make money by maximizing their clothing utilization. Each garment or accessory should be rented as many times as possible *and* be maintained so as to maximize its "life."

Key to maximizing utilization is understanding which piece is used for what purpose by which customer. In becoming a data insight power-house, Rent the Runway came to use data not only for itself but also for its suppliers, the fashion brands. Indeed, it leveraged the data from its customers to inform suppliers about usage and to give them ideas about what designs would work best in the future. For most fashion designers, this was detailed and timely information they had never had before, which helped Rent the Runway strengthen their cooperation with the brands.

The right metrics should enable you to run the business by under-standing *how* you are performing and *when* to get in front of any dis-turbing trends in the numbers. Thus the numbers inform how you end up spending your time as a CEO. Indeed, you don't want to get lost in day-to-day stuff in which you can easily drown. A good rule is that you should spend your time on the top 10 percent (major strategic issues) and the bottom 10 percent issues (what needs fixing). The middle can be delegated.

The key lesson here: know your metrics. If you're going to scale, a lot of things are going to happen. You're going to be extremely busy. A lot of positive things, a lot of negative things. A lot of day-to-day stuff. But you need to be extremely clear on what your key metrics are so you can take a step back from all that business and growth, and really be sure that you're on the right path of scaling.

BERI MERIC, IVY

REVENUE IS NOT CASH

There's a very big difference between revenue and cash. That's one of the things you learn very much and very quickly the hard way—booked revenue is not recognized revenue, nor is it cash. That's something that took a bit to sink in.

We had a very quick sale cycle. From conversation to close, about ninety days to 120 days, which is superfast for an enterprise sale.

Compliance and procurement can take three to six months. And then we generally are subject to sixty- to ninety-day payment terms.

You add all that up and you're like, that's great, you sold a company in three to four months. But you're not getting that cash for at least another six months. That's really hard as a business.

ANNA AUERBACH, WERK

Of all the key metrics, one should always be cash. If you run out of cash, you run out of business. And if you realize too late that you are running out of cash, there is a true probability that you will have a hard time raising more. You do not want to raise funds in a situation where time is not on your side.

When it comes to cash, one common mistake is to think that when you make a sale, you immediately get the cash. Anna from Werk realized late in the process that her projections to receive payment were off, because sales cycles were longer than anticipated. Werk ended up raising a bridge round for this reason. You may wonder how somebody might miss this, but we see it happen all the time.

"Conversation to cash" was a new metric we hadn't thought about. Which is different from conversation to close or discovery call to close—we had to think about conversation to cash, about how we anticipated market adoption, in addition to the conversation-to-cash cycle.

ANNA AUERBACH, WERK

While Anna learned the hard way that cash would take nine to twelve months to reach their accounts after contract signature, other business models allowed entrepreneurs to receive the cash from customers up front, before incurring the expenses or before the customers got the product. This is the case for subscription-based businesses like

Blue Apron or Plated, which get paid up front on subscription and pay their suppliers on thirty- (or more) day terms.

Blue Apron was incredibly capital efficient until about 2016. We had built a negative working capital cycle into our model where we got our customers to pay us with their credit cards a couple of days before we shipped them. And we paid all of our suppliers on credit terms. So as we were garage fast, our suppliers were basically floating the capital for our business, which was a really nice thing.

MATT SALZBERG, BLUE APRON

Monthly Burn and Cash Flow Metrics

As CEO, you want to make sure that you install a simple mechanism to know how much money you have in the bank, how much money you expect to flow in the next X weeks, and, even more importantly, how much money you "burn" every month. These metrics are absolutely key and need to be top of mind. In addition, managing your accounts payable is a key lever that you need to master early on.

Pay as late as you can and negotiate those terms up front. Get paid as fast as you can and negotiate those terms up front.

Entrepreneurs often ask us how much time should be spent on financial scenarios and planning. For many, the question is when to move from unit economics to business planning. We loved the advice from Justin of Henry the Dentist on that front:

I have a theory that a company should plan as far as into the future as the age of the company. Your first year, you should be focused on the next twelve months. You should know the next twelve months really well. When you're in year three, you should have a thirty-six-month plan. And when you're in year ten, you should be thinking about how to get to Mars. Jeff Bezos should be thinking about how to get to Mars because they're at a stage to be thinking about that. But when you're a popcorn kernel of a company that's pre-million dollars, you should be hyperfocused on the next twelve to twenty-four months.

JUSTIN JOFFE, HENRY THE DENTIST

Independent of how long you plan for, if your metrics look bad—your losses are mounting, your cash reserves are dwindling, and you aren't able to raise financing—then having an "oh sh-t strategy" or Plan B is important for survival.

One thing that comforted me—and our investors—was knowing that if the online advertising market stalled, we could always slash our marketing spend for audience acquisition and thereby get to break-even fast. We didn't have a large amount of fixed costs. We could restructure fast. And that's exactly what we had to do to survive the Covid-19 pandemic.

JIM SHERMAN, SHERMANSTRAVEL MEDIA

THE TENSION BETWEEN GROWTH AND PROFIT

Another big topic for entrepreneurs is at what stage you need to be profitable. Although there seems to be somewhat of an evolution on that front, many U.S.-based scale-ups (and even unicorns) favor growth over profits for a long time. There are many examples of companies who IPO'd based on their revenues or user base, rather than on their profits. Think of Uber and Airbnb. In many of these cases, it is even unclear what the path to profitability would be. Despite their fast revenue growth they remain significantly unprofitable, but they continue to scale with enough cash flow from investors.

European entrepreneurs, on the other hand, tend to favor profit above growth. Catalina, who coaches European scale-ups in the U.S., is constantly surprised by European entrepreneurs boasting about the fact that they are profitable in their second or third year of existence, while U.S. companies tend to emphasize fast growth while underplaying losses.

It is clear that aiming for profits early on in the life of a startup or scale-up can have a taxing impact on growth. It is okay to go without profits, especially as you invest in growth, but you need to assess the timing for eventually getting to profitability and how much cash you'll burn along the way. Miscalculating this timing is dangerous.

In addition, a relentless focus on growth can also have negative consequences. Beri from Ivy, the leadership community for professionals that organizes events, learned the hard way that focusing on growth can get you in trouble.

My huge mistake or key learning is that top line is a terrible indicator of success, because it's great while it lasts, but if you can't weather a storm with your top line, if the cost base is not variable with your top line, it will get you in real trouble.

BERI MERIC, IVY

Focusing on growth came with a cost for Beri. As growth stalled, the company got in trouble because of its fixed costs. He had to launch a major restructuring to survive. Beri nevertheless acknowledges that there is pressure to show growth, which seems to stand for "success."

There are so many examples of unicorns that make you think you're supposed to grow fast if you want to have success. I'd actually say, I wish someone pushed me to grow without hiring people and without spending more money. And if I was going to burn money, force me to burn money on things that only correlate to growth. Variable cost that's just to fuel growth.

BERI MERIC, IVY

The other issue with focusing on revenues instead of profits is that at some point, the markets can turn against you and the financing windows close. This is particularly the case if you can't put forward a path to profitability.

So, entrepreneurs should regularly ask themselves the question: *When should we shift from growth to profit?*

The question is, are you going to feel like you'll have more success if you remain as a growth company? Or do you believe you'll have more success as a nongrowth company?

ANTHONY SOOHOO, DOT & BO

So, what is the right answer? When do you shift from revenues to profits? As investors, we strongly believe that every entrepreneur should have a view on how to ultimately reach profitability.

It is usual to go through a phase of investment and losses, which will require additional financing, but there should be light at the end of the tunnel. It is also a natural process to invest in areas such as marketing, technology, or logistics, in order to experiment and grow. Without those investments, you can't grow. HBS professor Jeffrey Rayport refers to this phase as one where you need to shift from proving product/market fit and growing revenues to proving "profit/market fit."

For many companies, the economics only start working after reaching a certain scale. In other words, you must grow to a certain volume of activity to get your unit costs down so that you can start making a profit.

We believe that if you know your metrics and have a cogent view on investments, then you should have an estimate of at what volume you will reach profitability. The longer that time horizon is to reach profitability, the greater the risks.

Whether you're pursuing profitability in the short or long term, the metrics that show you *how* to scale are only half the story—the *who* is the other half. Scaling won't happen without you and your team.

10

MORPH YOUR TEAM
AND YOURSELF

> Few entrepreneurs excel as managers.
> You are likely not the best person
> to scale your business.

We just kept outgrowing the team; we had to upgrade and get the right people in the right roles. Someone rolling up their sleeves is a lot different at $2M than when you're an organization that is about to hit over $100M in revenue.

ANTHONY SOOHOO, DOT & BO

Throughout your scaling journey, you will face the continual challenge of making sure you have the right people in place to handle the growth. Since you will not be able to anticipate all the things that go wrong, the people on your team will be key to making sure you tackle the problems and handle the situation.

You will need to hire more people, acquire new skill sets, and grow into an organization with new faces where not everyone knows everyone.

As the company evolves, the founders will need to evolve, too, as they make the tricky transition from entrepreneur (who does a bit of everything) to manager (who leads others who do everything). Not every founder will like it and not every founder will be able to do it. That's because the early phases require creative skills and extraordinary passion, while the later phases require strong operations and management skills. Few people can excel at both.

As a matter of fact, history has shown that most often the initial founders are not the best leaders for their scaled organizations. According to *Harvard Business Review*, the founder-CEO is more valuable in a non-CEO role after six years.

The team transition is a tricky one but is key, since it is the people who will ensure you will be able to handle all the challenges associated with growth.

HIRE. HIRE. HIRE.

I think the key to a young founder being successful is getting the right people below you, getting the right diversity of skill sets, and having the right team members involved.

MATT SALZBERG, BLUE APRON

Growth requires hiring new people. Very often, a lot of new people and fast, which makes hiring in the scaling phase a true challenge. Finding the right people is far from given and hiring mistakes will have a negative impact on your financials and your culture.

As we will see later in chapter 17, culture plays a critical role in your ability to both attract and retain talent, which will make a true difference when you need to hire fast.

Being able to both identify the right talent and then convince the talent to join your startup is a crucial skill set. Many entrepreneurs would put it at the top of the list, after coming up with the right business idea. The power of the founder CEO to persuade talent to join the team cannot be overestimated.

Besides the plain challenge of adding more people, what happens with growth is that a current role will likely transform into one that exceeds the person's skill set. The person you hired as head of marketing to get going is different from the one you now need as CMO. The same issues bubble up in other departments, like technology, operations, finance, etc.

A lot of people that are good at managing large scale suck at doing stuff small. They don't have the mindset for it.

In the field of innovation, for example, the definition of innovation is different as you evolve, because we need to start innovating around things that are already working and not working. For that you need folks who have more experience managing large teams.

ANTHONY SOOHOO, DOT & BO

The HBS founders showed us that hiring has three overlooked aspects: it's about knowing whether to bring in talent from the outside or to promote from within, knowing when exactly to pull the trigger on hiring, and recognizing that hiring matters for senior and lower-level roles.

A key question as you add people is, do you choose somebody from the outside or make an internal promotion? Experienced external managers can bring a wealth of expertise that the team needs. But outsiders might demotivate young high-potentials who were hoping to get the promotion. Bringing in people from the outside at a high level can also be tricky from a culture point of view.

In terms of hiring the more senior team, we routinely had the pain points of having to decide if we were going to give a more junior manager a stretch

position and rely on them, or hire and bring in someone who was more ex-
perienced. In some cases we brought in people who were more experienced.
And in other cases we let it ride on internal folks. We were correct more often
than we were wrong, but we made mistakes on that. That caused big problems
when we made mistakes that we had to correct. That was a big challenge.

You have to make that decision on a case-by-case basis. In general, given
how fast we were growing, I sort of wish we had brought in a little bit more of
those external, more experienced and specialized people sooner. And there
were probably certain management roles that we kept less experienced
people in for a little bit too long. That caused certain problems.

I felt a sense of loyalty to some of the people who had gotten us to where
we got. Even though they didn't have the experience operating at scale, I
wanted to give them a shot, because I would give myself a shot at it, too. I
hadn't done it before, either. Getting the right mix of that was a challenge.

MATT SALZBERG, BLUE APRON

Finding the balance between internal and external hires is difficult
and is more an art than a science. Many aspects come into play and,
since you're dealing with people, emotions will always be involved.

Overall, we would argue that if you have somebody with the required potential in-house, an internal promotion offers big advantages:
it is cheaper, probably less risky, and less disruptive for the team and for
the company's culture. But it assumes that you support that person in
the transition.

The big point is to help them change roles proactively. If you're suddenly go-
ing from an individual contributor to a manager of the group, you go to sleep
Friday as an individual contributor. Monday you come in as a manager. Like,
you're not going to be automatically different. You didn't wake up a different
person. Just be really thoughtful about how do you set this person up for
success and give them the space to grow into that new role.

ANNA AUERBACH, WERK

Favoring the best profile will always be your right choice. Alexandra from Gilt gave good advice when she explained that she always tried to surround herself with people who were better than herself.

I always want to hire people that are, in some ways, smarter than I am. I always want to learn from others.

ALEXANDRA WILKIS WILSON, GILT

It is a known capability of leaders to attract and hire A-level talent. If you surround yourself with a very strong team, the likelihood of you being able to attract additional talented people will increase, as A people work like magnets to other A people.

In that sense, it makes sense to carefully consider each top hiring position and not rush into things. Knowing *when* to hire is itself a skill. You might have heard the saying "hire slowly and fire fast." Dave from Yumble Kids explains well how growth can put immense pressure on hiring fast, but—whatever the pressure—take the needed time to make the right hiring decision.

I've been accused by some people of hiring too slowly. We're having explosive growth, we need to start building out a big team. I agree with them, but I want to wait until the last moment until we find that awesome rock star. And until we felt that pain point firsthand ourselves, to know exactly what skills this person needs to have and what they need to be better at than me.

DAVE PARKER, YUMBLE KIDS

Beyond your top team, you will also need to hire at lower levels, and sometimes very fast in order to face the increasing pressure from growth. This adds to the complexity, not only to find the right people but also to onboard them.

A consistent misconception among entrepreneurs is that finding skilled hourly labor is easier than filling the C-suite. This is clearly false.

It's actually hard to find people who are expert seamstresses. It's often a trade that is passed down from generation to generation in certain communities. The same thing with spotting, the same thing with dry cleaning. The talent recruiting and retention is even more important as it relates to my hourly employees than to my corporate employees.

JENN HYMAN, RENT THE RUNWAY (HOFFMAN PODCAST)

As you scale, hiring will be one of your key challenges. Not only is it difficult to find the right people for the job, but any mistake will create pain. It is therefore interesting but not surprising to note that many HBS founders decided to remain involved in hiring even when their companies had become much larger.

I'm still pretty hands-on recruiting because I do think that's one of the most important things and one of the best ways I can get leverage for my time. Just the payoff on hiring the right person is so high, compared to almost anything else that you do. I think that's a worthwhile area to focus.

JAKE CUSACK, CROSSBOUNDARY

Tips to Hire

Anna Auerbach joined Egon Zehnder, an executive search firm, as a consultant after selling Werk. In one of our interviews, she shared insightful tips on how to hire the right people.

BE AWARE OF BIAS. You tend to like people that are like you. Within five minutes you will like or not like someone. But whether you like or don't like someone doesn't mean they're the right person for the job.

FOCUS. Your mindset when you're interviewing and hiring is very important. You cannot be looking at emails. Even if you're on a Zoom, shut everything down. Shut it all down. Be present.

HIRE FOR CURIOSITY. Curiosity underpins everything. How much are you actively seeking different perspectives? How much are you actively asking for feedback? How much are you actively working on yourself? Those are the people that will scale with your company.

SPEND ENOUGH TIME. Spend an hour. Nobody likes hour interviews. People want to do thirty-minute interviews. There's nothing you're going to get done in thirty minutes. I think thirty minutes is a waste of time. Really take the time. Leave the space. And the answer kind of comes out.

LOOK FOR THE HOW, NOT THE WHAT. What people should be looking for is not what people did, but how they did it. This idea of potential is a way to sort of frame what drove them, how they accomplished the things that they did.

CHECK UNPROVIDED REFERENCES. The last bit is referencing. Try to trace an unprovided reference. That is the most important thing. So, not just references your candidate provides. Ask for the real story.

BE KIND BUT BE A LEADER

One of the challenges I had as an inexperienced CEO was holding people accountable. That was something that I, and other inexperienced managers, tend to struggle with.

It was compounded by the fact that the business was growing so fast and so well that it was hard to hold people accountable for certain things when everything was going great.

MATT SALZBERG, BLUE APRON

As you grow the number of people on your team, you must ensure that everyone steps up to their job. It's easier in the beginning: when the team is small, everybody is involved, they know what to do, and things just flow. But scaling means some employees' responsibilities need to expand as the company grows, and not everyone can rise up to that automatically. So, aside from promoting and hiring, as we discussed, there's more that you can do.

You have a natural inclination to say, "Clearly everybody just should show up and work. You just figure it out. You were hired to do this, so that's what you'll do, that's it." But that's not how it works.

STEVE SZARONOS, BESPOKE POST

You must learn how to communicate, create accountability, and delegate so that people understand what is expected from them and know where they stand.

The advice we heard from entrepreneurs encompasses the following: be tough and set goals (and don't mistake that with *not* being nice), and if people do not perform, first find out what *you* can do differently.

In the early days, you are involved in everything and tasks are typically assigned among the team in a very fluid way. As you grow, you assume that people know what to do, because this is how it has worked so far.

But this isn't always the case. You have to make sure that you communicate individually and collectively so that they know. This requires that you start thinking about specific job descriptions and making sure that there is enough communication with employees so that they truly know what to do.

Most young CEOs are not used to setting goals and being tough. As is true for many things, we heard that the transition to more delegation and accountability is a learning process. And a critical one to go through.

As you grow, you have to make sure that you communicate individually and collectively so that your team knows what is expected of them. This requires that you start thinking about specific job descriptions and making sure that there is enough communication with employees so that they have direction.

We're learning to be more direct with people in terms of performance-related things. People want to know where they stand. They get frustrated when you're not telling them where they stand, or when they think you're being nice.

We're trying to figure out how to let people know what they're responsible for, empower them to do a good job, and give them the authority. If we're saying that you're responsible for doing this, then we're giving you the real authority to do that, and they can actually make a difference.

MATT SALZBERG, BLUE APRON

Don't assume being clear and tough will make you a less nice person. People value directness. For example, even as a young CEO, you should be able to manage older people by very clearly stating what you expect from them.

You've got to coach people. You've got to have tough conversations. You've got to have heart, but you also have got to be a lion. Be kind but be a leader. It means being very clear on what you expect and what you want and being consistent, delivering it in a supportive, nice, good way. People will respect that. Everyone needs leadership and management and direction. We all need it. People also want to be respected and talked to kindly. If you do that you can manage any professional.

JUSTIN JOFFE, HENRY THE DENTIST

Holding people accountable with clear responsibilities will allow you to evaluate their performance. This in turn will be critical to subsequently promote and reward them, or possibly fire them in case of a lousy performance. You want to give realistic but stretched goals and preferably use metrics.

If people do not perform, try to understand why, and more precisely understand if their underperformance is driven by a lack of will or lack of skill, or possibly both.

Your approach to help them will be different depending on the answer, ranging from coaching (when they miss the skill) to motivating (when they are not willing) or to firing/putting in a different position (when they are not willing to gain the needed skills). The best situation is obviously to have somebody who is skilled and motivated, in which case your best approach is to just delegate with clear expectations.

I believe if somebody is underperforming or having challenges, the first question is, What can I do to fix things? *What have you missed as a leader that is keeping them back from performing at their best? That's something I've always been passionate about from the first time I managed people. If somebody's not doing a good job, that's my fault. There's something I haven't done. There's something I don't understand. There's something I haven't taught them or some tool I haven't given them.*

Obviously, that's not always the case. It's not always your fault. And sometimes people are not a great fit for their job. But the first step is understanding that person's unique circumstances.

ANNE AUERBACH, WERK

BECOME THE CEO/MANAGER (IF YOU CAN)

I've certainly improved and developed my leadership skills as I went from managing zero people to managing five thousand people and being a public-company CEO. I had to evolve my skill set and leadership skills pretty significantly over that time.

MATT SALZBERG, BLUE APRON

One of the most difficult transitions when scaling relates to the role of the founder.

In the early days, the founder is an entrepreneur, a visionary, a creator—not a manager who runs a full-fledged business. Jim remembers an HBS professor who said that the "entrepreneur-creator" gets the business from 0 to 1, while the "entrepreneurial manager" takes the business from 1 to 100. The two require vastly different skills. Which are you as an entrepreneur? And can you make the transition?

You outgrow your founders at some point. In the early days founders are great in terms of thinking about things in a small way, doing things quickly, when you could break a lot and it didn't matter. Later on, getting them to change a mindset that things can't break when you have a running business like this was a little more challenging.

ANTHONY SOOHOO, DOT & BO

When the organization grows, the founders need to start worrying about running a larger organization, including hiring and managing people. It's no longer about getting something off the ground but about running a business. That is substantially different. With a larger organization, the CEO role is about goal setting, people leadership, conflict resolution, etc. As a result, the CEO needs to move from being involved in everything to focus on the 20 percent most important items (the good and the bad), and leave the remaining 80 percent to managers.

Many founders do not like the new situation, because it involves a more formal organization wherein risk-taking is more limited and you need to spend a lot of your time managing people.

Alexandra from Gilt acknowledged that when the organization had grown, she wasn't having the same fun as in the early days.

I kept myself stimulated by being involved in so many other startups, just advising them and angel investing, but I was bored in the sense that Gilt was kind of a big company and I felt like we'd lost a lot of that early magic.
ALEXANDRA WILKIS WILSON, GILT

In the end, she decided to quit before Gilt was sold to the Hudson's Bay Company in early 2016. Her cofounder Alexis left even before she did.

Even if as a founder you still enjoy it, you might not have the right profile to make the transition. It is a very different thing to be an entrepreneur rather than a manager. Just because you are great at creating something new and bootstrapping it, that doesn't always translate to being great at managing and growing a formal organization. That is a different ball game.

So it is not surprising that many entrepreneurs do not survive the transition, as exemplified by numerous examples where the cofounder(s) left the company. Think of companies like WeWork, Twitter, Uber, Oculus, and many more. All of them were asked to make room for a true manager by their board of directors.

So, how do you know when it's time to leave? It is rare to have founders who decide for themselves that they don't fit the bill or that they are not enjoying it anymore, as Alexandra did. These founders do exist, but they are the minority. More often, it is the board of directors or investors who decide.

In that sense, it is always good as a founder to have a sounding board, one or many advisors, which helps you to assess whether you and your top team are still the best people to lead the company.

A great way to preempt and solve the issue is to consider a few things:

- Identify for yourself where you stand on the spectrum from entrepreneur to manager. Be honest (and seek the opinion of others).
- Get a coach to help you transition from the creator to operator role. This can be a formal or informal relationship, whatever works best for you.
- Hire a COO. Even if you don't have the perfect profile to run a business, you can second yourself with somebody who does and still remain very much involved in areas where you do excel. Think of Mark Zuckerberg, who seconded himself with Sheryl Sandberg at Facebook.

A note of caution: If you or your board do end up bringing in a new CEO, you should find an "entrepreneurial" one. Otherwise you run the risk of losing the creative passion that is crucial to continued growth.

11

YOUR BUSINESS MODEL
IS NOT CAST IN IRON

> Change your business model whenever
> you sense significant weakness or opportunity.

A lot of times, the real scale comes after the fake scale. And then you do a reshuffle of your business model and how you offer your product. Then you can grow faster.

BERI MERIC, IVY

As you scale up the venture, you will likely encounter issues to keep on growing or encounter new situations and uncontrollables. As we will see in chapter 16, you are never safe from unforeseen events that can destabilize you and require changes to your business model. The one thing entrepreneurs can be sure of is that, at some point, they will need to modify their business model.

The HBS founders were no exception and faced multiple challenges and changing circumstances and—at some point, needed to re-address their business model assumptions on their quest to experience sustainable growth.

As such, it's your job to make sure you sense the signals to change and anticipate. The best entrepreneurs are the ones who constantly seek to strengthen their business models knowing that success and continued growth will only come if you are ahead of the curve.

There is a saying that as an entrepreneur, *you want to be in love with the problem you solve, not with the solution you offer.* If you are in love with the problem you solve, you will likely pivot along the way and not be beholden to only your initial solutions.

It is rare to find a venture that hasn't had to pivot. As a matter of fact, most successful companies have pivoted their businesses to find their path to rapid growth—or to find a new path to growth after an older one became stagnant or declined. They may pivot at the ideation phase, at the outset of scaling up, or at a later stage.

For some entrepreneurs, the challenge will be to fix one or two elements of the business model, such as marketing or operations. For others, the pivot is more extensive and requires the launch of a new product or service in your industry. Finally, there is what we call the *extreme pivot*—which is when the business just isn't working and you must start over with a new product in a new industry.

ANTICIPATE OR FAIL

We watched Google carefully because they bought an airfare software company, which to us meant that they wanted to eventually serve up flight search on their search results page. That would be a big problem because we relied on that traffic—as did others—to bring users to our own search tool.

To manage the risk of a potential new entrant in this market, we needed to ensure that we never became too dependent on that product line. We ended up diversifying with a couple of other new products. A few years later

Google then did in fact enter the market, and many firms that relied exclusively on airfare search saw their business drop by 90 percent. The upshot is that you have to manage risk in a business and always have a Plan B. You have to keep an eye out for threats.

JIM SHERMAN, SHERMANSTRAVEL MEDIA

The name of the game is to stay ahead of the curve. The only way to strengthen your position is to do so proactively. If you wait until you experience problems and obstacles, the odds will be against you to the point that you might have a very hard time turning things around. It is crucial that you sense signals early on so that you have the time to correct core challenges to the business model—to correct things before you run out of money.

Similarly, you cannot be so buried in the day-to-day operations that you miss opportunities. If that's the case, then you won't maximize your venture's prospects.

So, how might you sense the signals?

- Carve out time to speak regularly with industry leaders and advisors.
- Keep abreast of the news that could impact your business.
- Have a pulse on your core business operations, staying attuned to what risks you face.

It behooves you to consciously take a step back and observe, ask questions, and connect with others in an effort to track the pulse of what's going on today or what may impact your industry and company tomorrow.

In the case of SkyMD, Eric realized there were signals he could have sensed to change his business model. While the dermatology app itself was a strong product, he faced ongoing challenges in finding a strong revenue stream for the business model. The metrics showed that the model in terms of "who paid" was flawed, and their ideal app user was hard to reach.

The strongest signal was in how dermatologists used the app differently depending on whether they were based in an urban or rural location. After deciding to focus on urban doctors, multiple attempts to engage doctors and onboard patients failed, which should have been a strong signal to Eric.

What we had found were two types of dermatologists. There were dermatologists in urban areas who had a hard time keeping their schedules filled. And there were dermatologists in rural areas who were overwhelmed with demand; they just didn't have time to do anything else. They had a forty-day wait to get in to see them, and they didn't have time to think about something like this app, although it could have saved them time by allowing them to provide diagnoses remotely. But it was just very hard to get them to pay attention to us.

So we said, "Let's focus on these urban doctors." The ones who don't have enough patients. We said, "Let's see if we can use this tool as a way to acquire patients for these practices."

So, we started testing paid acquisition. We found, however, that the cost of acquisition was extremely high compared to the value we could get from them. It didn't work.

ERIC PRICE, SKYMD

You have got to be ahead of these signals and have a plan to address them *before* they present lasting harm to the company.

As a leader, sensing the signals means keeping an eye on what is happening around you. From early-stage startup into scaling, if you haven't built up an organization that allows you to do this, then you run the risk of being blindsided.

...

WHAT IS YOUR 2.0?

Initially, we were creating a business that was effectively based on the mistakes of the brands and the people that they sold to at full price—so miscalculations of how much inventory to produce. And so, leftovers, and we were there to save the day. But you can't build, plan for, and scale a business when it's all about other people's leftovers. We realized we had to get ahead of the supply chain.

ALEXANDRA WILKIS WILSON, GILT

Good entrepreneurs keep questioning and pushing their business model not only in the early days as they find the elusive product/market fit, but also as they scale. They are always on the lookout for a "2.0" that will strengthen their position and ensure growth.

Indeed, the best entrepreneurs are always looking for weaknesses that may emerge in their business and for new opportunities. They don't wait for an external event to happen.

Even if your core business is doing great, it is important to keep an eye out for the next opportunity. Major companies like Google even encourage their employees to devote 20 percent of their time to exploring and testing new opportunities that will benefit Google. Be sure to create space for strategic experimentation despite the everyday work pressures in managing your ventures.

Our business was coming at a really nice clip. And yet, we continued to question, like, what was coming? What was next? How could we get more usage out of our customers? How could we stay fresh and relevant as a brand and scale more quickly once we did have that capacity at our warehouse? How could we use inventory more efficiently? So, could we turn around our apparel the same day so that we could enable more usage of inventory, more utilization of inventory, which meant things like build-

ing dry cleaners in our facility and really taking ownership of the tech-nology to power reverse logistics because no one else was doing that before?

Thinking forward and ahead of where customer behavior is going.

JENNY FLEISS, RENT THE RUNWAY

If sales go up fast, you as a leader should know why, yet always think of your next move, which may include a change in business model. If you don't do that and instead stand still, you might lose your competitive advantage and eventually stall your growth.

Good times inevitably end, and uncontrollables strike when you least expect it, so it's not a good idea to sit on an existing product and milk it. It's your job to be looking out for the "next big thing."

With the HBS firms, some founders had a clear idea from the very beginning how they wanted the business model to evolve and what their 2.0 would be. They took it step by step, first focusing on finding product/market fit and in a later stage altering and strengthening the business model to support scaling.

For example, with Henry the Dentist, Justin had clear milestones in mind when building out the business. He started off with mobile clinics only and he always intended to expand from one geography to another. However, he also expanded his services by later offering a brick-and-mortar location for more complicated dental needs, for what could not be done in the mobile clinics. He refers to his 2.0 as a "hub and spoke" system, with the "spokes" being the mobile clinics going out to office buildings. The brick-and-mortar "hub" office became the next natural evolution of his service for patients.

For others, the 2.0 was not part of the initial vision but developed over time because of market opportunities that emerged or challenges encountered with the initial business strategy.

An HBS lecture by Professor Rayport on scaling up noted that an entrepreneur should exploit what is working while keeping an eye on exploring. You are also more likely to discover your business's long-term edge on day 500 than on day 1.

At CrossBoundary, the consulting firm that had grown fast to offices in multiple countries and fifty-five employees, Jake explains that at some point they decided to expand their core model and began to set up investment vehicles so that they could directly invest in specific opportunities abroad in developing markets. Their 2.0? Becoming a private equity investor, which was an extension of the consulting project work with which they'd started the firm.

At the time of writing, they had set up two investment vehicles: one focused on solar energy for African businesses and one for rural communities who don't yet have access to electricity.

For many entrepreneurs, the 2.0 became clear as they grew and got feedback from their customers. In some cases it resulted in systematic expansions of the business model around the same core basic strategy.

In the case of Rent the Runway, for example, the 2.0 was a set of business model expansions, including their product offering, the distribution, and pricing.

We had a website first that rented dresses only. Then we added accessories: necklaces, earrings, bracelets, rings, handbags. Then we tested out retail, where we offered those items together, both in an online setting as well as on our mobile app. But then you could also have the option of either picking up your order at retail or placing an order at retail.

We added subscription most recently. Subscription has two types. There is an option where you rent four items for an entire month and you keep those four items the whole month. And there's another option where you can swap your items out as many times as you like.

JENNY FLEISS, RENT THE RUNWAY

For others, the 2.0 resulted in a sharpening of the initial strategy and vision. In the case of RubiconMD, for example, technology emerged as a competitive advantage at a later stage in the company journey. Carlos explains how initially they saw themselves as a "clinical health company" but realized with growth that technology had become a big part of the competitive advantage. The team evolved to realize they are a "health tech company" instead of a clinical health company. Changing their perspective was important as they strengthened their market position.

I think it's been a journey where we've had to adapt to realize that we are a health tech company. And we have to be both. We have to be a really good tech company that also has all of this clinical leadership.

CARLOS REINES, RUBICONMD

Blue Apron similarly found that they could leverage their key asset— their customer base—to further strengthen their business model. Their subscription business is just one component. Matt explains how they strengthened their customer relationship by offering a variety of products, including wine.

We don't think about our business as a subscription business today. We think about ourselves as a direct-to-consumer brand that sells a variety of products in a variety of ways. And increasingly, we're in a variety of channels.

MATT SALZBERG, BLUE APRON

THE LIKELY PIVOT TO ACHIEVE SCALE

Even if you anticipate threats to your business model and have a 2.0 growth strategy, there is a high likelihood that something will not work out as planned.

Your growth or business model assumptions might not work out as expected. Growth does not kick in or growth kicks in but stalls after a while. Operational or financial problems arise and make your model unsustainable. Or something unexpected happens (for example, a new competitor coming into your market with deep pockets) that requires you to make changes to your model and pivot.

Every entrepreneur will face a moment when a pivot is necessary. A pivot is a substantive change to one or more components of the business model or product.

Each community manager got ten to twenty new members to join every month. With a $1,000 up-front joining fee, it was $10K to $20K in revenue per community manager per month. So, we had as many community managers as possible. Seemed like a no-brainer. We couldn't hire them fast enough. But the underlying lesson is it became a business that relied too much on one-off revenues. Soon I saw how dangerous it was. If you have a business that needs to sell a certain number of units every month and one month you sell less, just six months can kill you.

BERI MERIC, IVY

As an entrepreneur, you should be ahead of the facts, expecting to pivot at any point. This can happen at the ignition stage (before you have proven product/market fit), early on in the scaling phase, or during the later stage of growth. Your mindset should be that your business model is a continuous work in progress. Nothing stands still.

Depending on the type of problem, there are small or large pivots. The bigger the pivot, the more time and money you will need to make it happen. A big pivot is like starting over again and one should not underestimate how much effort is needed to make that happen. It creates substantial stress on the organization, not only because it can mean that you need new skills, but also because it can create nervousness and misalignment if you don't communicate well.

Most HBS entrepreneurs took a pivot at some point in time. In the case of Ivy, the college-like social community, Beri needed to pivot the company's marketing strategy because it had become unsustainable due to the nonfunctioning of the lead-generation platform they used. The resulting drop in revenues was nearly fatal because of their fixed cost structure.

As Beri learned that driving top-line growth with one-time up-front pricing and a fixed sales force was not a good model, he searched for an optimal pricing and overall sales strategy for his club membership. Ivy transitioned from an up-front membership price to a monthly fee per member. After a few iterations, Beri also pivoted recruiting, onboarding, and management of their events in order to reduce costs and increase his operating margins.

From September 2017 to almost September 2019, in these two years we basically went to quality over quantity, fewer events, once a week in each city. We made them excellent. We centralized all events and community functions. Automated all new member onboarding. We got rid of calls [by the community managers], we got rid of all of their functions. And then we went to a fully recurring monthly revenue model.

We removed the up-front joining fee of $1K. But we doubled the recurring fee from $40 to $80 a month. And we use a lot of SaaS [software as a service] tactics now in marketing. Now, with just two marketing people, we pick up as many members as we did with fifty full-time community managers!

We also launched digital events, which cost us nothing, which are already getting us more RSVPs than our physical events.

What's happening now is the stress we were faced with forced us to move into a totally recurring, low-cost base and an ultimately much higher margin operation. It's a variable or no-cost initiative that made it a lot easier.

BERI MERIC, IVY

One could argue that Ivy took a set of "smaller" pivots related to pricing, operations, and marketing, but the changes were critical to ensure the viability of the company. After the pivot, Ivy became a more agile and profitable organization that is less dependent on growth to cover high fixed costs.

Dot & Bo went through a different type of pivot, literally adding an entire business stream in order to keep up with demand. When Dot & Bo launched, they sourced their home furnishing products mostly from Asia. As the business boomed, they had trouble meeting all the demand, which couldn't be fulfilled through their existing supply chain. So Anthony decided to shift gears by investing in manufacturing operations in China. He decided to become a furniture manufacturer instead of just a media and e-commerce company. This was a significant shift in the business model that allowed them to tap into faster growth and also helped them to expand their margins.

In terms of demand, we outgrew our supply chain. People couldn't supply us product because we'd basically capped out the vendors that could give us product. We were growing faster than they anticipated. We had to start developing our own products ourselves. We became furniture designers and set up factories in China to learn how to be a furniture manufacturer instead of just a media company that was monetizing through commerce.

That was a shift and a big change from what we were expecting.

ANTHONY SOOHOO, DOT & BO

For many entrepreneurs, the pivot needed to get on the explosive growth curve requires a change at the core: a change of product or service you offer.

A company that exemplified such a pivot, moving from an opportunity that had some traction to a much larger opportunity, is Anna's venture, Werk.

Werk started as a job platform or marketplace for flexible jobs. But Anna fundamentally shifted the business model when the team realized there was an unmet demand—one that they could not have spotted when founding the firm. Their business was doing fine, experiencing growth, but she realized it could do much better if they changed their model.

One thing we realized very quickly was that companies were having a hard time communicating what it was that they meant by flexibility. We'd say on the job board, "Flexible face time, flexible hours, telework." But telework doesn't actually mean anything to anyone. Telecommute? I don't know what that means as part of a job description.

So we locked ourselves in a room for two days and came up with a taxonomy for work flexibility that was, in McKinsey terms, MECE—mutually exclusive, collectively exhaustive—and which had never existed before. All the flexibility types we had seen before were overlapping. So, how do you search for a job and how do you get any information if it's overlapping?

We came up with what were essentially filters for the job board. And within months we realized we were onto the tip of the iceberg of a very large data set. For the first time we could say which types of flexibility were most searched on the job board, most offered, for what jobs and what kind of geography, and for what level of person. We could actually pinpoint where the market failure was for the very first time.

We realized fairly quickly that we could help companies better articulate what they were offering, and help people better articulate what they need. This ended up being the point of the pivot.

ANNA AUERBACH, WERK

So Anna and her team decided that there was an opportunity to create software for companies to better track the flexibility needs of their employees and to ultimately help firms to retain their staff. That opportunity emerged out of their listening carefully to their corporate clients for their job board. Anna realized that they could have an impact that went well beyond just helping a firm hire more people.

The pivot that we took came about when we saw a bigger opportunity to have a lot more social change. If we're just helping companies hire one hundred people a year on a flexible schedule, that's not actually going to change the way we all work. But if we can help companies provide greater flexibility to all their employees, not just the new hires, if we can help them take this seriously, if we can help them add this idea of flexibility to their strategic agenda, then we're going to achieve a lot more social change and a lot more market acceptance.

ANNA AUERBACH, WERK

Anna also realized that the pivot allowed them to strengthen their revenue model by moving to annual contracts, rather than just one-off job postings. In addition, it allowed them to offer something unique and strategically compelling.

The second thing is that the pivot allowed us to truly build a much more sustainable contract—ongoing contracts with businesses. Recruiting ebbs and flows. It ultimately is based on the volume of people you're hiring. That is not recession-proof. And there's some big incumbents in the space. How do you compete on a job board versus LinkedIn? So, the pivot changed the business model to be one that is subscription based—that is recession-proof also from a financial standpoint. We thought that was incredibly powerful.

Finally, the last piece of the pivot is that this had just never been done before. Job boards have been done. We suddenly saw staring right in front of us an opportunity to gather a completely new set of "people data" and to give companies "people analytics" that would make flexibility a top priority. There is nothing like this. The idea of taking on something brand-new, that's the third reason for the pivot.

ANNA AUERBACH, WERK

By sensing the market feedback, Anna ultimately stumbled into creating something entirely new—the notion of data-driven people analytics software to measure and manage flexibility needs. This led to a major pivot that enabled them to capture a new, more interesting opportunity. In the process of shifting to the new model, Anna and her cofounder realized that taking a large pivot is like starting over again. That has consequences, including for your team and for investors who initially joined and invested in a different concept.

We went from a job marketplace to selling a SaaS analytic enterprise solution, which was software. This is a massive pivot. It's a totally different business model. And it takes time. Even a small, nimble startup can't pivot overnight. The initial investors signed up for a job marketplace. They didn't sign up for a SaaS enterprise solution.

ANNA AUERBACH, WERK

Another example of a major product pivot is with ShermansTravel Media. Jim originally launched PDF digital destination guides in 2002 with targeted ads, which airlines and online travel agents like Expedia could email to travelers days before their intended trips, but later pivoted to become a publisher of handpicked travel deals.

The initial business was to offer people who had booked a trip relevant, timely information about their destination with ads from hotels, car rental firms, restaurants, tours, and activities. But the venture did not grow rapidly—not without a large pivot.

I soon realized the business model of targeted destination guides just was not going to scale up quickly. A key bottleneck was getting more airlines and online agencies to sign a distribution deal with me. Their interest was lukewarm.

The good news is that the online travel guides got me to focus on the overall online travel industry and the advertising market, which, I suspected, was going to explode. In my research, I stumbled onto a site called Travelzoo, which was publishing travel deals as simple text links in email and online, and making advertising money from travel suppliers such as hotels, cruise lines, airlines, and tour operators. They had deals but no other travel advice. I liked their monetization model and felt that companies paying for these text links would continue to grow. Text link advertising was pretty new back then.

I decided that there was room in this market for more than one player.

So, we pivoted the online product and launched ShermansTravel with our Top 25 Deals *newsletter and a website with rich editorial. I was sold out every week. It was a hit out of the gate.*

JIM SHERMAN, SHERMANSTRAVEL MEDIA

THE EXTREME PIVOT

Some of the HBS founders needed to completely reinvent their ventures. Several chose to exit an initial business and start a brand-new one in a new industry. Along the spectrum of pivots, starting over is the most extreme. As we have seen earlier, the founders of Bespoke Post and Yumble Kids decided early on in their ventures to take an extreme pivot, and start over again.

The same applies to Blue Apron and Henry the Dentist, which were born after the founders had tried other businesses. Each took their startup passion and chose to change industries entirely to go after something new.

Prior to launching Blue Apron, Matt had launched a crowdfunding site, Petridish, for science projects. So, when he decided to change industries entirely, he took the investor funding that remained for Petridish, told his investors he needed to pivot his business (they agreed), and launched Blue Apron.

I concluded that Petridish wasn't the right thing based on the qualitative "excitement" around it. I think it was definitely the right decision, but it was a very hard decision.

We had spent almost none of the money that I had raised. We were really scrappy. So it was easy to transition to something else.

MATT SALZBERG, BLUE APRON

Justin of Henry the Dentist has a similar story of making an extreme pivot. He was incredibly busy managing a network of beauty salons that he and his private equity partners had rolled up via acquisitions into one branded firm.

He began to have doubts about the future upside of this business because the margins were not strong, the daily execution tasks were incredibly challenging since these were mom-and-pop salons, and the cost to acquire new salons to add to their portfolio was becoming exceedingly high. The business model was looking increasingly challenged on several critical fronts, and he ultimately lost confidence in the business's prospects.

Justin also questioned his own long-term attraction to the beauty salon industry. He was not particularly passionate about hair blowouts. So he, similar to Matt, chose to jump into a completely different industry: dentistry.

For a founder, coming to the conclusion that you should start over is heart-wrenching. So much time, effort, and often money has been invested. Emotionally it is challenging because one does not want to think about "failure" (even though we should add that from failure comes the best learnings and often future success with the next venture). So, determining when to call it quits is exceptionally difficult. Typically, a founder holds on longer than he or she should. The founder is so busy developing the business, they may not be able to take the necessary step back to reevaluate.

PART IV

Financing

Fundraising Doesn't Equal Success

We raised way too early. We raised because we were strong personalities with a big idea and a big problem we were trying to solve. We were nowhere near product/market fit when we raised money. And I think in a way the timing of financing wrote, sort of, the story for our exit.

ANNA AUERBACH, WERK

12

HOW MUCH
(AND WHEN)
TO RAISE?

Fundraising doesn't equal success.
Wait to raise money, then wait some more.
Be as capital efficient as you can be.

There are certain business models that simply need large amounts of capital to get to profitability. There are other business models that don't.

JOSH HIX, PLATED

While startup financing is a popular topic in business schools, it is not fully appreciated until one actually embarks on the arduous road of raising money. Given the large challenge of getting other people to invest in your venture, you should reflect first on whether raising money is *necessary* or even *desirable*. There are many examples of boutique lifestyle businesses as well as large enterprises that launched without outside financing.

However, if you do need outside capital, there are several key considerations.

First, you should wait as long as you can before trying to raise funds. It's vital to reflect upon, what does the business truly need and how far can you go *without* external financing? It is in your best interest to hold off raising funds (bootstrap the venture), if possible, until you have proven out more of the business model and customer demand.

Once you decide that you do need to raise funds, then you should strive to raise the *right amount* and leave room for error. In the early stages, it is not always easy to know how much to raise. Raising too much will result in more dilution but raising too little might lead to continuous raising. By the time of your growth-stage financing, your milestones will help you define when and how much to raise. If you are doing well, it's possible that investors will be chasing you. In all cases, you should be careful not to raise too much. You should be capital efficient.

Second, there is a personal dimension to consider in this crucial question of how much to raise—and when. Do you want to be "king or rich"? With the former, you may raise very little and therefore own more of the business, but you might not raise enough for the firm's growth, which in turn may reduce your ultimate financial reward. Of course, your focus should be to raise what your business needs, but personal preferences are likely to influence where on the spectrum of possible capital raises you choose to land.

Finally, and this predominantly applies to businesses that are doing very well, you should consider what we call "exit optionality" versus "go big or go home." How much risk are you willing to accept? Raising huge sums of money at eye-popping valuations (what some refer to as seeking funding glory) might *not* be in your best interest since it closes off potentially attractive exit options at relatively lower sale prices, because investors expect to recoup their money—the more you raise at high valuations the higher the bar becomes to achieve success for them and for you.

WHAT DOES THE BUSINESS NEED? AND WHEN TO RAISE IT?

We designed an e-commerce business that could only be profitable at large scale. And to get there, we needed to raise, spend, and invest large amounts of capital in marketing, infrastructure, and so on.

JOSH HIX, PLATED

Assuming yours is a venture business, you are targeting a large investable opportunity and you must raise money from investors to fund your startup, then you must assess *how much* capital you believe your firm needs for launch, how much it will likely need over time to achieve profitability, and *when* to raise capital to meet those targets. The earlier the stage your business is in, the more speculative you will be in assessing how much capital it will need.

In our experience as mentors to startup founders, we see a lot of entrepreneurs who attempt to raise financing too early when they have little to show. They struggle and waste valuable introductions to skeptical investors because the founders have not proven enough of their ability to execute and of the business opportunity. While angel investors will take a flier on entrepreneurs and their ideas, the more data or proof of concept you have, the easier it is to close a deal. So you should go as far as you can without seeking outside capital. In other words, bootstrap as much as possible.

Should You Even Be Venture Backed?

The vast majority of businesses are not venture businesses. These are not talked about in the press as much, perhaps because they don't have the allure of the next unicorn. One such business that may not require funding is a lifestyle business, such as blogs, moderate-sized e-commerce/retail businesses, marketing agencies, and many others that have potential to grow without external investment and provide a good (or even great) return to the owner. What these all have in common is the potential to get to profitability either from day one or shortly thereafter, but their ultimate business size typically has a ceiling (multimillions but not hundreds of millions of dollars) to it that dissuades traditional venture capitalists from investing.

Josh Hix explained how he and his business partner understood early on that they were *not* building a lifestyle business, because his meal kit business needed funding for infrastructure and he expected it would generate venture-like returns by targeting a very large market opportunity.

One of the first decisions is: Is this a venture business? Is it a lifestyle business? That's a fundamentally important question that doesn't get enough attention. Many of the best entrepreneurs are lifestyle entrepreneurs. Family businesses with different labels for this category are sometimes used pejoratively by a lot of folks that are in the venture space. I think that is a mistake. A lot of very, very large, successful businesses get built without venture capital. Venture capital only works for a specific kind of business and is often toxic to other businesses.

If you're trying to build a multibillion-dollar technology business, it probably needs to be venture. If you're trying to build a $50M e-commerce business, there's a strong argument that you probably shouldn't take venture money. And that's a very, very successful business if you own 100 percent or near to 100 percent of it that you can run for your lifetime and pass on to your children. That is not a possibility with a venture business. Venture capitalists, any institutional investors, need their money back. They need liquidity. There is an implicit deal that *is often not made explicit in taking that capital. One of the first questions to get out of the way is what we're trying to accomplish.*

JOSH HIX, PLATED

The key upshot of a lifestyle business is that you remain in control. You may (or may not) have a board of directors. Even if you raised some money from non-VC sources (such as friends and family), you will likely still be in control. Plus, you can avoid the time suck of trying to woo VC investors and choose your own fate—whether to run the business for a long time or sell to a strategic buyer.

In addition to lifestyle businesses, there are other businesses that have the potential to be very large and may not require outside financing. If a business is not capital intensive and if there is a pathway to generating profits early on that can be reinvested into growth, then a founder may choose not to raise external funds.

In this situation, building it step by step and matching expenses carefully to revenue growth are crucial.

The advisory business has been entirely self-funded. Obviously, this kind of business is driven entirely by the people. There is no secret sauce of software that we have, algorithms or something like that. It's driven by the quality of the people.

JAKE CUSACK, CROSSBOUNDARY

HBS-founded examples of self-funded large opportunities include CrossBoundary and WestEnd New Media. One of the best non-HBS examples is email marketing software firm Mailchimp. Founded in 2001, it never took on outside capital and was acquired by Intuit for $12B in 2021. Other very well-known firms (for example, Patagonia, Spanx, and Tuft & Needle) also got going by bootstrapping, never raised any money, and went on to become large, successful businesses with revenues well over $100M. These founders valued profits over growth, and chose to retain full ownership and decision-making authority.

Early-Stage Funding: Bootstrap as Long as You Can

We raised on a problem, not on a solution. Lessons learned. Don't raise on a problem, raise on a solution. And the issue is, the clock starts ticking. You start spending money. You start hiring people.

ANNA AUERBACH, WERK

The advantage of bootstrapping during the early stage is that, by waiting as long as you can to raise financing, not only will you have greater chances of success in later raising your first round of angel or venture money, but it will also enable you to raise more and on better terms (higher valuation; less dilution to you) since you should have more evidence of the opportunity.

It is worth noting that building a large business does not automatically require your raising a ton of money early on. In fact, there are many examples of ventures that became large and scaled up significantly in the launch phase before choosing to raise a lot more capital in later stages. For example, Thrillist raised over $50M for the media and e-commerce business but only *after* it had achieved solid traction. The e-commerce site Shutterstock got going with 30,000 of the founder's photos, raised very little money post-launch, and today is worth over $2B and is public. Amazon raised just $8M of venture capital before going public and raising more.

Assuming that you decide that you do need to raise funds and have gone as far as you can with bootstrapping the venture, then in the early stage, we recommend that you carefully reflect on how much is needed to prove that you are going after a large opportunity, complete the minimum viable product you need to begin capturing customers, and prove out elements of your business model.

Knowing when to move down the path of fundraising and the amount to raise is tricky. Anna felt that since she was able to raise a good bit of capital early on, she would do that. But in retrospect, she realized it was not in her interest to do so. Even if you can raise a lot of money in the early stage, it may behoove you not to do so. There are several key reasons why.

First, you do not want to burn through capital on an unproven idea where the true potential remains murky. With all startups, there is a need to iterate on your product or service. If you have too much capital, you will be tempted to build it out too quickly and hire too fast.

We should have probably found a scrappier way to iterate and launch a version 1.0 so we could have gotten to these insights sooner without spending capital on the experimentation. We spent too much capital on experimentation, essentially.

ANNA AUERBACH, WERK

Second, having less capital, both during the ignition and scaling phases, forces you to be creative in building the business. A benefit of not having too much money is that you will stay hungry—keeping you sharp, focused, and creative. This is particularly true in marketing. You do not want cash to be a substitute for creativity, enabling you to paper over problems. In fact, it is the lack of resources that forces the entrepreneur to be entrepreneurial—to be efficient, and effective in finding not just "a path" but the "best path" forward. Finding that path is what will also ensure your competitive position in the market.

Third, you gather bits of crucial information that help you test your assumptions of the business model and learning what you don't know (unit economics, cost to acquire customers, staffing requirements, cost of any capital expenditure/R&D, etc.). This information will help you to gain a better sense of not only how much capital it will ultimately take to achieve your first milestone but also what it will take to get to profitability.

Finally, an advantage of raising as little as you can in the angel/seed stage—until the opportunity is proven—is that you can later better match the money (the right investors) to your opportunity (more on this later in finding "smart money"). Should you need to pivot, you will want to have investors that are on board with a change in your strategy.

The upshot is to avoid the assumption that you must raise a lot of money early even if you are targeting to build a very large business. Having said this—and it may seem like a paradox— it is also true that there is some tendency with entrepreneurs during the early stage to raise too little. You do not want to find yourself in fundraising mode too often.

If you have achieved what you believe is product/market fit or have a high degree of confidence that you will establish it and have some evidence to support your view, then be careful to raise a sufficient amount of capital to get to your next milestone. A seed round should be sufficient to provide you runway ideally for eighteen months. You should plan for unexpected delays and leave room for unexpected costs.

With hindsight, we were always too optimistic when deciding how much to raise. Existing investors would obviously favor raising a minimum, as it would be in their best interest so as to minimize their dilution. But that meant I ended up always raising money, spending my bandwidth going from one fundraising round into the next without enough time and energy to focus on the milestones and the traction.

CATALINA DANIELS, SWEETWELL

...

Growth-Stage Funding: Traction and Capital Efficiency

If you are fortunate to experience rapid growth, then you will want to fuel your scale-up with whatever capital is needed. For a growth-stage round, you should be able to point to traction and you should have a good handle on your metrics (gross margins, sales and marketing drivers, operating data, etc.). Your fundraising at these stages should be tied to milestones—that is, by taking in funding, you should be able to explain how and to what level you will grow the business. And each round should cover your needs for eighteen to twenty-four months.

You need to raise enough capital so that you do not find yourself exhausted of funds before achieving your next milestone, which will enable you to raise more, or end up without any cushion to absorb unexpected costs.

I've not stopped raising money since we started this company. It's continuous.
BERI MERIC, IVY

Series A and B institutional investors expect proof of customer demand and validation of business model assumptions. While the early money is looking at the dream and the team, growth-stage investors want to know that there is something smart and real to spend money on. In other words, the later the round, the greater the expectation there is by investors that you have already figured something out (compelling product/service and large opportunity), that your team has proven it can execute, and that you have a cogent operating plan to grow.

In particular, potential investors will evaluate whether you can keep up the growth, what the ultimate size of the opportunity is, when the business will be profitable, and what this may mean for a future exit for them.

In Josh's case with Plated, they eventually raised a total of $56M by the close of their Series B round. However, they got going with a mere $300K from angel investors to produce their site, hire a small staff, and purchase ingredients. They followed that with a somewhat modest $1.4M seed VC round, after the business was already generating over $1M in annual recurring revenue (ARR); they validated customer demand and began to understand their core metrics. Only after he had data on Plated's customers (cost to acquire, lifetime value, etc.) and cost of operations (warehouses, staffing, etc.) did he use that data to raise his next growth round. Plus, by the Series B, he had a much better understanding of how much the company would need long-term to scale up the business and ultimately achieve profitability.

For growth-stage financings, don't be surprised if potential investors ask for a detailed financial model as to how you will invest funds and grow your business. They will expect you to have a good grasp of your key business drivers, how these impact your top and bottom line, and how additional capital will help you to ultimately achieve your goals.

Finally, if you are growing like a weed (as VCs like to say) and your sector is on fire, then you may find investors throwing money at you—but do not take too much. You may be tempted by sky-high valuations as well, which we sometimes read about in the press, to raise a lot more than you need from others who want to be a part of your success story. But be careful in such a situation.

You should strive to be capital efficient. With overcapitalization comes a temptation to hire too fast, overinvest in unproven tactics, launch new products that are not adequately tested, and push unprofitable revenue growth, which then triggers large ongoing losses. There is a tendency to lose focus. So, just as you need to be careful with raising too little, be leery of death by overfunding.

Find the Right Balance: How Much and When to Raise?

- Too Soon: You lack a good handle on the market opportunity, the product/market fit is unclear, the business model's core metrics are unstable, and you can't competently estimate the ultimate capital need of the business to achieve profitability. In addition, the earlier you raise, the more expensive the capital is going to be in terms of equity dilution.

- Too Much: You run the risk of "death by overfunding" and expand too quickly, pursue suboptimal strategies and tactics, and aren't disciplined in marketing and operations. There is great risk should financial markets deteriorate in your industry and your venture continues to need capital.
- Too Little: You will need to be in fundraising mode all the time and you don't have the capital to experiment and to weather unexpected operating challenges.

Getting the right balance is tricky! One way to find the balance is to surround yourself with people who have been there, done that.

Even if the markets are such that you can raise a lot of money, it does not mean that you should. You don't want to raise too much unless you are pretty certain your growth can be sustained.

In the case of Bespoke Post, the firm grew to over $100M in sales and was modestly profitable while it had raised a total of just $8M in capital across their angel, seed, and Series A rounds. Talk about being capital efficient!

Could Bespoke Post have raised a lot more to fund faster growth? Surely yes. And some of their investors wanted them to raise more. But the founders chose a more conservative path, preferring moderate losses while investing primarily in proven revenue streams for their growth. They would experiment but did not want to waste money on unproven ideas. After eight years, only then did they complete a Series B round for $35M, valued at over $300M.

There is a lot of media that exalts huge funding rounds at high valuations during the growth stage achieved by certain tech firms, but going for funding glory often creates future risks for the venture should conditions change. Valuation inflation can create a bubble. If the financing climate for your sector deteriorates and you have high fixed costs that prevent you from quickly getting to break-even, then the company's survival is at stake. You might face a fire sale situation (more on this in Part VI). Your financing strategy greatly influences the story of your eventual exit.

A tension exists among the amount of capital you raise, the company valuation at the point of capital raises, and equity dilution. The greater the amount of capital and the lower the valuation, the more dilution you will incur. So founders find themselves balancing these considerations—what the business needs versus what they are willing to give up.

Furthermore, you need to consider the fact that your ownership will be diluted not just by the first equity financing round but also by future rounds. A rule of thumb is that each round of capital dilution is approximately 15 to 25 percent. By the Series B round, the average founder owns less than 30 percent of company shares. As ownership declines, so does your decision-making authority at the board level.

As you think through the implications, bear in mind the words of the HBS professor Howard Stevenson, who once famously said, in regard to entrepreneurs and their financing goals: "Do you want to be rich? Or do you want to be king?"

It is exceedingly hard to be both. You can be a 70, 80, or 90 percent owner and retain control, but you may not have raised enough financing to fund your business's growth. Or you could maximize your fundraising, but you may lose control of your business.

Most of the time, you won't have a choice. The business requires a certain amount of capital, you need to raise it, and the market will determine the valuation (and hence the degree of dilution for you and others).

With the HBS firms, we've seen a range of situations, with some entrepreneurs raising a lot of equity without, it seems, concern about dilution, and others who strove to strike a very careful balance.

I'm a little bit of a weird entrepreneur in the sense that I'm less dilution sensi-tive than most. Joanna and I are both founders; we obviously have the big-gest piece of the pie. I'm not worried about our dilution. I want to maximize the probability of success. So, I would advise people to optimize for success as opposed to necessarily dilution.

DAVE PARKER, YUMBLE KIDS

As Dave says, optimizing for success rather than dilution is a pre-ferred approach.

Having said this, to the extent you can self-fund the early stage (the most expensive stage for the founder in terms of giving away equity) or raise not a huge amount of financing early on, the greater control and equity stake you will be able to maintain despite subsequent financing rounds. In other words, you might be able to still be king and raise a lot of money if you're able to raise it *after* the company has scaled up and commands a higher valuation.

EXIT OPTIONALITY VS. "GO BIG OR GO HOME"

I raised a total of $25M for the firm across two rounds (Series A and B). The first round was to prove out more of the business model. The second was to accelerate growth of a proven model. It was a good amount raised and enough to achieve the level of top-line growth, profitability, and ultimately business size that I thought we could achieve. Could I have raised even more? Yes. But I did not want to force upon myself more pressure such that the only way to have success was to raise the bar for a successful exit that much higher. It was the right financing amount.

JIM SHERMAN, SHERMANSTRAVEL MEDIA

Whatever your growth-stage financing strategy is today, it *will* impact you down the road—especially on exit. If you want to have flexibility or options for positive exit scenarios, and not just a binary, boom-or-bust outcome, then you need to reflect on your financing strategy. "Exit optionality" in financing means raising just the right amount of capital for your company's needs at a reasonable valuation (avoiding a valuation bubble) while still maintaining the option to exit at a more modest price (i.e., a "small exit") in the future, if necessary, and still see a positive return for all stakeholders. It means being capital efficient as you strive to validate the future before closing off lesser exit paths.

When raising growth financing rounds, you may be tempted, especially after reading so many stories about private company unicorns, to shoot for maximum capital at the highest possible valuation (think Uber, WeWork, Airbnb, etc.). Unicorn-hungry investors may push to invest more than you even want. Some very large VCs can only make big investments and must swing for the fences; in other words, smaller exit outcomes for them don't yield wins they need for their large portfolio. But don't assume this is your best strategy. It is a particularly risky strategy should the opportunity *not* be as large as you expect (which often occurs) and should you wish to seek an exit at a more modest price, or should your future financing dry up while you're still racking up losses and you run out of cash. Both situations can—putting it mildly—lead to a suboptimal outcome for you and your investors.

The more money you raise at ever-increasing valuations, the greater the pressure to grow—and the greater the pressure on the price at which you need to exit to make all investors, founders, and other equity holders happy.

Founders of efficient companies (or lightly capitalized firms) can sell their companies at any point along their development and get a great return. Heavily capitalized firms are targeting massive growth upside and have fewer exit off-ramps where all stakeholders can benefit.

There is a trade-off between the amount of capital/valuation and exit optionality. The key challenge is to get these aligned in a way that is right for the business and right for you personally. It isn't easy.

Our view is that you should preserve the option to exit at a modest level until you see a greater-than-not likelihood that the business will achieve a much larger exit with more capital. You need to be comfortable with achieving the kind of growth that is expected from the high valuation. Be aware that risks abound.

Let's look at the spectrum of financings—from raising nothing at all to raising a lot—and how the financing strategies impact exit optionality especially in light of changing market conditions.

With Jim's first entrepreneurial venture, West End Media, in 1998, he never intended to take on venture financing for the internet strategy consulting business. One key reason was that it was not absolutely needed—it was optional. He had been approached by VCs, but he was not convinced that the venture would scale to what their expectations were, and he had an even greater concern that the Internet 1.0 bubble could burst—which it did by 2001. As fast as the market went up, it came crashing down. Because he chose to run what was a highly profitable medium-size business, with twenty-five senior consultants, it worked well for him as the sole owner.

He wanted his exit to be steady self-sustaining profits, albeit with slower revenue growth, while still keeping open the possibility of a future sale. The companies in that era that chose to take on significant venture capital, if they had not sold for cash before the stock market crash in 2000, ran into troubles when growth slowed and financing windows closed. Most went out of business, resulting in losses for investors and little, if any, return for founders.

This is a common situation of startups raising money in a frenzied market only to see conditions change and growth stall. Continued financing dries up and the business is forced to sell at a price that is not particularly attractive to all the stakeholders.

For example, in the case of Gilt, the founders and investors believed in their goal of building a multibillion-dollar company. The founders raised $286M to fund it, with later-stage financing valuing the business at $1B.

Because of the amount of VC raised at eye-popping valuations, Gilt had to keep growing in order to meet those value expectations. Eventually the firm faced challenges, including rising competition and a strengthening economy which reduced incentives for brands to discount. It could have worked out fine as a solid medium-to-large business with more modest funding and valuation terms. Eventually they were sold to Hudson's Bay for $250M, which is a very nice exit but one that did not satisfy all equity holders given their limited exit optionality.

Some entrepreneurs only believe in the "go big or go home" mantra. That is, the only exit that matters is the home run $1B exit—doubles and triples worth a more modest $100M to $250M do not matter. For some, they wish to take that gamble. Other entrepreneurs do not and prefer to play a game that affords more options for exit, including smaller exits. You need to decide your preference, as it will impact your financing strategy, from whom to raise, and ultimately, your exit outcome.

Case Study: Plated vs. Blue Apron

Nothing illustrates the dichotomy of exit optionality versus "go big or go home" better than the financing strategy difference between Plated and Blue Apron. Both companies, operating in the same field, raised a significant amount of funds. However, Plated raised less and retained greater optionality.

With Plated, Josh wanted to retain "optionality" for different exit outcomes, so he raised enough to enable the firm to ultimately go public, but he did not raise huge sums (compared to other meal kit firms) at eye-popping valuations. He agreed to valuations that would not take them many years to grow into. This approach enabled him to preserve *flexibility* on a future exit that would appeal to investors, founders, and employees.

We wanted to always raise money to the extent that we had choices. We wanted to make the choices where our investors and our employees and us as one would all win together.

We didn't want to raise money at huge outsized valuations, huge out-sized multiples that would take us years to grow into in the best of scenarios, where the employees that join during that period would only make money if we not only grew into those multiples but then exceeded them.

So, raising money at ten times revenue, if you believe the business will ultimately be valued at three times revenue, means that you have to get a whole lot bigger before the valuation will increase. It is the only way that people who join the team during that period will make money for their hard work. I think it's a fairly technical concept, but it's something that both of us [Josh and Nick] always felt strongly about. That meant at certain points in time taking lower valuations. It meant fighting hard for "clean terms." No "participating preferred" stock. Reasonable "liquidation preferences." A bunch of stuff that gets very technical quickly, but I think it is very important.

We viewed that reasonable multiples were in the three to four times revenue range. That was always the range that we raised in and we felt acquirers would one day value us that way.

JOSH HIX, PLATED

Plated was ultimately sold for such a multiple and at an exit price well above their earlier valuations. The company raised a total of $56M, its last round was a Series B at a $150M valuation, and Plated was sold for over $200M. The decision to retain optionality was a wise one.

In contrast, Blue Apron approached its financing from a different perspective. Blue Apron's financing strategy reflected a more aggressive plan—aggressive in terms of the growth vision and the amount raised, nearly $200M, at high valuations, which meant exit options would be limited.

My financing philosophy had always been, from the earliest days of the company, to build the kind of company that could be a public company. That's how I set up the capital structure.

I've never been afraid of raising capital. We were able to raise it at increasingly good valuations because we had real revenue traction and real business traction from the earliest days. Pretty quickly our market became competitive after we launched. Even before other people launched, we were competing in the most competitive market in the world, which is grocery. There are a gazillion ways for you to eat dinner and get food. So I always thought that it would require a good amount of capital.

Whenever we saw an opportunity to get capital on attractive terms, we tried to be a couple of steps ahead of our needing it. The seed round was with First Round; the B round was with Bessemer, then we raised a round with Stripes. The Stripes round was Series C. And then we did a Fidelity round, a Series D round which was at a $2B+ valuation, all ahead of the IPO.

MATT SALZBERG, BLUE APRON

The upshot is that the large amount of capital raised at high valuations made it such that an IPO might be the only viable exit path if investors were to see a positive return. It seemed highly challenging to find a corporate buyer in the food space that was able and willing to spend north of $2B. And $2B and above had become their exit floor.

The amount of money raised and the valuation will ultimately determine what flexibility you have in the future—flexibility to finance ongoing losses and flexibility to sell at a price that makes everyone money.

When times are good, it is very tempting to raise as much as you can and at the very highest valuations you can get. Funding glory can be quite the sport. But be aware that good times are fleeting. Conditions can quickly change—company-specific performance, sector challenges, or macroeconomic factors can turn against you, and if you do not have exit optionality, then you won't have a successful outcome for all the stakeholders, including you.

13

GET INVESTORS TO
BELIEVE IN YOU

> Investors don't invest in an idea, they invest in you—
> so show them you're worth it.

All the investors who had invested in Petridish were not investing in the idea; they were investing in me. So it was very easy to get them to come along to Blue Apron. I raised a bunch of money from people who wanted to back me as a person, not from people who were especially passionate about that idea.

MATT SALZBERG, BLUE APRON

Whatever round you raise, *you* are the most important factor when going out to raise financing. Confidence in leadership makes the difference between those who had an easier time raising funds and others who did not. Investors know that, despite a founder's well-laid-out plan, success ultimately depends on how the founder and team deal with unforeseen challenges and grasp new opportunities.

Getting people to believe in you starts with networking and gaining warm intros to key potential financiers. Then you need to build the element of trust over time. Ideally, you have taken time to develop a relationship with your key financing prospects.

The build of trust then comes from demonstrating proof of your business model assumptions. The biggest proof is showing the progress of your business and hitting milestones or proof points. Doing so shows your agility to handle unforeseen events and successfully manage through challenges. Proof is likewise supported by passion—you need to show strong conviction in your idea.

NETWORK AND BUILD TRUST OVER TIME

When raising funds, the personal connection with existing investors was critical. Trust makes it easier, especially in the early stages when you don't have many proof points.

CATALINA DANIELS, SWEETWELL

In four HBS cases, the entrepreneurs were able to raise money without having anything beyond just them and the idea. The entrepreneurs successfully closed an early round due to the strength of the founding team and the idea paired with good connections.

The investors had gotten to know the founders for some time prior to their business launching. They worked together in some cases, and their decision to invest was not based on any traction, since they had yet to launch. Instead it was based on the belief that these entrepreneurs could pull it off. The investors *believed in the founding team*.

Unlike later stages—Series A, B, etc., when closing a financing requires some degree of traction—"angel" investors (and some seed investors) are willing to bet just on entrepreneurs and their ideas. It happens. But such a situation places an even greater emphasis on one's

network. You must have a strong network of folks that you have culti-
vated over time.

*The more important factor in being able to have raised the money was hav-
ing been on the investment side, quite frankly, and having a personal network. Having worked at Blackstone and Bessemer made it easier for me to
raise money because investors speak a very specific language. And I think if
you understand how to speak that language, it gives them more confidence
that you're not going to waste their money, that you're going to build something excellent.*

MATT SALZBERG, BLUE APRON

In particular, investors were backing Matt as a person. We see this
because they stuck with him even as he ended up switching business
ideas from Petridish to Blue Apron.

*Almost all the money I raised in the seed round was from people who just
said, "We don't care what you're doing, we just think you're going to be successful." These are people I'd known for a long time and wanted to be a part
of it.*

MATT SALZBERG, BLUE APRON

There was a similar situation with Anthony of Dot & Bo. He was an
"entrepreneur in residence" at Trinity Ventures, where he got to know
the venture capital firm's partners. They invested in him and his new
idea.

*There was nothing more than ten slides on a PowerPoint. I was an entre-
preneur in residence at Trinity Ventures at the time. My pitch was, "I've got*

these three ideas I'm thinking about at the intersection of content and commerce. I'm thinking about pursuing it. What do you think? Anyone want to participate and have interest? I'm looking to raise a million dollars." I ended up getting about $6.5M or $7M in commitment. And then I dialed that back down to $4.5M into a Series A priced round instead of a convertible-note round.

In the round, Trinity Ventures came in for $3.5M. The other million came in from some others. They all banked on the fact that the concept I shared with them was interesting. Also, the fact that I had a track record of work in startups being successful inside larger companies as well as smaller companies.

ANTHONY SOOHOO, DOT & BO

Building up your financial network does not necessarily mean you must have worked with VCs, as Matt and Anthony had for some years. Of course, that was a huge help for them. But you can find other avenues.

For starters, you should look at your network and determine if there are friends, family members, mentors, professors, and business professional contacts who could be potential investors. This is always the best place to start.

We raised our angel round, a small number of friends and family that were crazy enough to believe in us. That was fall 2012. In early 2013, we met our first institutional investor.

JOSH HIX, PLATED

Even if your network contacts are not likely to invest, you should leverage them to get warm introductions to other appropriate people whom they may know. Be sure to add on anyone in your life who you feel could make a relevant introduction. Press your contacts to think about financiers who could be good. Even if the financiers are not right for you, they may know others who are.

We relied on our lawyer to introduce us to venture firms that he knew. He was a critical piece of this. Also, our HBS professors were very helpful in making introductions to early investors.

JENNY FLEISS, RENT THE RUNWAY

Warm introductions are much more effective than going in cold to that sought-after meeting with potential backers. It behooves you to leverage *all* your contacts to find as many warm intros as possible.

We went to a host of people we knew—colleagues, friends of theirs, extended connections—and we raised our search capital to cover our costs while we searched for a business to buy.

We raised funds more through our professional network than friends and family. There were a couple of friends as well. There was also one of our largest initial investors and our largest equity investor in the actual transaction, who was a Boston-area entrepreneur who started taking an interest in search funds. He was looking to write checks to support this type of pursuit. We got connected to him.

GREG GERONEMUS, SMARTOURS

Warm introductions to investors can come from your own network, but they also can come from established accelerators, incubators, and boot camps (ERA, Y Combinator, Techstars, 500 Startups, etc.). These programs can be especially valuable to entrepreneurs who may not have a developed business network. Should you participate in one, as Plated and others did, then you will have potential investors coming to hear your pitch.

Finally, you can also seek advice informally from business mentors or advisors and build up a relationship with them. After a while, it is not uncommon for an advisor to want to invest in your journey.

In the case of RubiconMD, Carlos had the good fortune of establishing a relationship with an industry advisor. That advisor came to believe in them and their idea, and he decided to become an early investor.

We went to our first advisor and we asked for advice. "How do you think we should go about raising a little bit?" People say, "Ask for money and you get advice. Ask for advice and you get money twice." We weren't thinking of this person as an angel, but he suggested himself. And he said, "What if I put some angel money in?" We were like, "Well, we hadn't thought about it, but this is actually a deal. We already trust you. We've gotten a lot of value from you. And you are the perfect investor."

CARLOS REINES, RUBICONMD

Although some investors will make up their minds very fast, you should plan to build trust *over time* with most—especially if there is skepticism (as there usually is) with your idea. This requires building and maintaining connections with the folks in your network over time and growing that trust. Then it takes even more time to build trust in your new business idea.

There is a huge amount of personal trust that you have to build. You should be talking to people very honestly about what's working in your business and what's not.

ANTHEMOS GEORGIADES, ZUMPER

Well before you go out for a formal raise, it behooves you to try to keep VCs and other potential investors warm. One person on the team, ideally the CEO, needs to build trust directly with VCs.

One way to do that is to send VC prospects an occasional information email update. Or meet up with people one-on-one for a general update meeting. Then, when the day comes that you are seeking financing, it will be that much easier to tell your story and persuade them to come aboard. They will have already gotten to know you better.

When I started the business, I spent a lot of years keeping VCs in the dark, where you don't keep them too updated because when you're fundraising and finally show this big amazing pitch, it all seems very exciting and builds momentum that way. And in the early days, it worked. We always raised financing.

When I look back, I think it was wrong. It is a far better way to raise money when you know those investors already.

If you want to rely on venture capital to reinvest your revenue and grow unprofitably until you hit real market share, you have to have a portfolio of venture investors that you know, and more importantly, that know you and trust you.

We did an $80M Series B round about a year and a half ago. Now I'm going to fundraise again this year. When I think about fundraising, I'm talking to people now who I've spoken to for over a year. It's not like I've seen them every month, but every quarter I'll make an effort to grab coffee, get them into the office, give them the update with no ask. And so, when I do go raise later this year, even though it won't be this exciting thing because they know the story already, it's exciting in a different way. They know the story, but they've built a personal trust in me and we go off, we execute, and I come back. That's what we said we'd do.

And by the time you go pitch them for the round, the stuff that wasn't working should be working. And they should know that that's authentic because they've kind of been with you on the journey.

ANTHEMOS GEORGIADES, ZUMPER

...

MAKE A GOOD FIRST IMPRESSION

You typically have one chance in front of prospective investors, and you need to impress them quickly. It's always better to present in person if you can. But many prospects will merely ask you to email them a deck or to submit materials via their website.

While the purpose of a well-composed email is to grab attention and motivate someone to open your attachment, the goal of the pitch deck is to get the investor excited enough to want to proceed to a meeting and to engage in more meaningful, in-depth conversation.

Reading through your deck, they will assess the venture along these lines:

- What problem are you solving and is it a large opportunity? (i.e., the strength and uniqueness of the idea)
- The strength of the team
- Traction to date

In regard to opportunity, investors pay careful attention to one of two things. For high-tech or science ventures, a crucial question is whether the product works or will work. Has the entrepreneur sufficiently demonstrated that the new technology, scientific discovery, or software actually is or will be effective? We are amazed as angel investors at how often entrepreneurs claim to have invented a new product or service yet don't show enough validation of its effectiveness or uniqueness.

In the case of business model innovation (which is the type of venture launched by the HBS founders), early investor focus is less on "does this actually work" and more on what behavioral change is needed for this to work, is it realistic to expect that change, and what the competitive offerings are (which, importantly, includes the status quo, that is, the target customer choosing not to change behavior). We've seen many new products and services that claim to offer tremendous benefits yet don't succeed in changing the status quo. You will need to prove that your product or service is sufficiently compelling to change extant behavior.

There are other criteria, such as the go-to-market plan (how will you market the product/service), any unique IP, product strength, the competitive landscape, use of capital, and exit opportunities.

But remember that—in all cases—investors will want to understand what problem you solve, how large and unique the opportunity is, and why you are well positioned to capture it.

In regard to the team, the investors will assess "founder fit" for the venture—what strengths do you have for building the business into something hugely successful?

The pitch deck needs to convince investors that there is something worthwhile in pursuing continued dialogue—getting them to want to engage in a face-to-face meeting and ultimately a due diligence meeting. Since investors see so many opportunities, skepticism runs high on what entrepreneurs claim. So you need to excite and impress them, and a lot will depend on your storytelling.

To grab their attention, ensure that your first few slides surprise them. Perhaps you have serious traction, or patented IP, or a unique team. Lead with what might impress.

One of the things that I learned was that with a lot of investors you get very little time to make an impression. I wasn't prepared for how to impress these people. And you only make one first impression. If you burn that one, and if you embarrass yourself or don't have an answer that they think is important, you've lost that opportunity to get that investment. It's hard to come back and be successful with them.

ERIC PRICE, SKYMD

Even firms that don't have much traction can find ways to craft a compelling story with a pitch deck. You need to find evidence to support your hypothesis as to the attractiveness of the business opportunity. You also need to convey passion and optimism.

The early seed stage is about crafting a deck that sells the investor on your idea and the dream, the team, and whatever progress you have made thus far. But as you progress along the fundraising journey (e.g., by the time of series A), investors increasingly are going to look for fundable milestones. They want to know that you have something smart to spend money on. The pitch deck needs to convey progress—what you have accomplished. Nothing impresses VCs more than seeing an entrepreneur make progress with few resources.

Also, *how* you present is as important as what you present. Jim recalls a piece of advice from when he worked for Martha Stewart.

I remember how Martha Stewart once said to me before her company IPO, "You have to show a little leg. You don't have to present every company detail. Tell a good story in a memorable way." What she meant was that, of course, you need to provide investors with enough detail and be convincing in the strength of your business opportunity, but you also have to give them a dream.

JIM SHERMAN, SHERMANSTRAVEL MEDIA

DEMONSTRATE PROOF POINTS

Get traction. I don't care how much they like you, how much you charm them—they're not going to invest in you unless they actually believe that you can execute. And if they think that this is the last ticket to the train, all the more so.

DAVE PARKER, YUMBLE KIDS

The best way to get potential investors to believe in you is to demonstrate proof points, like data demonstrating the attractiveness of the market opportunity, the business traction to date, and your skills in execution. These points will build the trust that you are worth the investment. Which proof points matter the most differs depending on the stage of company development.

During the early stage, pulling a team together is for example particularly important. While building trust in you and the idea takes time, a critical proof point will be your ability to pull together a strong founding team. Investors won't believe in you if you haven't assembled what they view as crucial human resources needed for success. Investors want to know that you have the recruiting skills to attract the best team players.

With SkyMD, Eric looks back and recalls that he did not emphasize his team enough—partly because they were not in New York with him. This was a liability for many investors.

I didn't emphasize the team as much because I was the face of the team here. It was hard to bring them into it since I knew they couldn't be here with me, so I didn't want to shine too much light on them. But then I soon realized that I had to.

It led to other challenges where they wanted to meet these people—one was in Florida and one in India—but it ultimately was better to pitch a bigger team.

ERIC PRICE, SKYMD

As investors, we often see entrepreneurs not mentioning their team in their pitch. Even early on, it is critical to do so.

In addition, there is hardly any better proof of your business concept than actual traction. Getting people to believe in you means getting them to react favorably to what you have accomplished—what you have done. The extent to which you have made progress with limited resources is the best way to get VCs to take an interest in you and your company.

Raising the money was easy for us because, one, I had a background in raising money. And two, the business traction from a revenue perspective was always there. It's always easy to raise money if you have a fast-growing business with good unit economics.

MATT SALZBERG, BLUE APRON

While product/market fit is best demonstrated with actual customers, you can look to other milestones that can bolster your case before you have actual customers—especially in the earliest phase. These could be acquiring a key distribution or marketing partnership, winning a government grant, or completing a prototype of the site or product. Or it could even be as simple as a business survey of how much interest there is in your proposed product or service with your target buyer—that's better than nothing.

For example, Justin of Henry the Dentist knew that he had a major challenge convincing early investors to jump in and fund his mobile dental clinic. He could not show traction since there was no mobile truck in operation. He had to build his mobile dental clinic to actually test the concept. And because so much of the value of his product was not just convenience but also the overall experience, showing the actual product and having customers try it out was important. But it all costs money to develop.

So he approached the financing in a creative two steps. One was his push with the Small Business Administration (SBA), where he was able to secure a loan for $750K, which he personally guaranteed. Then he convinced angels to invest $750K. While his personal guarantee on the SBA loan helped him to secure that financing, he had to rely on his sheer power of persuasion and the strength of the concept to draw in angel investors for the other half. To push the $1.5M round over the finish line, the angels were ultimately impressed by his closing the SBA loan. The SBA was a strong endorsement and a proof point.

No one wanted to write me a check before I had a product. A lot of people were like, "Oh, can you do a minimum viable product and rent a dental truck or use someone else's dental truck or do it in their office?" I'm like, "The whole thing is about the experience. No." Unfortunately, my minimum viable product was a PowerPoint presentation that I had to sell to companies based on a rendering. Exaggerating the truth, a little bit, but I had to go hustle.

I got the SBA loan. That's how I got the business off the ground in the beginning. I personally guaranteed it. Other investors followed on that.

JUSTIN JOFFE, HENRY THE DENTIST

For Rent the Runway, demonstrating traction came from early consumer tests of their service through their college "pop-up stores." They proved that their target customers loved the rental service, which helped convince some skeptical investors of the business opportunity. It was the necessary proof point to get investors to believe in the founders.

We had several of our pop-up stores on college campuses, which showed customers loved the idea of renting designer clothes. We wound up raising money, $1.75M from Bain Capital, before we had much of anything other than those MVP tests at the undergraduate schools.

JENNY FLEISS, RENT THE RUNWAY

The team, market opportunity, and traction are the trifecta of proof points that's needed to get people to believe in you and ultimately win funding.

Depending on the *stage*, the weights of these proof points vary. The earlier the round, the more investor focus there will be on the vision, the size of the opportunity and the team, especially you.

Meanwhile, for any post-angel or post-seed-stage investment, data and traction will be absolutely essential. By the time of the Series A and especially Series B, it is crucial to master your key performance indicators (KPIs) for the business model and to understand how additional growth capital will be used productively in a clear growth formula for the business.

The Series B is probably the hardest. It's a tweener round. You can fake your way and sell a vision maybe to a Series A. The Series B, you need to be showing serious traction.

CARLOS REINES, RUBICONMD

Dave illustrates how the content of investor conversations shifted as they moved from the startup to scale-up phase.

This is an amazing story of just literally what a difference a year makes. Originally, the questions were all about, "Is there really a need? What makes you different?" All of the foundational types of investor questions. "Is this really a problem? Do you really have a solution? And who is your team?"

Now people are coming to us because they know we're different. Now it's, "We like the problem, we like the solution, we like your team, so we want to invest in you, provided your metrics are close to what we think they are."

DAVE PARKER, YUMBLE KIDS

By the Series A round, there is a focus on customer or user traction; have you sufficiently shown proof of product/market fit by this point? For a growth Series B round, investors want to understand how exactly you will be able to scale up the business with the use of funds—a clear financial road map to how funds can be productively put to use. Of course, they will still want to assess the team, the overall potential market, and the business model, but product/market fit, by this stage, has already been established and there is a road map for continued growth and ultimately profitability. The questions now become: How can the team rapidly scale the business? How big can it get? What market risks might exist?

For these later stages, knowing your key drivers of the business and proving out the core metrics is essential. People won't believe in you if you do not have a solid grasp of them. Don't be surprised if you are asked to develop a financial model that quantitatively demonstrates exactly how additional capital will help you grow the business and what that financial pro forma will look like. Investors will also assume that you have already made mistakes and have figured out what works and what doesn't.

There was a point where we got our paid marketing to work. That's what led us to raise our Series A. Paid marketing started to work and we could show a payback period. We could show all of the numbers. Then it becomes really more about an analytical approach to raising funds. And the conversation was less about, "Okay, do these two guys know what they're doing? Do I think there's a market here?" And more, "Do you know your numbers? Do you know your stuff? Can this all work?"

We got to a point where we had a good handle on the unit economics. And we felt that we could scale the business if we had more money, essentially.

STEVE SZARONOS, BESPOKE POST

With Bespoke Post, the growth rounds rested on the founders being able to demonstrate how a dollar invested in marketing would yield a positive return over a customer's lifetime value. The metrics were compelling. With other HBS entrepreneurs, the metrics were different but no less weighty in helping to close financing.

For example, Zumper needed to show traction with their site traffic as well as rental listings. But they couldn't easily grow the traffic without having sufficient apartment listings. It was challenging getting the landlord listings until they had a large volume of user traffic—a classic marketplace problem. So they focused first on the landlords as a proof point for their Series A, and then focused on site traffic for their Series B.

The product/market fit of the vision, we always were absolutely convinced was there. It was always a story of "Can we show investors enough to fund the next round that will help us get that?" That was always the frame.

In terms of measuring success, the first two years was in how many landlord accounts could see sign up. And I think by the time we get to the Series A, we had signed up 30,000. By the Series B, we wanted to take 50,000 visits on the consumer side a month to make it into 4M or 5M. And we delivered 4M for the Series B. And now we're doing 8M a month. These were the clear metrics the first two years. The first number measured landlord activity, the second was consumer visits a month.

ANTHEMOS GEORGIADES, ZUMPER

Lastly, Henry the Dentist illustrates well how the business's proof points changed with successive financings. In the pre-seed stage, Justin needed to show that customers would come to his mobile clinic and that they liked the experience. For the seed stage, he developed his "hub-and-spoke" model of operation. Then for the growth stage (Series A round), he demonstrated how he could take his initial hub-and-spoke delivery model and expand it geographically with additional financing. At each stage, he could provide proof points and successively reduce risk for the investors.

The pre-seed was to get the first product out and see if people would come from their office to the chair. The seed was to grow it into a hub-and-spoke model. The vision here was to create a brick-and-mortar hub-and-spoke with three mobile clinics that serve as tentacles. The Series A round of

$10M would open up two new geographic markets to build more hub-and-spokes.

JUSTIN JOFFE, HENRY THE DENTIST

Proof points will define your ability to raise funds. Since investors will be looking for different proof points over time, you should be attuned to what is key at your stage of development.

14

DO YOUR PITCHING
HOMEWORK

> Don't shoot in all directions. The right investor may be
> difficult to find but easier to land.

*I wasted a lot of time talking with VCs that would never invest at this
stage. Theoretically that's not a bad thing, because you can build relationships with those who at a later stage may want to invest. But I
was pitching hard for an investment* now *from companies and firms that
would never have considered something this early.*

ERIC PRICE, SKYMD

Success in raising funds starts with a plan to reach out to many people—it is a numbers game, to a large extent—as you leverage your network. And it will be easier and time better spent if you target the *right*
people and VCs. There are many who will not be in your sweet spot of
likely investors.

If you can, it behooves you to target *smart money,* because there is nothing better than getting not only money but also access to a network and smart advice—a luxury, especially in the very early stage.

As you reach out to investors, it's crucial to be aware of skepticisms to overcome, to pick up on the key objections and preempt the issues in future meetings by modifying your story and being ready with answers. While skepticisms may very well be unique to the VC or individual you're pitching, it is also likely that some issues will emerge as common. As the HBS founders did, you should absorb the feedback, iterate, and improve your story as you forge ahead.

A NUMBERS GAME AND THE RIGHT TARGETS

You have to kiss a lot of frogs. It's a numbers game.

JUSTIN JOFFE, HENRY THE DENTIST

In the ideal world, you have already developed a strong network, and you can leverage this network either as potential investors or for them to make intros on your behalf to other investor prospects. The best approach is focus and quality. Matt and Anthony were able to do this with Bessemer Venture Partners and Trinity Ventures, respectively. They nurtured quality contacts from their network and succeeded in closing financing rounds fairly speedily.

In reality, however, most entrepreneurs do not have funders waiting in the wings. Most entrepreneurs do not spend enough time building trust with investors, and even so, raising funds ends up being about the numbers. Most HBS alums pitched to hundreds of investors; few had a limited list.

There will be a lot of "no's." Many of the "no's" might come from meeting the wrong investors for you, but "no's" also happen from meeting the right people at the wrong time—or by being ill-prepared.

The typical startup founder needs to kiss many frogs before finding one that agrees to invest in his or her vision. This is because it is hard to know who is right for your opportunity. So, the more people you meet with, the more likely you are to eventually gain introductions to the *right* people who could be interested. This is particularly the case during the angel and seed stage.

While warm introductions matter greatly, it is critical to plan your outreach to be far and wide, since you never know which initial contact could lead you to an ideal investor.

For example, Plated raised $380K in their first angel round, but that was only after pitching more than two hundred people! In retrospect, it seems hard to believe that they had trouble raising money, given how successful a business Plated became. But the reality was that raising the first round was very difficult.

We started pitching angels, everyone and anyone who would listen. Like a lot of businesses, we had a very long road. We pitched something like two hundred people before anybody said yes. Honestly, I don't think that's too unusual. It's the reality for most people, certainly when you're doing it for the first time at any scale, and also if you're doing something that is new. We had a hard time, not necessarily harder than average, but several months' worth of pitching anyone who would listen and having a lot of doors slammed in our faces.

JOSH HIX, PLATED

Justin of Henry the Dentist counts around seventy-five potential investors with whom he met in his early fundraising. He had to pitch a concept that, to many, seemed fairly mundane—dentistry. He didn't have any IP, and the service—dentistry—was not new. But the convenience in how it was delivered to the consumer was new.

I'm literally bringing the dental clinic to your office. I'm removing all friction. But we're doing dentistry. I have a dental clinic for all intents and purposes.

Zero IP. No patents. No trademark. Nada. I'm a dental clinic in a Winnebago. Then I went out and probably met with seventy-five investors that all said no. Every single investor said no.

JUSTIN JOFFE, HENRY THE DENTIST

However, as we mentioned earlier, Justin did ultimately win over angel investors but it was only after he had closed an SBA loan for $750K.

To increase your odds of success, you should do your homework as to which potential investors are the *right* investors for your venture. Angels and seed/VC investors typically specialize in a few industries (health care, climate tech, retail, fintech, edutech, etc.), type of business (B2B or B2C products/services, marketplaces, deep tech, etc.), or even type of founder (women, POC, LGBTQ+, etc.). They have a preference on check size, and stick to a particular stage of development (some won't look at pre-revenue companies).

Also, there are VCs and angels that only seek investments with potential for billion-dollar-plus exits, while others are fine with more moderate but potentially lower-risk exits of $100M to $500M. You should find the *right* type of investor for your company.

I think there's a Venn diagram that needs to overlap. An investor looks at the check size, the industry, the founder, their portfolio weighting, the timing of their fund. They have a whole investment thesis for what they invest in, when, the stage, all that. And the company has to fit into that.

I walk in every investor meeting assuming it's not going to be a fit. The majority of cases, I'm not hitting that Venn diagram. I'm too early or too late. I'm cap X (require capital expenditures) or I'm tech or the wrong industry, wrong founder, wrong relationship, wrong-size check. I'm too small. I'm too big. Who knows? I'm unlikely to fit.

You have to hit the right fund that wants New York–based, health care, doesn't mind retail, doesn't mind brick-and-mortar and capital intensive businesses, likes to write a check at that stage, has the fund resources for that, doesn't compete with their existing portfolio. I didn't take any of it personally. No problem. Qualify. Meet with you. Great. Here's the pitch deck.

I had to sell the vision. But mainly the big funds turned me down. I get that. They need billion-dollar exits and they didn't believe this could be a billion dollars. They didn't believe you created a moat that had some network viral effect. Okay, no problem. There are other investors that totally saw the potential and were more than happy with this being a $500M company in the next seven years.

Some funds are designed to only need a Google or Facebook to make the fund economics work. Totally fine, not my type of investor. But today, people are pounding on our door and I have a wait list of investors and we're turning down people and we're oversubscribed every round.

JUSTIN JOFFE, HENRY THE DENTIST

Key Factors for Lining Up the Right Investors

Getting in the door will be a challenge unless you match these and other criteria:

- Industry. Are you in an industry that truly interests these investors?
- Stage of development. Are you too early for them? Are you matching their ARR (annual recurring revenue) threshold?
- Check size. Do you meet the minimum investment size?
- Potential upside matching investor expectations. Some investors only seek $1B+ exit opportunities while others are open to lesser exits. Do you fit their expectations?
- Type of business. Are they aligned with your type of venture— software, service, physical product, capital intensity, etc.?
- Market entry barriers. Do they require IP or some other moat?
- Type of founder: women, POC, LGBTQ+, affinity groups (e.g., university alumni), etc.

FIND SMART MONEY

Some of our investors played a critical role in introducing us to prospects. It made a world of difference being introduced at the right level with the right intro. It truly increased our odds to close [customer] contracts.

CATALINA DANIELS, SWEETWELL

Raising money is not easy, and the temptation will be high to take *any* money you can find because it is money and will allow you to continue. But *smart* investor money will provide you strategic and operating advice along with their network of contacts to help you with hiring, customer development, partnerships, marketing, fundraising, and more. This is especially helpful during the early phase of a company's development because you cannot afford to hire all the talent that you may need and your company has not achieved much brand awareness yet. Smart money is also more than likely to be more patient with you when you hit the inevitable bumps in your business startup and scale-up journey.

For Rent the Runway, Jenny recalls how important it was to have their early-stage venture partner from Bain help their team to focus on operations and logistics. He helped them realize that what was an operational challenge for them would end up evolving into an enduring competitive advantage—one that would also help them to lure additional capital.

Carlos of RubiconMD mentioned how their first angel investor was incredibly important as an early advisor in helping them to better understand the complex health care industry and how to best scale their idea. He also helped to attract other angel investors.

He became an awesome mentor for both of us. He's a physician. He's an MBA. He's been CEO of one of the largest insurance payers in the country for twelve years. He's making sure that we're developing in the right way.

He became our investor with a little bit of seed capital and then a few other angels followed.

We love all the investors that we brought on board. They're great people. They're a real value-add. They have a great brand.

CARLOS REINES, RUBICONMD

We noted in chapter 2 that many great new business ideas come from entrepreneurs who don't have industry experience in their chosen market. While this can be helpful in allowing an outsider to rethink how things are done in an industry, it can be an impediment to raising funds, since investors want to validate from industry experts that the idea is a good one. Thus, having an industry leader, as Rubicon MD did, as an early advisor and investor not only helps with industry expertise but can also prove to be a great lure to attract other investors.

Eric describes how he wanted more strategic backers for SkyMD—investors with industry knowledge and contacts—but he was never able to make that happen. That lack of access to major insurance firms contributed to some blind spots that the team had in regard to the health care industry.

We did try to get strategic investors, but we didn't get the traction we needed with them. The investor base that we got didn't have a lot of experience in the health care industry. They were amazing. Every investor we had was supportive. But in terms of contacts, even our lead investor, who was very invested in our business, as much as he wanted to help, he just didn't know the right people. We didn't, either. We didn't have people around us who could get us into some of these places like insurance firms. And we didn't realize how important that was going to be. That was another lesson.

ERIC PRICE, SKYMD

Your early investors can also play a critical role in helping you to raise your follow-on rounds of financing. Your past investors help to make introductions to new investors that are right for your next phase. They also have deal-making experience, which is highly important as you negotiate future financings. Your early investors can be your negotiating partners as you close future rounds. You should leverage their expertise.

I use my board with regard to fundraising. My Series B was co-led by two funds that I originally met through my board members that I then developed a relationship with. But my board, when we get term sheets or when we want introductions, they've been phenomenal and go to bat for me.

ANTHEMOS GEORGIADES, ZUMPER

Finally, smart money will—more than likely—be more patient money that understands *why* a company's strategy may need to shift or why things are taking more time to develop than initially planned. The smart-money investors will be more empathetic and supportive when bumps inevitably occur in a company's development.

It took patience. The first million we raised, we said, "Hey, thanks for the money. This vision we painted for you is still our true north [where we enable transactions to lease apartments], but we're not going to start it now because if we start it now, we have no users on the platform. We're going to have to pay for all of our users. And then we just end up as a kind of tech brokerage. That's not the ambition of the company." Luckily, our investors were very patient with us to allow us to build the top of the funnel, where we generate qualified rental leads before we built the end-to-end transaction piece.

There was a beautiful naivety in how quickly we thought it would go. We thought getting to 8M visits a month, which is what we do now, would take maybe a couple of years. In fact, it took over four years to get to that number.

ANTHEMOS GEORGIADES, ZUMPER

Smart investors are likely to behave differently when you hit a serious bump. For example, Yumble Kids hit a major problem when one of the key operating partners who helped with meal prep and packaging needed to drop their account. Dave was distraught, but his chief financial backer understood and gave him confidence that Dave would work it out. Your financial backers can provide you the emotional support and confidence you need during strenuous periods.

I called Steve, the head of Apple Core. And he said something I loved. "David, this is going to be a footnote in an amazing story. You're going to figure this out and you're going to tell the story one day of how you were able to figure this out." And he was right. That helped give me the confidence to make it happen fast.

DAVE PARKER, YUMBLE KIDS

Smart money will also be more willing to accept not just tactical changes but more fundamental shifts. In the case of Werk, Anna recalls how important it is to have the right investors if you need to pivot the business. She had raised the first round early (before the company achieved sufficient product/market fit) as a marketplace. At a later stage, she and her cofounder decided to pivot to a SaaS platform. The company's investor base was not ideal for that evolution. Anna sums it up well: "Money should match the opportunity." Anna ultimately decided, with her investors, to sell the firm partly because her investors were not on board to invest more in the business pivot (more on this in chapter 20, on exit).

Smart money matters at all stages—whether it comes from smart angels, VC partners, or corporate venture folks. While you want to try to find it early on, when it is most critical, you also should strive for it in later stages.

In the case of Yumble Kids, Dave recounts how he looked at the issue of smart money across the phases of his company's development. For his angel stage, he found friends-and-family angel investors betting on him and the vision. However, in the second round, the seed stage, he found a VC with relevant food industry expertise from having been an early investor in Seamless and then a couple of others who had experience scaling a venture from the seed to Series A stage. For his Series A round, he was ideally seeking a more strategic investor who understood brand marketing. By that time his business and its growth were already catching the attention of others, and Dave wanted a strategic partner who could bring more than money.

The value that we're looking for in this new round is going to be brand, nutrition, and other food-related expertise, ideally with kids, or direct-to-consumer or subscription. Any of those things I'd say adds value in a way that we can tap into.

DAVE PARKER, YUMBLE KIDS

Dave ultimately closed a Series A round with Sonoma Brands, a growth-equity financial investor with a portfolio of food brands and direct-to-consumer businesses.

LEARN FROM SKEPTICISM AND REJECTION

I moved very quickly. I had a good network and I set up tons of meetings within a short period of time. Maybe if I had spread out the meetings more so I could absorb my learnings from things that I was not delivering on, that would've allowed me to be more successful in those later ones.

ERIC PRICE, SKYMD

To help you craft a strong pitch, you should approach your friendly contacts who can first give you honest, valuable feedback on your deck before you head out to pitch investors.

Since it's exceedingly unlikely that you will get a "yes" in your first meetings, try to just learn from the feedback, then incorporate that into modifications of your pitch deck and how you present the opportunity. Rejection is not only normal, it is typical. Learn from the feedback and move forward with persistence. As Eric wished, he may have improved his communication with investors had he had spread out his meetings more so that he could have taken learnings from one meeting to the next.

Most of all, doing your homework includes learning from your rejections and dealing with investor skepticism throughout the fundraising process. Remember that there are different kinds of "no's." There are some "no's" by those who are too busy or by those who just "don't get it." However, you are also going to experience "thoughtful no's" and from these you should learn.

The advice I try to give entrepreneurs is when you get rejected, try and capture as much feedback as you can, if they're willing to give it to you, because they're all thinking things. Might as well understand what they're thinking. It could help you refine your pitch for the next person.

And sometimes it has nothing to do with you or the business. They could be conflicted out. It's the wrong-size check. There are many factors that are out of your control.

JENNY FLEISS, RENT THE RUNWAY

Jenny learned along the way that it was difficult to convince male investors of the value of a female-focused business. She came up with a unique approach to convincing skeptical men at VCs about the value of her new clothing service for women. She and cofounder Jenn filmed their initial customers on college campuses and recorded the joy they had in being able to rent designer dresses from their pop-up racks—before even spending money on a website. The video captured not just the fact that women liked the opportunity to rent designer dresses, but that they *loved* doing it. After her first few venture meetings, Jenny anticipated the expected objection that men at VCs would have and proactively countered them at subsequent pitches.

Not every pitch went well. There were certainly pitches that men didn't get. You're pitching a very female, emotional connection to fashion, and most VCs are men.

We very quickly figured out how to overcome it, which was to show videos of these MVP tests. To show videos of customers that we interviewed talking about how they feel when they put on a dress, to show rather than tell. A woman puts on a great dress and immediately her mood and her energy and her spirit is transformed. We showed that to these groups of investors. Their eyes opened. Otherwise they might not have got it.

JENNY FLEISS, RENT THE RUNWAY

Interestingly, they did not find that investors were overly concerned about their lack of fashion industry experience. Their early investor meetings did not suggest it to be an issue, but just in case, they prepared by having ambassadors who could speak well about their venture.

I don't think it hurt us that we didn't have the fashion background. Maybe that was a good thing, that these investors didn't necessarily realize how incredibly hard and crucial the operational side was. They didn't necessarily ding us for it.

And we had found a slate of ambassadors, people like Jim Gold, who was the president at Bergdorf Goodman at the time . . . whose name we were able to drop and talk about.

JENNY FLEISS, RENT THE RUNWAY

Steve and Rishi of Bespoke Post had to overcome investor skepticism that men don't buy a lot online outside of tech products. They faced a battle convincing early investors that men would sign up for a monthly subscription to well-curated men's products—none of which were "essential."

Investors would say that men don't buy a lot of stuff online, except for tech. People would say, "It's not a real need," which is kind of true. It's discovery.

STEVE SZARONOS, BESPOKE POST

The way that Steve and Rishi managed that objection was to show potential investors their early data from Facebook marketing. They showed them strong retention data of their early subscribers, demonstrating that men liked the products, along with a very low cost of customer acquisition via Facebook. They argued that they could scale up the business with greater Facebook marketing. Many VCs didn't believe they could get subscriptions beyond 5K or 10K. At time of writing, they are north of 300K.

For SkyMD, Eric's challenge was likewise about convincing potential investors about the market size. But in his case, what he thought was large was actually not big enough for the VCs with whom he met. He misjudged his investor audience and failed to modify his pitch accordingly.

I didn't realize when I was pitching to the venture capital firms how big was "big." What I thought was big was too small for them. I talked about market sizes of a few hundred million; that wasn't interesting to them as much. But I thought that sounded like an amazing, huge business. I framed it incorrectly. I had the opportunity to tell the story of something much bigger, but I didn't do that. I think I lost the interest of a lot of those people.

I didn't always know my audience and I didn't always tell the story tailored to that audience. Of course, over time I learned and got better. But for those people, the ones where the opportunity was too small for them, I lost them.

ERIC PRICE, SkyMD

It behooves you to capture investor feedback along the way, learn from rejections, and know what are the perceived weaknesses that you need to proactively address. Then tailor your story according to your audience's concerns.

15

SET THE DOMINOES

> Don't underestimate momentum, herd mentality, and
> the snowball effect in fundraising. Investors can fall
> like dominoes.

*Trail Mix Ventures was my first check. It was the shortest meeting I had
and the first check that they wrote, and it was the best check that was
written. And it started the dominoes.*

JUSTIN JOFFE, HENRY THE DENTIST

Raising money is both art and science. While science is the numbers or
the logical analysis of a new business idea, the art aspect is more about
process and the role of psychology. You can help steer that psychology
to your advantage.

The HBS founders showed us that creating either a real or perceived
herd mentality, and in turn, the fear of missing out among investors,
along with your deal-making skills in running the financing process, is
paramount.

MOMENTUM IS YOUR BEST FRIEND

Momentum is *the* most important factor. After all, if you have it, then you are likely to create a herd of interested parties, and you will have that much more confidence in your terms and tone. Even if you lack a bit in deal-making and negotiating skills, momentum can make up for a lot.

Momentum derives from your own company's traction *and* your sector's appeal. This and a compelling formula for continued growth are key.

As long as we keep growing like this we're going to keep raising money, because who doesn't want to invest in a company that's almost doubling every year and there seems to be a very clear formula for growth?

BERI MERIC, IVY

From your perspective, you likely are thinking that all you want to do is bring in needed money to fund your MVP in the seed stage or to scale up your business in the Series A and B stages. You just want to get it done *now* so that you can move on to other critical business priorities in growing the venture—that is, hiring, verifying strategy, expanding marketing, building out logistics and operations, etc.

Meanwhile, potential investors are evaluating how they are going to get outsize returns on their investment. Seed-stage investors are seeking at least a 10X return. Series A are seeking a 5X to 10X return. Series B are in the 3X to 5X range. They want to invest in *momentum companies* and *momentum industries*, but they know that the bloom can come off the rose at any point. You need to convince them you're worth the risk. Nothing does that better than current traction and both industry and company momentum, along with a big vision.

It was always about showing that we could build enough traction with users. We had to show the means to that end, which was our core search platform for apartments. What is big enough for investors? If we have 8M visits a month, is that big enough? Is 2M visits a month big enough? Is it 20M? It's always so unclear what that number is. Typically, it's more about momentum and fundraising than it is about an absolute number. It's more about showing a six-month curve than it is about showing one absolute number in isolation, in my experience. It is a momentum story linked to your vision.

ANTHEMOS GEORGIADES, ZUMPER

For Dot & Bo, tremendous momentum around their company's sales growth led to several successful financing rounds at very healthy valuation levels.

We always had more demand than we could fulfill. It never felt in the first eighteen months that we knew we would survive. That's because we didn't know if it was a passing fancy or if it was going to be a durable business. It took probably eighteen to nineteen months before we realized as it was working that people do want to buy this, they can't get enough of it.

I think that the first round, based just on the idea, was priced at $13.5M. It was probably a little far-fetched. I think the second round was even crazier. We're at $2M of revenue, and we raised $15M on about a $95M valuation! Then, the later-stage Series C round—this was to be our big growth round—that was a $25M to $30M round to be valued at $200M to $300M.

ANTHONY SOOHOO, DOT & BO

With Rent the Runway, investor interest derived from growing interest in the fashion industry moving to online. Some investors felt that they had missed out on earlier opportunities in an attractive sector.

We had a lot of appetite. I think there were a lot of stars aligned from an industry perspective. It had been a moment when many investors had missed out on Gilt Group and they were primed toward the fashion retail space. People were starting to embrace the idea of fashion coming online. They wanted to make investments in that category.

JENNY FLEISS, RENT THE RUNWAY

If there is industry momentum, then the question for an investor is which one or two players will win in that space. In these cases, sometimes an investor has missed out on an earlier opportunity with a hot firm in the sector, and they don't want to miss out again. FOMO, or fear of missing out, is running high in this situation.

If you are fortunate, your growth rate will itself demonstrate a momentum story and it will be even more impactful if your industry is viewed as a momentum industry. That's when the herd comes running.

HERD MENTALITY

When I got USA Today/Gannett to invest in our Series A, all of a sudden I had inquiries from a great many other investors. They assumed that USA Today would provide tremendous strategic value to us. Plus they obviously are a great brand name.

JIM SHERMAN, SHERMANSTRAVEL MEDIA

Most investors act like members of a herd. It's that simple. They want to follow other smart investors. If you get a well-known angel investor or seed VC, this will attract other investors. If you get a well-branded Series A investor, they will attract more top investors to ride along.

There are also some bad examples of how investors can blindly run afoul. In the infamous case of Theranos, the blood test diagnostics bio-tech firm, one investor after another assumed that a prior blue-chip investor had vetted the veracity of the founder's claims as to what the Theranos diagnostic machine could do. After all, with investors in-cluding Tim Draper, Rupert Murdoch, the Walton family (founders of Walmart), Betsy DeVos, and a who's who of Stanford alumni, who wouldn't want to invest?

That is an extreme case. But the fact remains that investors are hu-man and rely on their instincts. Those instincts are naturally influ-enced by observing who else has invested. After all, they figure that if a prominent investor has gone through the effort of due diligence and made a decision to invest, then it makes for an easier decision for them to follow along.

Steve observed this herd mentality at Bespoke Post during their first round. It was hard to get investors in, but after a marquee name jumped in, others quickly followed.

There was an inflection point. Once 500 Startups went in, then the round closed very quickly. They had a brand name. And also, our traction was good. At that point, we were getting close to a million-dollar revenue run rate and we hadn't spent any money on marketing.

A couple of weeks later, after 500 Startups went in, then a bunch of other people jumped in. We cobbled together other investors. We ended up being oversubscribed.

STEVE SZARONOS, BESPOKE POST

Herd mentality also applies as you seek to secure a lead investor—by lead investor we mean a VC, an individual investor, or an investing or-ganization (for example, an angel network) that leads a funding round and negotiates the key terms. The lead investor is putting in the largest amount of the funding round. Other investors, assuming there is room in the round, may then follow on with the same terms.

In a perfect world, you ideally want to get competing term sheets from potential lead investors that put forth key terms, such as the type of security, amount of investment, and their valuation of the business. This is easier said than done, but if you can create a competitive "process," this will create some herd mentality and it will force players to act.

What's in a Term Sheet?

A term sheet is a nonbinding document that outlines the basic terms and conditions of an investment. It serves as a template for more detailed, legally binding documents once parties come to an investment agreement.

In the case of a *priced equity round*, the term sheet includes the company valuation, amount to be invested, type of security, protective provisions such as pro rata rights and anti-dilution rights, voting rights, and other key terms and conditions of a deal.

For the early stage angel/seed financings, *Simple Agreements for Future Equity (SAFEs)* and convertible notes are common. These do not require the legal complexity that arises with priced equity rounds. A convertible note is a loan agreement which is intended to convert into equity. A SAFE, on the other hand, is not a loan but an agreement on future equity to be awarded. A term sheet for either will typically be limited to amount invested, valuation, and a couple of simple additional terms. It is common to negotiate a valuation cap, which then is the price at which future equity is awarded upon a qualified equity financing event. Presumably the cap is lower than the future valuation.

With a priced equity round, besides the core economic rights, the investor documents are more complex than convertible notes or SAFEs and will include a shareholder's operating agreement and a stock purchase agreement, which are negotiated after a term sheet is accepted.

These agreements include a variety of economic and control rights, such as drag-along rights, rights to approve a company sale, rights to approve additional financings, anti-dilution provisions, and various other protections for shareholders.

Since VCs do deals every week and you don't, you need a good understanding of terms that might seem innocuous on the surface but can come back to bite you. You need a good lawyer to advise you on these matters!

To give an example, we want to flag "liquidation preference" which can, depending on the terms, come back to harm you, the entrepreneur. The liquidation preference and its structure (which is all about who gets paid what upon an exit) specifies the preference stack, the multiple, and participation rights (if any).

In a priced round, the investor typically receives preferred shares and a liquidation preference which determines the order (e.g., preferred securities come before common shareholders such as yourself and your employees) and amount VCs get paid on an exit. A 1X liquidation preference is the most common term. It simply means that, if the company has a liquidity event (e.g., is sold), then the investor gets paid back the full investment before other shareholders that are lower in the capital stack (including you). Should an investor's pro-rata share of ownership on exit not return their invested capital, then the 1X liquidation preference provides downside protection. This is typical. However, some investors negotiate a 2X or 3X multiple paid on their investment (this is not common) to give them even more protection. Furthermore, some investors seek to negotiate "participating preferred" stock. This means the investor receives their liquidation preference AND participates pro rata (their percent ownership) on the remaining proceeds in any exit. The liquation preference and structure can lead to a situation where the investor takes the lion's share, if not all, of the proceeds depending on the exit price. So, even though an investor might have what appears to be a reasonable 25 percent stake in the business at the time of the financing, a liquidation preference can yield a much greater percentage of the proceeds on an exit. In the downside case of a relatively modest exit price, the entrepreneur (as well as employee equity holders) gets squeezed and can end up with nothing.

Also, an investor with a complex liquidation preference and structure can make it difficult to raise additional funds. New money coming in later (should you need to raise more financing) won't want an earlier investor's preference sitting in front of their preferred equity position. Or new money coming in would want the same liquidation preference structure.

Another crucial term to understand is voting rights. In particular, this can come back to bite you if you or your investors wish to sell the company. You should understand who has what rights and for which decisions. Anna of Werk points out, "Control of the board is not control of a transaction." In her situation, the preferred shareholders had more capability to control her firm's future exit than she had understood at the time of financing.

The bottom line is to be wary of deal terms. They often lead to serious misaligned incentives between you and the investor(s) when it comes to raising additional funds or pursuing an exit at a more modest price.

Competing term sheets is the ideal situation. But be aware that the party who has given you their term sheet does not like it when a founder is using it to "shop around." In fact, it is a reason that whoever provides a term sheet may do so with a time limit for consideration and with a nondisclosure provision.

Textbook-wise you're supposed to have multiple competitive term sheets, right? And use one term sheet against the other. I don't think reality fully pans out like that. We had several term sheets on the table. One fell out. And then once you sign a term sheet, you have to negotiate all the rest of the terms. And you are prohibited from pursuing other term sheets during that time.

And then terms can change on you, as they did for us. Not the core valuation and amount, but some of the key things like liquidation rights, board composition, those things that are generally outlined in a term sheet; once we did the docs some things changed on us. And by then you can't do anything, right?

ANNA AUERBACH, WERK

Thus it is rare that you can manage optimal timing of multiple term sheets all coming in around the same time (unless you are a particularly hot startup and have many investors coming your way). Even if you don't end up with multiple term sheets, as long as an investor knows you are running a "process," then you can often extract better terms given their perception that you might have other options. Try to set the dominoes.

Jim ran a process where he managed to drive two investors to put forward competing term sheets for his Series A. The competitive process no doubt led to a better deal.

I had a business development partnership discussion going on with USA Today *and when I happened to mention I was raising a Series A they became very interested. So I literally flew down two days later to meet their corporate development staff and when they asked about the terms, I told them— and that I needed an answer within a week.*

They could sense some firmness—and that tone can only come through if you have a viable alternative. Tone should not be underappreciated. I ex-

plained that I had another term sheet on the table and I could not delay that much further. However, I expressed my preference to do a deal with a strategic partner such as USA Today.

JIM SHERMAN, SHERMANSTRAVEL MEDIA

DEAL-MAKING SKILLS

I've developed a strong respect for the art of the deal through the Series A. Then I saw it again in the Series B.

GIL ADDO, RUBICONMD

The art of the deal goes well beyond just being able to showcase traction or fundamentals. The power of personal persuasion and telling a good story, acumen in managing an investment process, and being savvy with creating and presenting powerful presentations matter tremendously. You also must have top-notch negotiating skills, passion, effectiveness in building trust, and good instincts as to who has interest and who does not. All are crucial while setting up the dominoes.

Just as crucial as getting investors to believe in you is honing your deal-making skills as you set the dominoes. It's as much psychological as it is about substance. Eric explains his view that deal-making is best learned by doing; it's hard to teach it.

Raising money was a big eye-opener for me. I come from a product management background, which is kind of the opposite of raising money. We're not business development people at all. We're not deal-makers typically. That was a big learning experience.

The ins and outs of making a deal is something that I studied to some extent academically, but you just don't know how to do it until you've gone through the process a few times. It's hard to teach, right? A lot of it unfortunately is mind games and things like that. A lot of it is a psychological understanding of where to push and timing and all that kind of stuff.

ERIC PRICE, SKYMD

Carlos and Gil from RubiconMD came to understand how challenging it was to close their Series B. The fundamentals were great, but they needed much more than that: a great story and having an investor who could pull the deal together.

Our deal probably would have fallen apart if our Series A investor hadn't started pulling the right strings and pushing all the parties in the right way to get everybody to the table.

The business fundamentals are great. But the Series B deal could have fallen apart and we could be in a very different position now. It's all about telling the right story and getting the deal together. I can think of the specific weeks when if he hadn't placed these calls and told these people this thing, it wouldn't have generated the momentum to get it finished. And it had literally nothing to do with the fundamentals.

I think the reason the Series B came together is because we did have the Series A investors in there. They brought a skill set, in my mind, that helped us around how you get a deal closed.

GIL ADDO, RUBICONMD

When discussions move along from interest to real negotiations for a deal, you should bear in mind the relevancy of speed. While of course you want the best terms (a good valuation, board control, etc.), the fact is that fundraising is long and arduous. And if you believe that you can complete a round much faster by demonstrating flexibility on terms, then it may behoove you to do just that.

Fundraising is a huge time suck. Speed is important. That's how I designed the first round. I gave the first-round investors what I thought was an amazing deal and what they thought was an amazing deal. And it was fine because I literally wrapped it up in a week and I was able to start executing my business.

DAVE PARKER, YUMBLE KIDS

While Dave closed his early round quickly, this is not common. More common is a strung-out process over months, where it can become challenging to discern who is truly interested and who is not. After you get some meetings and interest progresses toward a second meeting and eventually due diligence, if a prospect wishes to proceed, you need to be careful to *pick up the signals* as to whether the investor is truly likely to pull the trigger to support your venture.

Nudging and nurturing prospects is easier said than done. Prospects that take a long time to move to close are unlikely to ever close. Some companies, such as Plated, endured a rough period when even a signed term sheet for a post-seed round did not result in a deal. Be wary of this and always have a Plan B in case the dominoes don't fall as quickly as you hope.

We got three months into the process, with about three or four weeks left of cash in the bank, [and] they changed their minds, despite having provided us with a signed term sheet.

Around about Thanksgiving of that year, the VC person called me one day and said, "Thank you but no, we're out of here."

We had until New Year's Day before we missed payroll and went out of business. We spent the time between Thanksgiving and Christmas of 2013 raising an emergency round of financing, which was less than fun.

JOSH HIX, PLATED

For Bespoke Post, the founders had a similar experience. They were trying to close an angel round of about $800K. They had one VC who kept moving the goalposts on what milestone might convince them to invest. It's tricky, but you need to know when to move on if you are sensing signals that an investor cannot pull the trigger.

We kept hitting the metrics, but then they would come up with another reason not to invest. "What if you do returns differently? Bake that into the financial model and then come back."

We kept doing all of these fire drills for them. Redoing projections. They ended up never investing. I remember that specifically. We finally made the decision to say, "Look, we feel at this point you can make a decision if you're in or out. If you're out, that's cool. We're still friends. But we have other things we need to focus on."

Your natural instinct is to want to continue the conversation. And we realized with some people that it was just taking a lot of time. Too much time.

STEVE SZARONOS, BESPOKE POST

One of the challenges when raising funds, especially a first round, is that investors sometimes won't give you a firm "no." That's partly because they may want to see how your business evolves. Or maybe they want to see if you succeed in bringing in a well-known angel or VC that can give them more comfort. There is some tendency to keep the door ajar, which may be good for them, but isn't at all ideal for you. You need to be aware of this and pick up on such signals and plan in case an expected financier does not work out.

At the same time, be careful to differentiate between those who are just never likely to get to "yes" and others who genuinely want to keep the door open. With those types, momentum and herd mentality may be the factors that knock them from a "maybe" to a "yes."

PART V

The Underappreciated

Uncontrollables, Culture, and Governance

*One is so focused on making it work and keeping mul-
tiple balls in the air that topics like culture and governance get way too little attention, especially early on.
Yet, and especially as you will face many unexpected
challenges, it is the culture and the governance that will
keep it all together.*

CATALINA DANIELS, SWEETWELL

16

MANAGE THROUGH THE UNCONTROLLABLES

> Uncontrollable events are unavoidable—
> what counts is how you manage them.

We live in a world of uncontrollables, sort of a constant stream of uncontrollable events.

GREG GERONEMUS, SMARTOURS

The uncontrollables are *the* reason why startups and scale-ups are roller-coaster experiences. You might think that you have it all under control, but unfortunately that is never the case. Even if you do everything right (which is unlikely), you will face unforeseen events you must deal with. This is when the resilience of the entrepreneur is most tested.

During our discussions, we discovered multiple examples of events that destabilized the companies and sometimes resulted in a crisis or a near-crisis.

At the other end of the spectrum, we learned of unforeseen events that helped companies to survive in difficult times or provided an unexpected opportunity to change the business for the better.

For example, we wrote much of this book while under lockdown because of the Covid-19 pandemic. The pandemic and lockdowns took most of the world by surprise. For many, Covid-19 has been a hugely trying period, while for others it has brought unexpected opportunities. Think of Zoom, which benefited tremendously from the fact that there were lockdowns, preventing people from being able to go to work and meet.

The point is, unforeseen events will happen; what counts is how you manage them and navigate them as much as possible to your advantage. Here again, in the face of adversity, one might find a creative solution that actually results in a better outcome. But HBS entrepreneurs shared with us additional advice, which we summarized as follows: embrace the mindset that nothings lasts forever—always assume that things will change, and ground yourself—make sure that you are never taken off balance and that you keep your head cool.

NAVIGATE TO YOUR ADVANTAGE

The HBS entrepreneurs faced an impressive number of negative (also sometimes positive) uncontrollables. We've listed a few examples ahead.

Josh from Plated faced a sudden pricing change on social media, which had a huge financial impact.

Once upon a time, when you could reach 80 percent of your audience for free, your customer acquisition cost was zero. Your CAC was the hourly figure to pay a person to write the content. And then all of a sudden that be-

came tens of millions of dollars in a media budget to buy the same media that was at one point in time free.

JOSH HIX, PLATED

Beri from Ivy had to surmount an external lead-generation tool that nearly bankrupted the company.

The company essentially scaled up by increasing the number of community managers and events. We went up to fifty community managers. It was expensive on payroll, but they were all very profitable on a unit basis. We couldn't hire them fast enough. I think in one quarter we hired twenty-five people. It was crazy. Then we hit a bump in the road, our ability to generate leads. One of the external tools that we were using stopped working. All of a sudden these community managers went from being able to generate ten to twenty members a month, ten to twenty thousand dollars a month, down to generating on average five to six. Our model instantly collapsed, overnight.

BERI MERIC, IVY

Greg from smarTours contended with the outbreak of Ebola, which threatened their operations in West Africa.

It wasn't until year three that we had an issue, Ebola, that was quite disruptive to us. Africa is our single biggest destination.

GREG GERONEMUS, SMARTOURS

Steve from Bespoke Post overcame the sudden pulling out of an investor that could have been the end of the company.

There was another investor who we thought was going to be in, and then they were out. That was very devastating. I remember sitting down in a conference room with Rishi and saying, "What are we going to do? Are we going to be able to continue?"

STEVE SZARONOS, BESPOKE POST

We could go on and on. Uncontrollables will happen but what matters is how you navigate them and even turn them to your advantage. One of the key skills of an entrepreneur is to make the very best out of circumstances, and that is what HBS entrepreneurs did.

When Plated was faced with the change in pricing in algorithms of social media that we mentioned, they decided to in-source part of the capability to minimize the financial consequences they faced. This decision later turned out to be a major asset.

We built the competency in-house and viewed it as a competency. If you're not assuming that your paid media acquisition tactics will shift, then you're going to be dead in the water, because they will. That was a large notable shift. But those shifts continue today, and every month, every quarter we need new tactics because the old ones cease to function.

JOSH HIX, PLATED

David from Yumble Kids explains that when his co-manufacturer pulled the plug, he initially thought it would mean the end of the business. But in the end, he found a solution that turned out to be even better than the first one.

I don't know that I ever experienced more trauma professionally than in that moment. I wanted to just break down. We had no plan to find another co-manufacturer. Literally, every other co-manufacturer before that had said no to us. And we only had ninety days.

I didn't believe it, but for some reason I was able to convince myself. We hustled a meeting with every potential co-manufacturer. We actually got a few offers, fortunately. We were able to convince one of them in one shot to take us on. And we negotiated the terms of their investment. We gave them what turned out to be an amazing deal for them. And I had our lawyers whip it up like that. And we got it turned around in weeks.

That's the proudest moment of my professional career.

DAVE PARKER, YUMBLE KIDS

CrossBoundary, which has faced challenges linked to the economic and political instability of some emerging countries, saw the opportunity to diversify more.

We've diversified more, so now we're not overly concentrated in one customer's geography. If there is a bad election or something like that, I think the business is resilient to that.

JAKE CUSACK, CROSSBOUNDARY

When faced with an unexpected event, the first thing you want to do is explore how you can manage the situation to your advantage. Besides that, your mindset will greatly matter and influence your capacity to deal with the situation.

ACCEPT WHAT YOU CAN'T CONTROL

In hindsight, it would have been better for me to just accept the things that I could not control. I was not going to be able to clear up this misunderstanding for our end market. It would have been better to focus my energy, our team's energy on taking travelers who would otherwise be going to South Africa and get them excited about any number of other destinations.

GREG GERONEMUS, SMARTOURS

Greg from smarTours faced an important uncontrollable when Ebola broke out in Western Africa in 2013. Indeed, many smarTours trips were organized to Africa, more specifically to South Africa. While Ebola was not an issue in South Africa, customers *perceived* it to be an issue and it crushed smarTours' South African business. Greg's initial reaction was to fight that perception but he soon realized that he would not succeed in doing so and that he should accept that he was facing an uncontrollable.

Thirty percent of our business was to this one region, this one country. And we had this massive misunderstanding from our consumer about the risk of going to that destination. Our business in South Africa dropped dramatically.

My inclination was to try to push back against this exogenous, uncontrollable event. Try to educate the consumer and almost by sort of sheer force of will push back against this very strong, uncontrollable event. I think in part because I was annoyed that it was driven by a misunderstanding about geography.

GREG GERONEMUS, SMARTOURS

As a founder, your mindset needs to be that, no matter what, things change outside your control and you need to accept it. Especially when all goes well and it feels best to "continue as is," change will often happen and have drastic consequences.

While at Sweetwell, Catalina had to learn the hard way (and accept) that the core of Sweetwell's business model, its strategy, did not hold due to an unexpected event.

Sweetwell followed a dual strategy to scale the company: for the B2B market, the sugar replacer would be sold directly to manufacturers of cookies, ice cream, and more; for the B2C market, which is dominated by large players with deep pockets and huge marketing budgets for product launches, the sugar replacer would first be licensed out to a U.S. player for the Americas. The U.S. license would bring up-front cash and recurring revenues, which, together with the B2B revenues, would enable Sweetwell to launch the product itself B2C in Europe. The strategy and resulting cash flow were key to avoid going back to shareholders for additional funds.

The strategy made a lot of sense, and more than one U.S. player showed interest for the B2C license, so negotiations started in parallel with two key players.

After a few months, a first external event happened: one of the players, Merisant, entered into Chapter 11 bankruptcy and stepped out of the discussions. Negotiations and due diligence nevertheless continued with the other player, a subsidiary of Johnson & Johnson. After multiple months of due diligence, all signs were positive. Then a second unexpected event happened.

We were in the final stages of negotiation when, for some reason, things slowed down. Questions were left open with no definite answers. It sounded as if something was off.

And then I found out why: the CEO of the subsidiary had announced that she was quitting. With her departure, the replacement CEO search and hiring process dragged on for months until they appointed an internal candidate as CEO. The new CEO had always been a big supporter, but felt it was too risky a project for him as brand-new CEO.

As a result and against all odds, the deal got aborted.

CATALINA DANIELS, SWEETWELL

This resulted in a major pivot for the company. The board did not want to raise funds, but still wanted to pursue the B2C strategy. It ultimately decided to move operations to Central America, where a B2C launch without a partner and without fundraising sounded realistic. As a result, B2B efforts in Europe were put on hold. The changes and financial pressure created substantial shareholder disagreements. All of this ultimately led Catalina to leave the company since she disagreed with the new strategy and with the actions of some shareholders.

In a span of a few weeks, everything changed. What seemed to be going well, with a sound strategy being well executed, was entirely reversed.

This example might seem extreme but the point is that, as an entrepreneur, you cannot take anything for granted and you sometimes need to accept what happens. You just cannot fight it.

In most situations you will have room to maneuver. The more you know and have invested in your strengths and competitive advantage, the better off you will be, even if (or when) an uncontrollable event destabilizes you. As we have discussed earlier, this is when you might have to take a light or more serious pivot.

GROUND YOURSELF AND DON'T LET IT GET TO YOU

If someone could have told me maybe to care a little bit less. I don't know if that's possible. But I think I cared too much. And my identity was too attached with the brand.

ALEXANDRA WILKIS WILSON, GILT

When facing an uncontrollable, it helps to accept the situation and ground yourself so that it doesn't get to you. Accepting the situation won't solve anything per se, but it will help you get over it mentally and start managing whatever you can to cope with the new environment.

Having created a startup before is also the best training to be able to handle the uncontrollables in your next one. Experience in similar circumstances can help you to accept things and get the needed distance.

I think the first startup for so many people is so emotional with the highest highs and the lowest lows. At Gilt, we met Madonna, we met Gwyneth Pal-

trow, exciting moments like that. But then we had tough challenges, too, in terms of scaling and growing.

My second startup, and all the ones after, they're just not anywhere close to being as emotional, the good and the bad. I don't get as excited about the wins. But I definitely don't let the down moments affect me as much. They roll off my back.

ALEXANDRA WILKIS WILSON, GILT

Alexandra found grounding in her life outside of the startup, especially with her family and her children.

Once I had a family, that was very grounding in the sense of helping me manage my stress. It's not that I'm not passionate now; it's just that I have children now, so I have to leave that level of emotion, and be more even-keeled and more businesslike in the startups.

ALEXANDRA WILKIS WILSON, GILT

Not everybody will have a family to ground them. But you should find what works for you at that point in time. It might be sports, meditation, a peer group to talk to, a personal coach you can openly discuss issues with, or something else.

Find ways to ground yourself so that the uncontrollables don't stand in the way of your ability to solve the problem.

17

CULTURE IS YOUR COMPANY DNA

> Culture is what people do when you're not around. Hire and fire not only for skills and IQ, but especially for culture.

Culture is everything. Culture is key. You do get told that, but it's impossible to smell it until you see it. The only way you do it, you take the plunge and have to go build your own culture, make mistakes.

ANTHEMOS GEORGIADES, ZUMPER

When talking to the HBS entrepreneurs, we had not anticipated that so many of them would mention culture, how important it turned out to be in their journey, and how much effort they put into bringing it to life. It is typically a topic that is underappreciated, especially early on.

Culture is intangible, which makes it difficult to describe, more so than other more obviously impactful fields like marketing and operations. In our discussions, we sought to interrogate "what" culture is, "why" it matters, and "how" culture is built.

In defining culture, the HBS entrepreneurs mentioned a handful of related terms, such as *norms, values, vision,* and *mission.* But the *underlying* consensus was a succinct and simple definition: culture is what people do when you are not around. At its best, it's the DNA that ensures everybody points in the same direction.

It is the crucial ingredient that helps to explain why some firms outperform their industry competitors. In an effort to be the best, this is why culture matters so much.

The definition might be simple and the reason that it matters is compelling, but the message we got from entrepreneurs is that it's not easy to bring to life. Part of the problem is that culture is one of these topics you can read about, or learn about, but it is only *on the job* that you realize what it truly means and how to deal with it. And by "on the job" we mean starting from day one.

At its most fundamental level, culture starts with you—the norms, values, and vision of the founding team. Before you add people to your team, your culture is taking shape. In your earliest days, how you behave and what perceptions you validate are what establishes the company culture.

So, contrary to what many entrepreneurs think, it becomes critical to work on your culture at an early stage. Every company ends up having a culture, whether by design or not, and you don't want to be the founder who puts it on the back burner until a day when you wake up and realize the people in your company do not act the way you want them to.

Managing culture is not as simple as telling employees to change their behavior. It requires more to get everybody in your company pointed seamlessly in the same direction. While it takes some doing, a strong company culture helps you keep it together when the going gets tough and is paramount to reach your objectives, especially when you grow fast.

WHAT IS CULTURE? MORE THAN WORDS ON A WALL

Culture is how you make sure everybody's moving in sync toward the right North Star.

GIL ADDO, RUBICONMD

Again, culture defines what people do when you are not around. But what does that mean concretely?

Culture describes *how* you want to realize your mission. Not in terms of the business plan or strategy you follow, but in terms of the behavior and mindset you and your team maintain as you execute.

Culture, in practice, can only exist in the actions and speech of your people. It's all the big and little things they do day-to-day to achieve your mission and vision. In that sense, it is clear that culture is not something merely written on a wall behind the desk of your company's reception area.

I go to so many companies where they have the word "Courage" on the walls or "Vision" or "Work Hard." It doesn't mean anything.

ANTHEMOS GEORGIADES, ZUMPER

Putting words on a wall might reinforce your culture, but it won't make it. People don't do something just because you write it on the wall.

To build your culture and create your company DNA, you first want to define what your norms and values are. This will take some careful thinking, sometimes in an iterative process. What is important, though, is that the values you choose need to match your own values and be relevant to your business mission and strategy.

Founder Driven

No matter what, culture ends up being driven by the founders. It's all the things you do and everything that you don't say. You have a culture. It is happening no matter what.

GIL ADDO, RUBICONMD

Founders have a constant impact on the culture of their company by what they say and what they do. In practice, even if founders don't explicitly talk about values, their actions and words signal what is right, what is wrong, what is expected, and what is not. For that reason your company's values only make sense if they are in line with your own values.

You must walk the talk. Are you sending (harsh) emails late at night? Do you berate junior staff in front of others? Are you a coach? What do you do to encourage social interactions among staff? Do you encourage informality? And how does any of it tie back to the business?

Alexandra from Gilt explains this well. While at Gilt (and later in her subsequent role), she would interact with people in ways that were in line with her own beliefs, clearly sending signals about what the norm is. She wanted to empower younger people and create a "flat" hierarchy where she, as a founder, would be close to her employees. Alexandra's attitude and choices send a message to the rest of the organization, which supports a culture of openness and humility.

I like to give junior people a taste of the top. I bring them to important meetings. Here [in my current job at Allergan], I'm literally the only person glob-

ally at my level who sits on the floor. And that's because that's the approach I've taken since 2007. This big meeting room could've been my office. I didn't want that. I wanted to sit with the team.

ALEXANDRA WILKIS WILSON, GILT

At Adore Me, the company culture emphasizes team belonging and internal promotion. It results in many of the employees being friends with one another and hanging out together outside of work. Morgan reinforces the core values of team belonging and promotion with his own actions and attitude.

Team members are very close with each other. They hang out with each other all the time outside the office. They're roommates with each other, sometimes they date each other. It's a very, very tight and very genuine connection. The resulting happiness is superhigh. They have a tribe that they belong to and that they're excited to be a part of.

I am very close to my team and very supportive. In the early years, I was literally sitting at the same desk as my team, helping to do pretty much anything they needed. We have a culture of upward promotion. We take people that have usually pretty low experience, which is very McKinsey type, and we promote them upward when they succeed. And we give them pretty much every tool we can to succeed. In the early days, the tool was my time. I've taught people everything I could.

MORGAN HERMAND-WAICHE, ADORE ME

The message here is that as a founder you should be well aware of the impact of your actions and attitude. You should make sure that you yourself act by the values you set for the company. Because if you don't, people will pick up conflicting messages, and you will not succeed in creating the culture you want.

You cannot fake a norm—it just needs to fit who you are as an entrepreneur. David of Yumble Kids describes key elements of their culture as "scrappiness" and "data-drivenness." These values very much reflect who they are as founders.

I like a scrappy culture. Dan, my cofounder, is incredibly scrappy and he will get stuff done. I am incredibly data driven, and also get stuff done. I think we complement each other well. We're piecing that culture together from our own values.

DAVE PARKER, YUMBLE KIDS

One could assume that founders will only choose values that they "naturally" feel comfortable with, but it is always good to pressure-test, especially in the case of multiple cofounders. It's important to spend enough time carefully reflecting on values that fit well with you personally.

Business Relevant

Beyond the personal match, values and norms need to be relevant for your business. They need to have relevance to realize your mission. If they don't, it's likely that nobody will care.

Blue Apron has been a mission-oriented company since early on, with *learning* as a key element of its culture. The vision of the company was to make home cooking accessible to everybody and, by doing so, to improve people's lives. With learning a key pillar of home cooking, it also became a key pillar of Blue Apron's culture.

The reason we call the company Blue Apron is because chefs around the world wear blue aprons when they're learning to cook. And so for us it became a symbol of lifelong learning in cooking. And lifelong learning was one of our most prominent company values. It created a learning culture at our company where we had a speaker series and opportunities to connect with experts about the food system, including our suppliers. But also, we invested in coaches for everyone at our company because we had a lot of young people. We had a lot of professional development opportunities that we made available to them.

MATT SALZBERG, BLUE APRON

Zumper has *resilience* as one of the key pillars of its culture. Although all startups need a good dose of resilience, for Zumper it was particularly important because they had to spend years building a marketplace in a market where there were already large, successful competitors. Anthemos knew that it would require what he calls "delusional optimism" to build Zumper. By making resilience an explicit part of the culture, he made it clear to the organization that resilience would be the norm and required from everybody. With hindsight he acknowledges that it has been part of why they have been able to keep the team together and ultimately reach success.

Resilience is a massive part of our DNA. There were weeks and months in the first two years where it was very, very unclear if we would get to the Series A, let alone the scale we're at now. And that's where you need to surround yourself with talented, resilient entrepreneurs—and basically somewhat delusional optimists because you have no resources and you're going up against companies that have four thousand employees.

You have to lead from the front as the CEO. We'd be very honest in our weekly all-hands meetings about the stuff that was working, the stuff that wasn't working. But it was always wrapped in this frame of we know it's going to be hard; it's going to take time.

ANTHEMOS GEORGIADES, ZUMPER

CrossBoundary has two core values: mission driven and outcome driven. These values are critical for the company and define the behavior of CrossBoundary's team and how work is delivered, that is, how consultants work in practical terms.

We are mission driven, which means that we will turn down work that would make us more money if we feel it's not aligned with the mission and the impact that we want to have. It also means that sometimes we'll do work for free if it's aligned with the mission and the impact that we want to have.

Another core value is that outcomes matter more than hours. We have a policy of unlimited leave. We didn't want to be a firm where it's like, "Who came into the office first? Who's the last to leave?" That's irrelevant and not healthy for work/life balance. We want to be a firm where you're judged on what you have gotten done.

The reality is the excuses are irrelevant. And we didn't want to have a culture where people came up with this elaborate narrative of why this didn't work out or not.

JAKE CUSACK, CROSSBOUNDARY

In terms of how you go about defining the values, the most typical approach is that the founders (or at least one of them) make them explicit. This will rarely happen in one go and will typically lead to discussions and adaptations.

In the case of Blue Apron, they chose to follow a different, interesting approach involving everybody in the organization early on to define the values. Needless to say, this bottom-up process can only work if the founders and early employees already share a set of implicit values.

We did it in a way where we got everyone's input. We had some exercises where people said what they thought the company values should be, what they want. Then we took all that feedback from different focus groups in the company and adopted them in a set of formal company values. And they, coincidentally, were the values that we wanted them to be because we already were practicing those values. That happened pretty early on in the company's life.

MATT SALZBERG, BLUE APRON

START EARLY AND ALLOW FOR CULTURE TO EVOLVE

I knew that it was important to develop a strong mission, vision, and values early on because, obviously, as the business grew quickly, I couldn't do everything myself. So, we built a good training and onboarding process for corporate leaders. The idea was to help the company scale by empowering folks to know the guardrails and be able to make their own decisions.

MATT SALZBERG, BLUE APRON

Many think that culture is not critical in the early stages of a company, when you're focused on the MVP, product/market fit, money, and other tangible results. The less intangible "stuff," like making sure that your values are explicit and lived by, is often put on the back burner.

Contrary to this common belief, as a founder you want to focus on culture early. Indeed, having a strong culture from the outset is self-reinforcing for a number of reasons.

A strong positive culture helps you hire the people you want to hire. New potential employees will sense whether the company feels right for them or not. This will give you an edge in a very competitive marketplace, where, as a small company, it is difficult to attract great talent and compete with bigger names. The beauty is that if you are successful in hiring A-level people with the right values, it might be the beginning of a virtuous circle. They in turn will attract more A-people with the right values. You fortify your foundation and strengthen your position with each step of the way.

We found it wasn't easy, but there are really good people who are attracted to the mission and the culture of the firm. We have successfully been able to take good people out of jobs at McKinsey, Goldman, and top private equity funds, and who are interested in taking that skill set and applying it in areas where they feel like they're having more impact.

If you're working in those bigger firms in somewhere like New York, you feel like, if I left there are ten people here to replace me. You wonder, "What unique impact am I having?" We've been able to attract people to even take a pay cut but have more impact.

Being really disciplined in our recruiting process has paid dividends. A-players only want to work with other A-players. Nothing saps the morale of a team more than having a B-player around you. Other people have to pick up their slack.

JAKE CUSACK, CROSSBOUNDARY

At the other end of the spectrum, if you are not proactive about culture early on, norms and values will start to spread based on the type of individuals you have hired and how they behave. If this does not match the culture you have in mind, then things become difficult to change.

Because we were traveling so much, culture ended up getting driven by a couple of poor fits or bad apples in the company that we didn't address early on. And that led to meaningful turnover at periods.

GIL ADDO, RUBICONMD

The magic number to start working on your culture varies depending on who you ask but seems to be once you have ten and before you have thirty people in the company.

Rent the Runway made its core values (still published on their website today) explicit as of thirty employees. At CrossBoundary, Jake explained that they started explicitly working on culture when they were very small, probably fewer than ten people. At Yumble Kids, which was still a small company at the time of writing with eight employees, Dave was working at building the company culture. He realized that it would be critical as they were growing toward twenty employees. Gil from RubiconMD shared the same thought but acknowledged that many companies think about it but fail to act.

I do agree with thinking about culture very proactively the entire time, and frankly making sure that the people that are in the organization are good stewards of the culture, especially at the early stage, eight, ten people, there's no way every person isn't just critical in impacting culture. And that's how you get from ten people to twenty people, twenty people to forty people productivity. I think everybody says that. Just nobody does it.

GIL ADDO, RUBICONMD

It is important to realize that your culture will evolve with your company growth and maybe even differ by department in the company. It is a slow process, typically taking years, but as you add on activities that require different mindsets and as you hire more people from the outside, values and norms grow.

Culture at scale presents challenges. You may find a breakdown—with many new hires, mistakes get made, while forms of management that worked on a smaller scale no longer have the same effect. Breakdowns also tend to happen with leadership change, such as when the founder gets replaced by an outside CEO.

So, as you grow, you must remain proactive about adapting your events or programs to reinforce your culture, evolving it to meet your new needs.

As we hired more and more people, especially in the fulfillment centers where they were less connected to the corporate office and we were hiring hundreds of people at a time, it was challenging to continue to train everyone and induct them into the company in the appropriate way and maintain that strong culture as the company got bigger and bigger. And we had to continuously evolve those programs to address gaps where we saw them and add new things to keep that strong.

MATT SALZBERG, BLUE APRON

Growing also means that you might evolve to a situation where your employees live by a common set of values, but the working environment and norms can differ in smaller groups of the organization.

Basically, there are clusters. It's not two hundred people hanging out together, it's six clusters of twenty-five, thirty. The clusters are based on office location first, people together physically, location based. And based on what their passion is.

We have our distribution center in New Jersey. It's a culture of logistics. They have a very different look on things than the IT team, which is made of developers. But they both have in common the value of caring for each other, which is one of our big values, the value of helping each other, promoting upward, the value of celebrating success.

MORGAN HERMAND-WAICHE, ADORE ME

Culture, like other topics we covered, is one of those areas that are a continuous work in progress. You are never done. Founder-driven norms, business-relevant values, starting early and allowing culture to evolve—this is only half of it. The other half of culture is in *how* it's applied to your team—the hiring, firing, and promoting that you do to build your company.

HIRE FOR CULTURE, NOT ONLY FOR SKILLS AND IQ

There are various ways to pull the levers of culture, but the biggest two are hiring and performance management. You have to screen for culture. IQ is table stakes. The cultural fit is why they should be hired. When I look back on it, a mistake we made, we didn't necessarily screen for culture in the early days—again, because of the mayhem of how difficult it is as a seed-based company to compete. We actually just made hires purely based on ability and IQ. It's a very short-term strategy to rush the hires and not screen for culture.

ANTHEMOS GEORGIADES, ZUMPER

All HBS entrepreneurs said loud and clear (with hindsight) that ultimately what defined their culture was the people they hired, the people they fired, and the reward system they put in place.

It all makes sense. If culture is defined as the norms and values your employees follow, then it is important to hire people who fit those norms and values and to let go of the ones who don't.

Anna from Werk goes one step further and advocates that people you hire for culture will also be best positioned to grow with the company.

Do you hire the right tool for the job? Or do you hire people that fit the culture that are just generally smart people that can do anything? I think that's one of the biggest tensions of startups. Even if you're hiring the tool for the job, I think the underpinning of what energizes the person, how they fit into the culture, is important because the role will morph regardless. And there's a bar of technical competency, particularly for engineering product roles. The most important is somebody that can grow with the organization.

ANNA AUERBACH, WERK

In the early days of a startup, it's easier to hire for culture, because the founder or one of them is typically involved in recruiting and will meet all candidates. The founder will tend to select the people who best fit the culture, even if that culture is still implicit.

These early hires will be critical, not only because, as a small team, you want everybody to get along and look in the same direction, but also because your early hires will themselves hire others as time goes by. If their values don't match your company's values, you will end up hiring more people with a mismatch.

Hiring for culture becomes more complicated as you grow because there is a need to hire fast. You won't always attract the best candidates, as you don't have a name yet, but you still need to fill the positions, so you end up compromising, which is a mistake. You may end up investing in people who shouldn't stick around.

As you grow and you hire twenty-five people in a quarter, the standards aren't the same across the board. The managers are like, "Hey, you want me to hit this goal? We need to hire these five people. These are the five, they're good enough. Let's go." You start making small sacrifices.

We were still, by and large, hiring people I thought were awesome in the first place. But the quality gets diluted. And then they don't get the founder's attention.

Then you have a middle management tier, and all of a sudden the flag passes from the founder being the culture maker to these middle managers. "Middle manager" sounds negative, but they're divisional leaders. They're the people you trust the most. But they're not the founder or CEO. They're not the entrepreneur. They have different varying skills of how to create that cohesion that you used to create. It's very difficult to maintain culture at that point.

BERI MERIC, IVY

Growing and hiring fast, as well as the pain points that come with it, is a problem that all scaling startups face and is difficult to cope with. Ideally, you want to find the right pace of growth that allows you to balance the market opportunity with what your organization can handle, including in terms of adding new people to the team.

It was making sure that we always were able to grow at a pace that felt aggressive enough to capture consumer demand. And knowing that we had the underlying kind of margins and economics, that we were able to grow, yet have a stable base.

We also hired at a pace that was fast but not blitz-scaling fast. So, it was quite useful for Jenn and I to interview and meet, I'd say, pretty much every-one for a long time before we chose to hire them.

<small>JENNY FLEISS, RENT THE RUNWAY</small>

When hiring for senior positions, ensuring culture fit is even more crucial, given the impact that senior managers have on the organization. Anthony from Dot & Bo, for example, argues that you should not bring in external professional people too early since it will have an important impact on your culture.

When you bring in new professionals, they always think that the people prior didn't know what they were doing. But they actually did and they had a lot more of a "can do" attitude. It's a fine balance, how many new people you bring in that are in leadership roles.

<small>ANTHONY SOOHOO, DOT & BO</small>

As we have seen in regard to scaling, hiring is a true challenge at that stage and often you will have to make a choice between promoting somebody internally or hiring an experienced manager. The latter can seem like a great idea (or even a relief) but can have true disadvantages if done too early.

At a certain phase, we did bring in experienced people. In small quantities it can be really helpful once the key elements of the business and the culture are pretty locked in. And that can help you scale, right, because a lot of these folks have seen scale.

I also think another piece that enables scale without necessarily inject-ing more experienced, longer-term executives is relying on advisors and mentors.

<small>JENNY FLEISS, RENT THE RUNWAY</small>

It is clear that getting senior professionals on board will impact your culture one way or another, and that you should actively test for cultural fit and carefully anticipate the impact on culture.

Hiring for culture is easier said than done. How do you really know if a candidate fits your culture, especially after a short round of interviews?

Many of the HBS founders remained involved or decided to reengage in the recruiting process even at a later stage in the development of the company. This allows the founder to implicitly favor more people with a cultural fit. Anthemos from Zumper, who described the importance of hiring for culture in the opening of this chapter, decided like many other entrepreneurs to reengage in the process when he realized that compromises were being made. Jenn and Jenny from Rent the Runway remained actively involved in recruiting for a long time.

In addition, some companies made hiring for culture an explicit part of their recruiting process. This means talking about your values in the interviews and ideally rating candidates on their cultural fit.

We talk about culture in the recruiting process. I just had a letter from somebody we recently hired who hasn't joined yet, and they said, "I was really impressed by how every person I talked to brought up the values."

We also look for people that we want to work with. There are going to be a lot of things that go wrong. We're traveling often in relatively austere conditions, or you get stuck in airports with these people. The airport test that people talk about is very real. We look for people who share the same values and mission orientation.

JAKE CUSACK, CROSSBOUNDARY

What applies to hiring also applies later to evaluations and promotions. You want to promote people who do a great job and have the potential to grow, but you also want to take into account their fit within culture.

In our employee performance review process we emphasize not only what you accomplished, but how you accomplished it, and tied that back to our values.

MATT SALZBERG, BLUE APRON

Indeed, your future managers will play a key role in embodying (or not) the culture. Promoting and rewarding the right people in itself reinforces the importance of culture and ensures that it will be strengthened. The promoted will radiate the culture, helping to find and attract the right candidates, make the right recruiting decisions, and retain the best people. With them you'll create a more stable team and environment.

There are lots of talented people at Zumper. Lots of people work hard. Lots of people achieve their goals. But the people we want to promote are the ones who exhibit to us the most resilience (one of our core values) and the most determined resilience to succeed. They should become the people we celebrate and promote ahead of time to embody the culture.

If someone doesn't exhibit the cultural traits, it doesn't necessarily mean that you fire them, but if they don't embody the culture that you need at the executive level, you can't promote them to that level. And you should work with them to find a better fit.

If you build a great, collaborative, fun, self-deprecating internal culture, it makes it easier to retain people. People are very loyal. Of my ten reports, nine of them have been with me for several years now. We retain pretty much all of our best people.

ANTHEMOS GEORGIADES, ZUMPER

Performance management is not only about promotion—it's also about demotion or firing. The reality is that no matter how good a job you do in recruiting, you will still end up hiring people who turn out to be the wrong (cultural) fit. Keeping these people in the company will have a negative effect. Even if they perform okay, it is probably better to part ways.

The hard part is that sometimes you have to let B-plus or A-minus players go. You have to tell them that they need to transition out of the business, even though they're quite good still, but they're not at that bar where you want everyone in the organization to think, "Wow, I'm lucky to get to work with all these people." And if you have someone who's not meeting that bar, it's corrosive to the team.

JAKE CUSACK, CROSSBOUNDARY

Firing is difficult, especially your first time. And letting somebody go when you have a small team has a tremendous impact on the rest of the team. But if you let somebody go who does not fit the culture, the benefits will be tangible and positive in the sense that it will reinforce your values.

For all these reasons, and the importance of hiring and firing on culture, it is often said that you should "hire slow and fire fast."

COMMUNICATE AND ORGANIZE FOR CULTURE

When you're at fifteen employees, you don't need to do any effort because it comes naturally. When you're a bigger company, we need to set up processes to make sure that the culture flame keeps going.

We now have team-wide events, where the two hundred people in the company go celebrate together. We do this three times a year. One is a summer retreat of three days. One is a holiday celebration for New Year's time. Another one depends on the year.

MORGAN HERMAND-WAICHE, ADORE ME

268 | SMART STARTUPS

The founder's commitment to the values should be a natural and implicit thing, but you still want to make sure the company's values are explicit. That's why, as a growing company, you want to communicate and organize around your values, so that everybody is on the same page.

Of the many ways to communicate your values, the onboarding process is, after the interviews, the first major opportunity to make sure your new hires understand the values you expect them to live by. It is for this reason that many founders also decided to remain involved in onboarding.

At CrossBoundary, in the beginning every partner would sit down for about an hour with new hires to walk them through each of the values, talking through examples so people would understand them. Now that they have grown to a different scale, it is harder to do in person, so they have a two-page statement of values, which they share with everyone who joins the company.

Other opportunities to communicate your values include team gatherings, town hall meetings (where people get to ask questions), and—yes—posters on the office walls.

At Blue Apron, they organized multiple types of events to talk about and communicate around the mission and the values. The communication was not limited to employees but also included clients and customer feedback. All of it was meant to reinforce the values and ensure that, by celebrating successes, people would feel good, motivated by the mission and values.

We had town hall meetings routinely where we talked about a lot of the good work we were doing and the positive impact we were having on the food system. Routinely, we had emails go out every week showing the customer impact we were having. We had a daily "feel good" email that went out rounding up the customer feedback and with people telling us we changed their lives and saved their marriages.

MATT SALZBERG, BLUE APRON

As you grow, there will be more room and need for other members in your organization to play a role in further magnifying the norms and values. This can lead to less conventional ways to communicate and talk about values. At CrossBoundary, with offices in multiple locations, the founders partly rely on others to maintain the culture. When Jake traveled to their Johannesburg, South Africa, office shortly after it opened, he was surprised to discover new ways to spread values.

One of the team members had put up the values in the bathroom, on the wall. Whenever guys are going to the bathroom, they had to read the values. And every week they have a session and each person goes around and says, "Here's an example of how I either saw somebody living up to a value or not living up to a value," which can include themselves.

JAKE CUSACK, CROSSBOUNDARY

But as you hire more people, you should also be aware that as founders or as a management team, culture will require more of your attention. For some it meant spending more of their own time. For others it meant adding somebody to the team for culture. For all it meant more structuring of initiatives.

It is something I spend a lot of time obsessing around because we now have one hundred people who are not all in San Francisco. And the values can easily get lost. People can forget we're not building a search platform; we're building something much more disruptive. It can easily get diluted as you hire more people and as I have less time with each of those people.

In the early days it was something that I made sure came across in every weekly stand-up, every daily huddle. But it was something we actually formally structured.

ANTHEMOS GEORGIADES, ZUMPER

An interesting way to deal with the growth of your organization is to create smaller "tiger" teams and keep innovation at the core of everything you undertake. This is what Rent the Runway did for years. As a result, initial key players continued to play their roles, even if the organization became much larger.

At some point, things start to get a lot bigger. And that's where it's sometimes important to create tiger teams or smaller groups who can work on certain projects and still feel that level of innovation and energy that they really come to a startup for. And the more you can then take some of those initial leaders who were part of the founding team and make sure they're helping to be these culture carriers and injecting that energy becomes really, really powerful.

JENNY FLEISS, RENT THE RUNWAY

Many founders chose to hire somebody to help them with culture and other organizational matters. Some created a function around HR and culture. One should be careful, though, since creating such a position will deliver results only if implemented well. The challenge for a startup is to know when to bring on a head of HR. Some do it during the scale-up, which may be waiting too long. Others bring in someone to handle HR but then the founders lose their focus on culture.

One example we loved is the "chief of people and culture" at RubiconMD. The founders decided to create the function as the company was growing. Interestingly, they did not delegate culture and people issues to the CCP, but rather spent a lot of time with her to understand what exists in the company and what they, as founders, should focus on to reinforce the desired culture.

We take a systemic approach. Once a week I sit down with her and I ask her who she's meeting with. She's supposed to touch everybody systematically at some point. Like at the coffee machine. And then I want her to tell me the things that I need to know about what's happening with people. And she'll give me, "Here's a thank-you card. Write this thing for this person so they feel appreciated. This person needs you to go talk to them about this. This person is really annoyed about that laptop policy you rolled out that you thought was no big deal. Hear them out." All those little things that she's gathering. And she's not betraying people's trust, she's helping to impact the culture in a positive way by collecting those informal pieces and creating a formal process around them. That's the piece that was missing and needs somebody who's doing it.

GIL ADDO, RUBICONMD

As the companies grew, all HBS founders further invested substantially in events to bring people together and talk about the company's status, goals, mission, and values. We were impressed to hear that many companies organized company-wide retreats, sometimes more than once a year.

At CrossBoundary, they organize a company-wide retreat once a year. As part of that, they have sessions on the values and the mission, and the history of the organization, so that people understand how hard it's been to get to this point and what they're being entrusted with.

At RubiconMD, they invest in "team weeks" once a quarter, where they bring together the entire team to discuss company direction and allow for personal interactions. In addition, with the help of the "people manager" they invest substantial time and energy in making sure that people interact with one another all year long.

We create opportunities for people to casually interact. Water-cooler type interactions. We're doing a happy hour once a month. We do a thing for people who have anniversaries. And we try to be very creative. We did a scavenger hunt through the city last month. We try to make those opportunities fresh and new.

GIL ADDO, RUBICONMD

Hiring, firing, promoting, communicating, and organizing are all key levers of culture. While conventional wisdom may undervalue the role of culture, the HBS founders all agreed it was one of the most valuable contributors to their overall results. The same goes for governance—underappreciated yet essential to success.

18

GOVERNANCE IS
UNDERRATED

> If you delay defining your board until it's time to
> fundraise, then you're too late.

*Spend time reflecting early on what is your ideal board. You should seek
at least one—and perhaps two—independents that know your industry
and have functional expertise. You have to work at this and not just let
things happen.*

JIM SHERMAN, SHERMANSTRAVEL MEDIA

Governance is the system by which a company operates and is controlled. The board of directors, whose members are appointed by the shareholders, is responsible for the governance. The board typically decides on the company strategy, approves budgets and compensation of senior staff, supervises and evaluates the CEO and management, enacts controls such as an audit committee (for larger companies) to ensure accurate and legal accounting, and reports back to shareholders. Most entrepreneurs worry about governance when they raise funds and need to put investors on the board.

Yet governance is much more than just the board of directors. It's an opportunity for you to surround yourself with great people who can help you make the right decisions. We believe that governance should be developed early on and in part independently from the fundraising process. While it can happen throughout the fundraising process, governance should not be limited to the investors, as we will see later in Blue Apron's case. In that sense, governance is underrated.

However you approach it, the key is to develop a governance model that works for you and your company. Start early on. Then remain in the driver's seat while developing great relationships with your board members.

YOUR BOARD IS AN OPPORTUNITY

We always had board meetings. Board meetings were initially every month, which was quite time-consuming. And then eventually every quarter. But for us as first-time entrepreneurs, we knowingly picked a board member who had recently been an entrepreneur himself. And so we actually viewed all those meetings as a chance to learn from him. They were often working sessions, or we left with us giving him assignments of things we needed for him to do. It was time-consuming, but I also felt like it was a good thing, ultimately, for us.

JENNY FLEISS, RENT THE RUNWAY

Governance is typically seen by entrepreneurs as something that arises from raising funds. Most startups only start worrying about it when they get investors on board—which leads them to create a board of directors or expand it with the latest investors.

Along these lines, it is widely accepted that governance is key when companies reach a certain scale. Think of companies that prepare an IPO, for which the board plays a vital role, ranging from the actual decision to go for the IPO to overseeing the whole IPO process.

Contrary to what we witness as angels, most HBS founders managed governance proactively and early on. They showed us how the board could provide wisdom, expand networks and establish contacts, and help you turn around a tricky situation in a very short period of time.

Our board member who was a VC let us run the company. He's not a super activist. But he's been very supportive. And he certainly provides advice. He sees stuff from his other portfolio companies. He'll say, "Oh, well, you should be thinking about this." We did a rebranding exercise last year. He introduced us to the firm that we ended up going with because one of his other portfolio companies had used them and had great things to say. A lot of things like that are helpful. He makes introductions. He's been super helpful, super supportive. But I'd definitely say he says, "All right, you guys can make all the operational decisions."

STEVE SZARONOS, BESPOKE POST

Many of the HBS entrepreneurs we met understood that the board is an opportunity to attract and work with people they could only dream about. They saw it as their opportunity to work with and get advice from people whom they could never hire. People who have deep experience, a career behind them, and who have time to help you. People who like to do that and won't ask for money in return.

We found someone who is passionate about the issues and had recently retired, so he was in full capacity but now had more time. And he just wanted to help out.

CARLOS REINES, RUBICONMD

In the case of RubiconMD, founders Gil and Carlos initially reached out to an industry expert for advice. That discussion was so positive that they kept in touch. The relationship organically grew into mentorship, investment, and finally board membership. This organic development is very often underrated.

Give thought to having an advisor early in the ignition phase—if you like them, they can become an independent board member even before formal financing. To appoint them early in the company's life cycle can be an unconventional, beneficial approach.

I am an advisor to many startups and sometimes end up joining their board of directors. It is a win-win for the startup and for the advisor to get to know each other before formalizing the relationship.

CATALINA DANIELS, SWEETWELL

With the myriad challenges of starting and scaling a company, you should aim for the luxury of being counseled by extraordinary people. Indeed, the right board and governance can make *the* difference when it comes to making the right decisions.

Rent the Runway, for example, had a board member from Bain who played a critical role in pushing logistics as a core competency of the company. The founders had not initially emphasized logistics—it took this board member's advice for the founders to focus on it and it became a key cornerstone of the company's success.

But beware: the impact of boards is far-reaching and can sometimes be negative, so make sure that your board is ideally composed and that you trust the members. Beri from Ivy explains how one of his investors influenced the top-line growth strategy, which at some point put the company into real trouble by pressing the company to grow and invest in fixed costs, without regard to losses.

We had one investor who pushed us on top line. Didn't care at all about bottom line. And he's not alone. A lot of investors are like this. They're like, "Go all the way, capture the market. And then you can optimize." "This was our revenue last year. Multiply that by two. This is what our revenue should be this year." They said: "Here's what we need to do to double our revenue. More events. More community managers. Increase the joining fee. Increase the ticket fees." Whatever it took.

If I had another board member who was like, "Just improve your margins," it would have been a very different story. I'm an inexperienced entrepreneur, to be fair. This is my first company. It's not like I've done it four times and learnt these lessons already. So we grew fast.

BERI MERIC, IVY

This is a great example of misaligned incentives. The outside investor may want to go fast for the home run, even if it's risky and the founder advocates caution. This is why aligned interests are so important when considering investors (as we discussed in Part IV).

Now, let us be clear: not every single situation and startup requires a board, but most do. If you are raising funds, you will most likely end up with a board. If you are not, the real question you should ask yourself is what input you need and expect to get from a board. If you feel you don't need input, you don't want to create a board just for the sake of it and with an additional administrative burden on the team.

We don't have a board. We've played around with the idea several times of "Should we get a more high-profile board? Some really good names?" And we've had some good relationships and names we could have gotten on it. We honestly felt like, and I hope this isn't overconfidence, but we kind of knew what needed to be done. We just needed to execute on it. And we didn't want to create a board for the sake of having a board and having a bunch of conversations when we felt like we could reach out for those kind of conversations in a more ad hoc way when we need them.

JAKE CUSACK, CROSSBOUNDARY

...

PLAN TODAY FOR THE BOARD YOU'LL NEED TOMORROW

The plane is off the ground and now we have to fly it—this is when we have to get buttoned up, by having a real corporate board that has different assets in every member.

DAVE PARKER, YUMBLE KIDS

In an ideal world, as a founder, you want to think of a board early on. Indeed, governance is a bit like "culture" in that it will happen no matter what (at least for all startups raising funds). So, the earlier you are proactive about it, the better off you will be.

As Dave hints at, to be strategic about it you must proactively think of the "assets in every member" and what your ideal board composition should be.

If I could rerun things, I would have tried harder to get an industry expert on my board a lot earlier. Of course I know the travel industry, but having another voice at the table in my industry would have been helpful, especially because my financial investors did not have any industry experience.

JIM SHERMAN, SHERMANSTRAVEL MEDIA

You should increase value not only by adding functional and/or industry expertise, but also by adding diversity. A diverse board is underrated and actually hard to achieve because VC investors tend to be white men. If your fundraising drives your board composition, then typically you will end up with a board of white men. It is proven by several studies, including from McKinsey, that a diverse board operates more efficiently (and is more fun) than a nondiverse one. And if somebody will tell you that you cannot go for diversity, because there is no talent around—we disagree. Look around and look better! You can get diversity without compromising the quality of your board.

My board was composed of older white men either coming from McKinsey or the financial sector; I can assure you that it made some discussions and decisions difficult as their notion of risk and doing business in general was not a perfect fit for a startup. As a female CEO, it would also have been nice to have a female ally on the board.

CATALINA DANIELS, SWEETWELL

Many will say that it is not easy to "get" the ideal board members in the beginning. And that is true. If you start early, you are still a small company and probably an unknown entrepreneur, so why would a top entrepreneur or top executive join your board?

That is why it makes sense to start with advisors, and possibly a *board of advisors*, who might later on organically become board members. One of the key advantages of such an approach is that you get to know each other (not only you the advisor, but also the other way around) and what you can mean for one another. Such relationships are invaluable. Plus, one of your advisors can become an independent board director in the future.

In the case of RubiconMD, Gil sought the opinion of the former chairman and CEO of Blue Cross Blue Shield, whom he met via a classmate at Harvard Business School.

It was expected to be a thirty-minute meeting and it turned into a three-hour discussion of the business concept and its viability. He later invested in the company as an angel investor and became a great mentor to Gil.

CARLOS REINES, RUBICONMD

As we saw earlier, the initial discussion led the man to become an advisor, a mentor, and ultimately a board member. This is an example of a board relationship that evolved organically and turned out to be very valuable to the founders.

Rent the Runway had a board of advisors *and* a board of directors. Some of the advisors naturally became board members.

It was me, Jenn, and then Scott Brand. We quickly after had Matt Diamond, who was at Alloy Media. That was pretty early on. And then we had our board of advisors. One of our advisors was Carley Roney, who is on our board of directors now. She was at the Knot Group and was one of the founders there. We were able to build a fantastic group early on.

JENNY FLEISS, RENT THE RUNWAY

You should not be shy about wanting to have your "own" members on the board. In the case of Blue Apron, Matt, who had quite extensive experience with governance given his own board positions when at Bessemer and Blackstone, made sure that he could influence the composition of the board proactively rather than wait until the financing rounds. As we will see later, this allowed him not only to get the input from additional board members but also to keep control for a long time.

When I did my first financing, I created a three-person board, added a VC, and kept an empty seat that I could appoint. So it was me, a VC, and an empty seat that I was able to control.

Then when I did another financing, I added another VC and then I added two extra seats. So then we had a five-person board where I had two VCs, me, and two empty seats that I could control.

And then as we were getting ready to go public, I had to start building out independents for the board. So a couple of years before going public I started looking for certain additional skill sets. And then I recruited the rest of our independent board members from my network and with help from others and help from people on the board. We built out the board to be a seven-person board at the time we went public.

MATT SALZBERG, BLUE APRON

Another critical reason to start early is that it will allow you to learn how to manage the governance process, which can be unclear and become complex. This is especially helpful when your board grows and you end up with board members who sit around the table with their own objectives.

We had a large and diverse cast. The formal board was eight. We had four independents, two with technology backgrounds, two with food backgrounds. And then myself and Nick as management and founders. And then two VCs. That was the legal board.

Then we had a number of observers, a number of junior people who also came with VC partners, so on and so forth. They made the effective board more like twenty. Then all the various legal distinctions of major and minor investors, and various people that have various forms of control rights and voting agreements and drag-alongs. It gets very, very complex very quickly.

You have the reality, for better or for worse, that what was one day a "grow the pie" mentality has become a "the pie is grown and fixed now, and everyone has to get their slice" mentality. Institutions, as represented by the people, have different needs and wants out of that event. And as management and founders you get to navigate all that.

JOSH HIX, PLATED

Governance is also one of those fields that are more an art than a science. You are dealing with people, group dynamics, and—especially in the later stages—critical decisions that can have important financial and other consequences. So, by the time you get to that stage, you want to make sure that you are up to the task. And the earlier you start, the more you will learn and the easier it will make your life.

I'm not sure how you prepare for something like this. We got all the broad leadership principles in business school, but you do have to learn by doing and practicing. Having the frameworks helped. Certainly, we had gotten some of the technical skills around CAP tables and understanding classes of securities and stock, those sorts of things. But the vast majority of it you have to learn by doing or reading, teaching yourself.

To say we were unprepared sounds more negative than it is. But yes, we were learning as we were going and managing large groups of smart but definitionally, and in a positive way, self-interested people. They're acting on behalf of institutions that manage, for instance, teachers' pension funds. They need to be self-interested. But it also means that you find people at odds with each other. It's an interesting dynamic.

JOSH HIX, PLATED

GET THE BOARD TO SUPPORT YOU

I use my board for two things. One is for keeping us true to our plans. The second is in regard to fundraising. The board gets us in front of everyone we want to meet. My Series B was co-led by two funds that I originally met through my board members who I then developed a relationship with. When we get term sheets or when we want introductions, they've been phenomenal and go to bat for me.

ANTHEMOS GEORGIADES, ZUMPER

We often meet entrepreneurs who see (and experience) their board as a controlling body that they resent, and that creates stress. Your board should be the opposite: it should *help you* on multiple fronts. While you should not expect your board members to put in more than a few hours of work per month, during that time they should play a critical role in giving access to their network and knowledge.

In terms of the role of the board, they were a great sounding board for us. We could have used the board more.

GREG GERONEMUS, SMARTOURS

In the ideal situation, the board "works for you," and not the other way around. You obviously want to regularly update your board about progress but you also want to seek their help and input where you encounter challenges or want to speed up things.

To get to the point where your board works for you, you need to manage the shaping of it in the right way, establishing trust and running a process that results in value-added outcomes for all.

Justin from Henry the Dentist has had multiple startup experiences and explains how he knew the kind of board and board members he was looking for.

I've now been through two different businesses, two different groups of investors, and two different types and styles of board governance. I know what motivates me and I know what stresses me out. I do not need anyone to apply any pressure to me. I don't need motivation from anyone else. I'm self-motivated enough. I need positivity. I'm a positive person. I don't work through the stick strategy. I work from the carrot strategy. I need nice, positive, supportive people around me. I don't deal well with the micromanaging, "Did we hit the milestone?" investor.

I have relatively high confidence that the investors that we have would deal well with bumps in the road. That's how we screen the investors. How will you deal with the bumps in the road? Because there will be. Things are going great, swimmingly right now. But I've been through my fair share of shit and there will be more that comes in this business. I feel confident that they are good people who are former operators who have the right incentives and the right beliefs, and that they'll be with me through thick or thin.

JUSTIN JOFFE, HENRY THE DENTIST

Once you figure out what kind of board you want, success then boils down to trust and managing the board. Developing a good relationship and trust is easier if you build it over time and get to know the individual board members one-on-one outside the boardroom.

I just had dinner with a couple of our board members last week. My wife and I went on vacation to Martha's Vineyard and hung out with our Series A lead. I actually love hanging out with our investors.

GIL ADDO, RUBICONMD

In the end, a good relationship with your board will significantly depend on how you run the meetings and the information you share. If you aren't the chairman, then your relationship with the chairman (who technically sets the agendas and is in charge of preparing the meetings) needs to be as good as it can get. You need to carefully plan your board materials and make sure there is time for board strategy discussions. And you must find the right balance in the information you share.

I'm very transparent. But I also control information. I don't hide anything. I don't say anything not truthful. I'm very honest. I also don't paint a rosy picture when stuff's not rosy. I'm careful with my information and my information flow so they don't call me every day. Too much is not a good thing, either.

JUSTIN JOFFE, HENRY THE DENTIST

When sharing information, there are obviously the facts, but there is also a huge component of "story" or narrative. How you share the information will be critical. This is a space where as a CEO you have a lot of flexibility and you might naturally be tempted to be positive.

Anna from Werk explains it is a fine line between trying to prove that all is good or will be good on the one hand, and sharing the challenges and asking for help on the other.

One of the hard things as an entrepreneur is you're constantly balancing the need to be incredibly optimistic to investors—eternally upbeat and everything's great, we're closing more deals, everything is awesome—you have to balance that with realism.

Obviously, we're fully transparent with our board and our board is incredibly helpful with everything. But where do you draw the line of being optimistic enough and positive enough about your future prospect, but then also thinking about the downside scenario? It's hard. As an entrepreneur I think you actually try to avoid thinking about the downside scenarios. Because if you thought about the downside scenario all the time you'd just stop operating, right?

The downside is the reality—the majority of startups fail. If I spent all my time thinking about what is the worst-case scenario in our cycle from conversion to cash, I would just quit. So, you can't think about that.

ANNA AUERBACH, WERK

As a CEO, you influence what gets presented to the board and what the underlying message is. As Anna says, it is not always easy to find the right baseline. You do not want to come with negative news or a downside scenario. That is difficult. It might make it easier to do so if you have a good advisor or mentor, who will help you to think rationally when you prepare the board meetings.

Although sharing challenges can be intimidating, if you have a good functioning board, your board members should help in fixing the problems.

I found I was petrified of communicating that we were having these challenges. It was unimaginable to communicate these things, and it felt much easier to fix it and tell them, "This is what happened, and this is how we fixed it. We're good." In the meantime, I didn't communicate. And the problem is it's hard to know when you should do it. If every time you have a problem you call your investors the next day, that's not feasible. But there is some cadence that's better than not communicating for three months.

I found the moment that I started communicating about the challenges, almost with no exceptions, all investors who had any business savvy, which is most of them, they're like, "Oh, you hit a bump in the road? You're restructuring? Yeah. It's business." It was normal for them to hear. They don't like it, the fact that you're having problems, saying, "Oh, this happened? What are you doing about it?" But they liked the fact that I had a plan and we did a lot. Communicating—you'd be surprised how with much employees and investors, the more you communicate, the better it is.

BERI MERIC, IVY

Given that most startup roads are bumpy, there is a high likelihood that you will need to share challenges at some point. While it can be intimidating (we see many entrepreneurs wait too long before they dare to share the "bad news"), a great way to do it is to not only bring up the problems, but proactively bring solutions.

Yes, we have difficult conversations about what needs to change to get back on plan. But they're always in the spirit of fixing things. It's never a personal thing or anything like that. Because of that, we've been successful to date. That level of honesty is really important.

My job is to bring trade-ups to the board and then solve them together. Never come with problems, come with solutions. And debate the solutions. That's how we use the board.

The board has also always asked us that if anything major happens—and luckily it never has—to give them forewarning, so they're never surprised. We're also good at communicating to the board if something changes between board meetings that is material; we're good at proactively managing that with them so there are no surprises.

ANTHONY SOOHOO, DOT & BO

BE IN CONTROL

I had always wanted to maintain board control of the company. And I was always the largest shareholder of the company, and still am the largest shareholder of the company. I never put either of my cofounders on the board because I thought that would be a complicated situation and I didn't think it made sense. And I never gave up board control.

MATT SALZBERG, BLUE APRON

Being in control is one of the recommendations made by the HBS entrepreneurs we talked to about governance.

It is probably not surprising given the importance of the board and its decisions. When mentioning control, it was not only about majority equity ownership (which you often lose as of Series A or B) but also about the process of "being in control." In other words, things like having a majority of seats on the board, the agenda you set, and the "narrative" you use.

Overall, there are two key factors that will influence your relationship with the board and make your life easier:

1. Having the majority of the equity or the voting rights, and
2. Hitting your objectives and delivering on the results

If you combine both, it's much easier to have productive board meetings and good individual relationships with the board members. The better the company is doing, the easier it will be to keep control—no VC will want to rock the boat if things are good. If you are not hitting your objectives, you can still own the narrative by presenting convincing solutions to address the issues.

I think our board status is good because the business is performing. I control the governance because I still own the lion's share of that equity.

JUSTIN JOFFE, HENRY THE DENTIST

As we saw earlier, Matt explains that expanding the Blue Apron board with new board members (other than the VCs) was also a way for him to keep board control. Independent directors can indeed influence board discussions and decision making. This, combined with the fact that the company was doing well, made it easier.

That allowed me to keep strong board control throughout the early days. It wouldn't have mattered regardless, because in the early days we never had any questions going on at the board level, because the company was always doing so well. And VCs, as you know, they like supporting management teams and don't like to break things that are going well. That was the dynamic.

MATT SALZBERG, BLUE APRON

A final key thought: what you do with your board does not apply to investors who do *not* sit on the board. You want to communicate with these investors and make sure that they are "happy," but you have no obligation to share information with them.

Are there lessons learned? I don't share a budget with anyone outside the board, with any other investors because I don't want them to hold me accountable to it if it doesn't happen. Of course, we're going to do the very best that we can do.

I allow other investors to get hindsight quarterly reports. I don't allow them to get forecasting budget reports. There's a lot of pushback on that. Nope. Sorry. Lesson learned. I don't need someone to hold my feet to the fire, quite honestly, if we miss a budget. No one can forecast five years out in the startup business.

JUSTIN JOFFE, HENRY THE DENTIST

PART VI

The Exit

Plan It from Day One

You're always planning for exit. You have to be. And obviously, the goal is to make it really big. But at every phase of your company, at every point of scale, at every pivot, you are thinking about, what are your options?

ANNA AUERBACH, WERK

19

TARGET THE EXIT THAT'S RIGHT FOR YOU

> An investor's primary concern, on day one,
> is your endgame.

Our goal was to run the business forever. That's what we were looking to do. We wanted to go public and provide liquidity to the investors.

JOSH HIX, PLATED

The HBS founders gave significant forethought to their endgame relatively early in their startup. Most were interested in an exit that would match the societal impact they strove to have on an industry and the world. The money factor, while important, was secondary. More important was leaving a lasting mark, in some cases by building a brand that could live on forever. However, an exit is about reaching your business goal and ultimately making a profit for you and your investors.

The exit is everybody's endgame. As such, while you may think it strange to start thinking about your exit in the first weeks of getting going, the topic is essential to the early fundraising process.

Investors—whether angels or VCs—have many questions about your business, and one of them will be about your long-term plan. *How do you view success and an eventual exit for yourself and for them?* Investors want some sense as to the path to liquidity, the potential value of their share on exit, and the implied return on invested capital this represents. In particular, investors want to know *your* perspective on the hoped-for endgame:

- What is your level of ambition and how much risk are you willing to take?
- Is an IPO the goal? Or a strategic sale?
- If a sale, then who are the potential buyers of your business?
- What valuation multiples of profit and revenue are typical in your sector?
- Who has the financial resources to be acquisitive, and has there been much M&A activity in your industry?

Investors want to know *your* preferences. They want to make sure you (and your cofounders) are committed to building an investable business—one that can yield returns as compensation for the risks taken. They also want to make sure that you are not interested in running it as a lifestyle business—one that may be excellent compensation for you, the founder, but not sufficient for investors. In other words, they want you and they to be aligned.

Determining your endgame early on is not just a priority; you also need to take early steps towards it by making connections and raising your antenna.

WHAT CONSTITUTES AN EXIT?

We define an exit with the broadest mix of possible outcomes that provide a return on one's equity (which can include your own sweat equity) or invested capital. Here are the four off-ramps:

- The Classic Corporate Sale—a sale to a strategic buyer, competitor, or private equity firm
- The IPO—going public (although it only qualifies as an exit if you, as a founder, sell your shares)
- A Sale of Secondary Shares—selling a portion of ownership during a financing round or tender offering
- Corporate Dividends—receiving regular cash distributions from the venture (although it does not qualify as selling shares, it is a path forward with income generation)

The most common exit is the first, the classic corporate sale. Meanwhile, for many founders an IPO does not technically qualify as an exit. It provides liquidity for shares and becomes an exit when they or investors decide to sell their shares.

Going public is not really an exit. It's just setting up the company to live on forever. It's a way to institutionalize and set yourself up for an even longer-term business. So in some ways, it is an exit in the sense that you could sell shares. But when you're a CEO of a public company it's not easy to sell shares actually. In some ways it's harder to sell shares.

MATT SALZBERG, BLUE APRON

The sale of secondary shares, often as part of a growth-stage financing, is another way in which founders and investors can exit or gain liquidity for some (or even all) of their stake. While years ago this was quite uncommon, today it is not so unusual to see insiders selling shares if the business and industry are attractive.

If you can take some chips off the table by selling a chunk of your shares during a financing round, in other words, a secondary share sale, then you should. Bankers would advise that it's wise to take advantage of the opportunity to gain liquidity for you and past investors this way. That's partly because you don't know when another exit opportunity will materialize.

JIM SHERMAN, SHERMANSTRAVEL MEDIA

For some entrepreneurs, their endgame may be to build a business that throws off sizable annual dividends—in other words, a cash cow. This is not technically an exit—at least not if you are carrying on running the firm—but it is a way to achieve potentially strong annual returns for you and, if you have any, investors. It is a means to achieve reward for your efforts or "a path forward."

Being self-sustaining is also an exit, right? It's not technically an exit and liquidity event. But it is a path forward.

ANNA AUERBACH, WERK

As you think about your exit, you have to reflect on the founding team's personal goals and the tension between growth and risk. Answer the personal questions listed above, which you likewise should ask during fundraising rounds. If you have cofounders, it is paramount that you are all aligned on goals and risks as well.

We hear a lot in the press about founders who believe the mantra "go big or go home." The founders of Slack, WeWork, Uber, Airbnb, Dropbox, and so many others have raised hundreds of millions of dollars at eye-popping valuations. They believe fully in their destinies to go public and become entities valued in the tens of billions of dollars, and they are willing to take on the high risks to get there.

Meanwhile, at the other end of the spectrum are entrepreneurs satisfied with exiting for a life-changing $10M or $20M. Such smaller exits are very meaningful to most and carry a lower risk profile because there are more buyers for firms under $100M, it's harder to achieve $1B revenue, and the passage of time increases risks with uncontrollable factors that can harm the business. But smaller exit scenarios are not what your investors are signed up for.

DETERMINE YOUR IDEAL ENDGAME EARLY ON

We've had various M&A approaches before in terms of inbound people. The way we think about it is we want to execute the vision. We've spent five years getting to this stage, now having a real shot at building the home run. It would take a lot of money to take us off the market now because all the work has been to get to this position.

ANTHEMOS GEORGIADES, ZUMPER

Founders should give serious thought early on as to their exit or endgame goal. While what you can achieve will no doubt change based on market realities, you need to start early with a point of view on what's your North Star. By North Star, we mean not only how big you believe you can become but how expansive is the product or service you are building; what's the core asset that you are creating.

There are several reasons to reflect early on these issues. For one, investors want to have a sense of the endgame because they are going to seek liquidity at some point. Second, you need to be prepared should an exit opportunity come forward unexpectedly. It is possible that a buyer may come along, as happened with Anthemos, and when that happens, you should be clear on how to react in line with your preferences. Third, your exit "plan" should influence your financing strategy—the amount of capital raised and at what valuations (as we discussed in chapter 12).

Josh and Nick of Plated shared the view early on that going public was the exit goal that they preferred. They wanted to start with meal kits but envisioned launching other products. They had a broad vision of where they wanted to go in the wellness space.

We wanted to go public, to be a stand-alone business, and run forever. We had big aspirations, broader aspirations beyond the current product in the health and wellness space, and lots of other things that we wanted to do, including making our meal kits available in all grocery stores.

JOSH HIX, PLATED

However, Josh further explains that he and Nick planned for the possibility of a lesser but still positive exit outcome—something short of going public. They wanted options. They knew that selling to a strategic buyer could occur and so their financing strategy was optimized to ensure that this could be an attraction option.

We always wanted to allow for the possibility where if we needed to or if we just simply changed our minds about an IPO, that we could sell. If we wanted to sell the business, we did not want to sell it for a price below the last valuation where people would lose money. We never wanted to have that happen. To the extent that you can control such things, we wanted to have more options.

JOSH HIX, PLATED

In the case of Blue Apron, Matt also always wanted to build a new brand that could live on independently forever. Going public would guarantee keeping the brand alive for a very long time. This was his goal from day one.

My philosophy on building businesses has always been that the most valuable businesses are ones that have strong independent company paths that can grow as independent institutions for decades because they're going after big, secular trends. And they've built great products and great brands and great infrastructure.

I'd always believed that it's important to build an independent brand that can live forever as an icon. That is the fundamental beauty of starting a company. It could live forever. It's an institution. A brand isn't tied to biology.

With the IPO, first, it was good to attract the capital that we did. Second, it allows us to position the business to be a long-term-oriented institution, which has always been my dream. The reason I like creating companies is because they can be immortal. Companies can live forever. That's one of the cool things about being able to create a public company, though it of course doesn't always work out that way.

MATT SALZBERG, BLUE APRON

Exit Optionality Revisited

We discussed in chapter 12 the importance of exit optionality in your financing strategy. Fundraising decisions impact the flexibility of your exit options—which options may lead to success and for whom. The difference between Blue Apron and Plated is instructive.

Despite the founders having similar goals (to go public), there were significant differences between Blue Apron and Plated in terms of their fundraising strategies and the impact on their exit options. This ultimately impacted the return for the investors. Blue Apron was more aggressive and raised a total of nearly $200M at a valuation of $2B before their IPO. It's unclear if all their investors did particularly well, since right after the IPO the public price per share dropped significantly, to a level where later-stage investors did not gain, based on their per-share price and the company's valuation levels when they invested.

We did our IPO at a slight discount to what our Series D was done at. The Series D was at $13.33 share price and the IPO was at $10 per share price. We did file at $15 to $17, but it got priced to $10.

MATT SALZBERG, BLUE APRON

Meanwhile, Plated, relative to Blue Apron, pursued a more conservative financing strategy. Plated raised a more modest $56M,
and while Josh and Nick wanted to go public—that was their ultimate goal and dream—they chose a financing strategy that afforded
them *exit optionality*.

Compared to Blue Apron, Plated lowered the bar on an exit in a
way that would still yield a good return for founders and all investors (from early to late-stage investors).

Plated sold the business for $200M to grocery chain Albert-
sons, plus another potential $100M in earn-out. With their rela-
tively more conservative financing strategy and more conservative
exit, the founders and all their investors made money. The financing
decisions they made allowed them flexibility to go down a corporate
sale path that would still be enormously successful for them and
their investors.

While Blue Apron and Plated had the ambition early on to reach the
required size to go public, Jenny from Rent the Runway relates how in
the beginning she had not considered whether or not they could become a $1B company. It was only *after* getting going that she realized
they had that potential.

*We realized very quickly, within months of our launch, that we were disrupt-
ing an entire industry and we were having an impact on both sides of the
industry, on the consumer and on the suppliers, the brands, and the other
retailers. That vision was materializing very, very, very quickly.*

*Then we scaled at a pace I never would have imagined or predicted, which
was exciting. I had no idea what to expect. I remember we brought in a CFO
at one point and she gave me the book, probably within the first year,* Blue-
print to a Billion. *And I was like, "Oh, thank you." She was like, "I want you to
read this because we're going to build a billion-dollar company." I remember*

rolling my eyes, being like, "Yeah, that would be great, wishful thinking." That was not even on my radar—that was a shock to me, just even hearing that. I had no concept that that's what we were building. I didn't have a goal of what size we were building to.

JENNY FLEISS, RENT THE RUNWAY

In Jim's case, he set investor expectations on a future exit to a strategic buyer, rather than any IPO, given the dynamics of the media industry and his risk preference.

For the amounts that I raised, with the Series B at an $80M valuation, I needed to make sure the exit opportunity was there to justify it. For us, that meant that I never saw the online travel media business as a $1B exit. There aren't many huge media startups that succeed in going public. I thought that was a huge stretch; possible but very risky. Could we grow the asset to be worth $200M to $400M? Yes. Might there be a lot of potential media acquirers in that range? Yes. That was what I targeted as our North Star and so the financing strategy reflected that.

JIM SHERMAN, SHERMANSTRAVEL MEDIA

While it may seem strange to think about such issues early on, it is important to reflect on your exit goals, your core business to start and product/services over time, your tolerance for risk, what's realistic in your industry, and your venture's overall potential.

The decisions you make in financing your startup, business strategy, hiring, etc., will come back to impact the kind of exit that fulfills your goals and those of your investors and employees.

...

TAKE EARLY STEPS TOWARD YOUR ENDGAME

You are always thinking about exit options. We were always thoughtful of who is on the field.

ANNA AUERBACH, WERK

If you believe that a future acquisition is a likely exit, then taking early steps by building relationships with prospective acquirers, making industry connections, and framing the strategic rationale for an acquisition makes sense.

You should start by keeping a pulse as to what is going on in your industry. To be well informed, you should not just attend the usual conferences and read trade media, but if possible also meet with appropriate bankers who more than likely understand the current industry and where it may be headed. They also may have insights into the strategies of relevant firms.

What you want to do is avoid being so focused on your day-to-day business that you ignore thinking about strategic steps that support your endgame. Greg, for example, suggests thinking about M&A possibilities quarterly. He kept tabs on his industry and the players in it.

It's something to put on your calendar to think about quarterly. And that could take the form of just checking in with market participants or other people in the industry that might be able to shed some light on M&A in the category. Talk with a banker who might be able to tell you some of the things that potential buyers might be looking for.

GREG GERONEMUS, SMARTOURS

Taking early steps to your endgame also means reflecting on *the right timing* for your exit. Is it in six years or two years? The company's performance will influence part of the story on timing, but other factors are key, including momentum and developments in your industry.

Competition may heat up, which pushes down pricing, increases marketing expenses, and compresses margins. Or you may need to invest more in product development and this may be in an area outside your core competencies, or you may not have the funds to invest, or you may need what a competitor is offering in order to satisfy your customer base. Or, in order to get to the next tier of growth, you believe you need to be part of something bigger, with greater scale.

Too often, entrepreneurs do not take this step back to reflect until it is too late. Yet it is crucial to think about the future and the challenges that may lie ahead in your industry (that which you cannot control) and with your firm (that which you can control).

Even if all is going incredibly well, you should be asking yourself if those good times will continue.

Finally, on top of market and company-specific factors, there may be personal factors—such as, are you burned-out? Do you like what you are doing? And what about your cofounders, investors, and staff? Are you aligned or are cracks emerging?

In addition, since it is hard to know when to make the move to sell, establishing relationships with potential strategic partners is vital. These could include marketing or distribution firms in your industry, suppliers, direct and indirect competitors, or any company whereby you feel there is an opportunity to create synergies from a combination.

You want relevant players to be aware of who you are and what you offer. Think hard about how you can add value to another company. Strategic buyers rarely buy a business just for revenue and profit—rather, there is interest to create something bigger and better together. You need to fit into their larger plan. Or sell them on your rationale for such a combination.

Taking early steps is important mainly because company sale transactions rarely happen out of the blue. They take time to come to fruition. A fast acquisition from first-time conversation to closing a deal is rare; more common is a situation where you have laid early groundwork, started a conversation, built a relationship, and taken other proactive steps.

Plated's Josh and Nick made it a point to meet some of their industry players years before any exit conversations took place.

We began deliberately and systematically meeting all the major players in retail early on.

Nick sought John Mackey (cofounder of Whole Foods) out at SXSW in 2013. We've talked to John pretty regularly for the last five years now, including through the acquisition by Amazon.

Starting with Whole Foods, and very quickly extending to all of the major grocery stores: Wegmans, Publix, Kroger, so on and so forth. We had been talking to them for a long time, both to get to know them—it's good to know people in the industry—but also because we've been looking for distribution. We wanted to have our product, our meal kits, in stores from the beginning.

JOSH HIX, PLATED

For Plated, the Albertsons deal likely would never have happened if Josh and Nick had not spent the time developing a prior relationship with the industry's major players.

SkyMD is a case in contrast to Plated. Eric was running out of time and he hadn't established industry contacts early on. By the time he decided to strike some partnership deals, he was already approaching the end of his financial runway. And driving a fast exit isn't typically easy. A potential buyer needs to get to know you and your business.

A lot of the same people we went to for strategic partnerships we later shifted to an exit conversation when we realized that we weren't getting where we needed to be in the business. With an exit, it's very difficult to approach the partner needing something at that moment. Right? It's much better if you built a relationship over a period of time and they've gotten to know you and your company.

Eric Price, SkyMD

Taking early steps is the best approach because what you don't want to do is overnight place a "for sale" sign on your business. Much better is for strategic acquisitions to evolve naturally after laying the groundwork by getting to know the players and having already discussed the rationale for a combination.

Having said this, it does not mean that sale events cannot occur from more random situations—if you jump on them. With SkyMD, Eric was emailing his customers to announce the wind-down of the business. Surprisingly, one of his contacts chose to make an offer to purchase the firm's assets.

We emailed all of our investors and all of our customers telling them that we were winding down the business. And one of our customers surprisingly said she wanted to buy it, which I would never have expected.

I never imagined that being an outcome. It teaches you how random these things can be sometimes.

Eric Price, SkyMD

20

ALWAYS BE PREPARED

> Whether next week or next decade, your exit can
> arrive at any time. Be ready to take it.

Simply put, you must always be prepared for an exit—it may arise when you least expect it.

Done right—with timing, smarts, and leverage on your side—the performance of your company is going very well, the general market conditions remain strong, and the industry's attractiveness continues to appear promising. That's when interested parties proactively contact you or when you'll want to look for an exit.

Done wrong—with timing, smarts, or leverage even just a hair off—a firm may struggle to secure needed financing and come to the end of its financial runway with no choice but to sell. In such cases, it is often a fire sale or no sale at all.

Attractive companies—those that can command solid prices when sold—demonstrate strength across several critical dimensions. These include financials (revenue, growth, and profits), the team, proprietary IP, unique product/service, a strong customer or user base, and competitive position. An acquiring firm will also be looking at the potential synergies that you bring for their business—a combination of two firms should be a catalyst to driving higher revenues and profits together. Additionally, higher valuation multiples are applied to those businesses operating in what are perceived to be highly attractive, fast-growing markets.

You, as the entrepreneur, have control over many of the variables. However, what you have least control over and what is of huge impact are external factors. A company can boast a set of numbers at one point in time that might suggest a particular value, and then, during a different point in time, the valuation can be significantly different—simply due to external factors.

External factors that might change your value at any given time include a strong competitor entering your market, a competitor that stumbles with its own financings, an unexpected acquirer showing sudden interest, or a rapid shift in investor sentiment for whatever reason against or in favor of your entire sector. There could also be a macroeconomic downturn that forces tough decisions about an exit.

Your exit is the result of not just your company's performance and unique assets, but the perceived attractiveness of your industry at a particular point in time along with the conditions of potential acquirers or the public markets. In other words, often the most important variable in determining the likelihood of achieving an exit and the valuation upon that exit is the *timing* of it. Timing is a factor that many entrepreneurs tend to undervalue. But because so many of the conditions for a sale or IPO are *outside* your control, you must always be prepared.

UNCONTROLLABLES REVISITED

The first time we encountered any challenges with raising money was actually the IPO. That was because we launched our IPO road show the day Amazon announced its acquisition of Whole Foods, which was incredibly difficult and one of the most grueling things I ever had to do in my life.

MATT SALZBERG, BLUE APRON

It is not uncommon to see an event (such as a challenged company IPO or the entrance of a major new competitor) shake up the perceived attractiveness of an entire sector—with your company caught up in the fallout. Such uncontrollable events may make it difficult or impossible to raise additional financing, and your own investors might turn sour on your company, which in turn may trigger discussions around a sale. You need to be prepared for this real possibility.

When faced with bad luck, what you want to avoid is maintaining the status quo. That is why the more prepared you are the better.

A great illustration of a sudden negative shift is what transpired in the meal kit space. As fast as that market went up in perceived value, it also came crashing down in terms of the market's perceived attractiveness. Amazon announced that it would acquire Whole Foods in 2017, which ended up having a major impact on the exits of both Plated and Blue Apron.

Amazon made their announcement just before the start of the road show for Blue Apron's planned IPO, when Blue Apron was going around to large investors to explain the opportunity to buy public shares. This hurt Blue Apron's IPO prospects.

Maybe this was just naïveté, but I was surprised by how confused a lot of the public market investors became because of that and the uncertainty associated with it, because it was so fresh off the press. They hadn't digested it, what it meant, whether it even mattered for us. So, I was surprised by how focused people were on something like that.

MATT SALZBERG, BLUE APRON

In addition to the issue of Amazon entering the market, a spotlight was placed on the unit economics of Blue Apron and all other meal kit companies. Analysts began to question the lifetime value economics of the meal kit customers, and increasingly wondered whether the companies could ever get to sustained profitability. Investors began to weigh business model weaknesses from the fact that customers, on average, did not carry on beyond a couple of months. There was growing concern about customer churn.

The uncontrollable event of Amazon buying Whole Foods was like an earthquake. It didn't stop the Blue Apron IPO, but the valuation of the firm dropped from a planned IPO value of $3.2B to about $1.9B.

This chain of events also hit Plated. Neither the Amazon acquisition of Whole Foods nor the weak performance of the Blue Apron IPO could have been anticipated when Josh and Nick launched and scaled up Plated. The whole sector, viewed favorably one day, was viewed negatively the next.

Josh and Nick had to weigh their options. While their dream had also been an IPO and they needed to continue to fund operating losses, raising a significant new round of money would prove too challenging. One strategic option for them was to slow down growth. They could raise a small insider round to fund losses for some time, restructure the business, and steer the business quickly to break-even with very slow growth. They believed this was a possible course of action. But it did not seem attractive to them nor to their investors.

We could have slowed growth down dramatically and probably gotten to break-even on the current cash, maybe with a small incremental investment from existing VCs and so on. Honestly, we didn't spend a ton of time doing the modeling on it because it just wasn't all that attractive of an option. To become a 5 percent a year private growth company is not particularly attractive.

We didn't think we could raise more money, not anytime soon. Not with what Blue Apron was doing in the public markets. That was the change for us. The change on their side, Amazon changed their world. For us, Blue Apron changed our world. They went public and immediately the stock price began sinking. Quickly and dramatically.

All of a sudden we had a public comparable, which we'd never had before. And it was a very negative one. Today it trades [public value] at .3 times revenue, something like that. And we'd been raising money in what we thought had been a prudent way, three times revenue.

JOSH HIX, PLATED

The sudden, unexpected bad luck forced quick decisions by Plated's founders. Josh and Nick chose not to raise more financing and instead swiftly pressed forward on sale discussions with Albertsons, the large grocery chain. They were extremely fortunate in having contacts with Albertsons from partnership discussions that began a couple of years earlier. They rekindled those ties and approached them about a possible sale.

Many other meal kit firms failed to raise subsequent financing, could not find buyers, and went out of business. An industry that boasted more than 150 variations of meal kits at their peak in the market over time dwindled to far fewer.

Another example of a fairly common uncontrollable that can lead to an unexpected exit is investor-founder conflict.

This happened in the case of Dot & Bo, when Anthony faced two challenges that ultimately led to a fire sale exit. One challenge came from the fact that an investor and board member from their prior round, for their own unique reasons, could not participate in the next round of proposed funding. This cast a pall over Anthony's efforts to raise the next round from new investors.

When you have a past investor that isn't participating in the next round, it creates questions. It made it difficult for us to raise the next [financing] round. We instead sought a company sale.

ANTHONY SOOHOO, DOT & BO

A second challenge came from a bad situation with another discount furniture and home furnishings company, One Kings Lane. (It was not entirely different from the Blue Apron situation that had cast a pall over Plated.)

At the same time, the market for e-commerce companies, because of what was happening with One Kings Lane, made it difficult to raise money. One Kings Lane raised $230M and later sold for $12M.

So, our prospective buyer, which was about to give us a big offer of about $110M, got cold feet. I told the bank [where we had a loan]. The bank then decided they were going to pull the loan. They froze our accounts, and then two days later put our company in limbo, frozen, and we all got booted.

The bank then sold the outfit to a firm which is owned by Alibaba. The experience and the ending were obviously not as successful or as happy as the first two company startups I was involved in.

ANTHONY SOOHOO, DOT & BO

Anthony had to deal with two potent uncontrollables. It isn't uncommon for a past investor's actions to harm your company's prospects. But the second factor—the dismal performance of another industry player, in this case One Kings Lane—negatively affected the whole sector. Investors will pile on like a herd to get in on great deals when they are perceived as hot, but they are just as quick to get out of a sector when sentiment shifts.

Dot & Bo tried to close a sale, but they did not have the luck that Plated seemed to enjoy.

Due to problems at One Kings Lane, our whole sector was put in a bad light. One Kings Lane didn't do well. They were about to go public. And they ran into problems. What happened there, they grew way faster than they needed to. And they never had positive economics on the way up.

What you'll find is investors try to figure out one company from the next and how each company is different. But when a sector hits a downturn like commerce or media in general, they just don't touch the whole area. Everyone got lumped in together.

ANTHONY SOOHOO, DOT & BO

Unfortunately, events such as these are outside of the entrepreneur's control. It's frustrating to the founder because you might do most things right only to suffer from some bad luck. Again, it is not uncommon when a weak player in an industry casts a shadow over all others even if some have strong fundamentals.

On the way up, positive sentiment for a sector can help you and your company as investors and buyers look at each firm individually and try to figure out how they differ and who will win. But on the way down, should investor sentiment turn against a particular industry or even just against one company, the investors and potential buyers don't tend to distinguish among firms. As Anthony says, they lump them all together.

Finally, general macroeconomic factors also can turn against you. For example, in 2022 we saw inflation and aggressive interest rate hikes by the Federal Reserve. This led to a significant drop in the stock market and public company valuations. In turn we observed a major pullback in private company financings and valuations. Such a weakening of the macroeconomy impacts the chances for startups to close more financing rounds, which can trigger forced sales.

Of course, predicting negative headwinds from the macroeconomy is challenging, but you should be aware that such an uncontrollable can hit you. In the case of smarTours, Greg chose to sell his firm in 2017 not only because a buyer approached him, but also because he had concerns that the economy would not hold up after years of expansion. As it turned out—and perhaps he got lucky—he sold the firm before the Covid-19 pandemic and general worsening of the economy.

By 2017, it was eight years after the last downturn. It was just a matter of time until there was going to be another correction.

GREG GERONEMUS, SMARTOURS

On the flip side, "good luck" uncontrollables can produce favorable conditions for an exit. This may include your industry's attractiveness.

We were lucky because, at the time, the overall deals space in our industry was viewed favorably. There was Kayak, Travelzoo, TripAdvisor, and us, all in the travel deals market. Investors looked favorably on the media model back in the mid-2000s. Plus we had grown our business 5X in three years.

The new private equity investor wanted to invest much more in us than I wanted to accept. To reach an accommodation, earlier investors and I agreed to sell a chunk of our equity ownership with a secondary sale.

As it turned out, by the middle of 2008, just a year later, the market crashed with the whole financial crisis. It would be a decade before the market recovered.

JIM SHERMAN, SHERMANSTRAVEL MEDIA

All executives need market-timing luck when steering to a successful exit. If these factors align positively after you have scaled up, then the chances of a successful exit are strong.

Sometimes—and this may seem paradoxical—negative market sentiment or industry events can trigger moves by larger companies to seek out attractive companies to buy. It is not uncommon that when markets turn south and financing dries up, it acts as a catalyst for young companies that require additional capital to seek a white knight to buy them. And to buy them on reasonable terms. Despite uncontrollable industry events, savvy founders can turn a negative situation into an advantage—assuming they have taken steps earlier to get to know the key players.

For example, while Amazon's acquisition of Whole Foods tarnished the prospects for many meal kit companies, Plated turned this into a positive. That's because Albertsons decided they needed a technology partner and a direct channel to consumers to compete with the likes of Amazon. Plated offered them a solution.

In a span of three weeks, which is the course of two things happening—Amazon buying Whole Foods and the Blue Apron IPO—the world changed dramatically. Traditional retailers had a newfound sense of urgency. They were really unnerved when Amazon bought Whole Foods and what this might do to their business. Meanwhile, we had a more pessimistic outlook on our ability to continue to raise money. Which meant we had two options in front of us. One, go it alone. We could have done it, but it would have meant slower growth, higher risk. We would have had to shelve a lot of growth and new product plans. There was a lot to dislike about that option. Or seek a sale.

JOSH HIX, PLATED

You should always be prepared because uncontrollables can come your way at any time.

SOFT-TEST THE MARKET

We were torn between raising a Series A or an early acquisition option.

ANNA AUERBACH, WERK

It is important to you and the business to ask the right questions, including *Is it time to seek an exit?* But how do you go about answering this?

A natural point to reflect on the exit question is when you're approaching another round of financing. This is a common tactic to test the waters for a potential exit. If you are like Zumper, you are doing well, have been successful in raising funds and have ample runway, you only are interested in an exit if someone offers you a very large sale price.

On the other hand, you could be like Werk. Anna wanted to pivot the business away from being a marketplace to instead offering a SaaS enterprise solution to businesses striving to reduce employee turnover. To grow the new opportunity required more capital and she faced a shortening financial runway. So she decided to use their financing round as a means to test the market for a possible exit.

Raising another round and continuing to operate is super-exciting in a lot of ways and allows us to bring to market a lot of the things that we have in our product road map. On the other hand, it introduces a ton of risk. Your valuation goes up. Your cost of doing business goes up. If you already think that being acquired by X, Y, or Z company is in your future, then you need to work toward that.

We sold it to a strategic—a startup that was a bit more advanced than us. Mom Project, which has since raised a pile of money. Their goal is focused on keeping women in the workforce. They do a lot of temporary work. It was a really nice fit and we had some mutual investors.

ANNA AUERBACH, WERK

Werk isn't unique in using a fundraising round as a dual path to also suss out interest in a company sale. It's a below-the-radar way to test the waters—a means to put out feelers without hanging a "for sale" sign. Many sale transactions of firms have resulted from what started initially as financing discussions.

For example, Bespoke Post has been fortunate because they don't have to raise any additional rounds of financing. It was optional because they have been profitable. However, they felt it would be nice to have more cash to invest in some new marketing channels and new product development.

In 2021, founders Steve and Rishi recognized that their company performance and market timing were good. They felt that they could run a dual process (financing round or sale) and choose to test the waters by pitching a Series B round for at least $10M but, in the process, they wished to explore whether any strategic buyers might be interested in acquiring them. They also explored a larger Series B round at $50M, which would include the sale of primary shares for growth capital plus the sale of secondary shares where earlier investors and founders could sell a portion of their equity. The business's strong metrics and the general economic conditions gave them options, including the one to exit, either partially or fully.

They also recognized that they personally, after eleven years of operating the business, wanted to take some chips off the table. As it turned out, they completed a $35M Series B round that included both growth financing and the sale of founder shares.

They decided to soft-test the market by running a financing process and used it to also get word around with some relevant companies (and private equity firms) that they "might" be interested in a company sale. They weren't "for sale," but they were not averse to a very good offer.

Another common way to raise your antenna is by seeking business development partnerships with a company or companies that you believe are potential acquirers. This can be a very effective way to lay the groundwork for a future deal. Management teams get to know one another, and they can map out together the case or strategic rationale for combining businesses.

These tactics are a smart way to soft-test the market, to explore whether there might be interest by potential buyers. If there is, then the board can consider an attractive exit option. If there is not strong interest percolating up, then they can continue on with their growth trajectory and raise additional financing (and perhaps include the opportunity for insiders to sell secondary shares) if the terms are attractive.

What you don't want to do is ignore the exit issue—especially if there's a chance you will run out of cash in twelve months. Don't be buried in the day-to-day such that you miss threats to your business model or miss the opportunity to exit if conditions are exceptionally good. Take a step back and reflect on the risks of continuing versus finding an off-ramp.

Hiring a Banker

It goes without saying that you need a good lawyer to advise on any transaction. However, the HBS founders were of different opinions as to a banker. It depends.

A banker can be helpful in finding prospective buyers, managing the sale process, creating a sense of competition, and building interest. Since it's unlikely you have managed many exit processes, a banker can also coach you as a founder to nudge values higher and provide psychological support during the emotional highs and lows.

Our banker helped me understand the psychology of pretending that you had somebody else looking at the deal, even if I didn't, and building up the sense of scarcity.

He taught me a lot of the tactics around how you build interest. He also taught me this 50 percent conversion that we got from initial cold outreach, which was so surprising to me. He helped me to draft an email that was very targeted toward getting the interest of an executive in a company, where it was three bullets focused on what we thought they would be interested in and then tailoring that message. He said, "You need to think about, for your industry, what are the categories, whether it's insurance companies, hospitals, skin care companies, and who are the biggest players in those spaces?" He gave me a framework, but then I came up with the names.

ERIC PRICE, SKYMD

For a strategic or financial buyer, coming up with the target list of potential buyers is critical. Like Eric, Josh agreed that a banker is not someone that they would look to in coming up with the names—the potential acquirers. He and Nick already knew the industry players. So, in their case, they didn't hire a banker.

There are two roles that a banker can play. One is running a process. Making intros. Putting the company on the block, so to speak. We didn't need him for that. We knew everybody in the industry. We had active and open and friendly dialogue. Two, a banker can run the financial side, the deal modeling, and so on. We had a very strong finance team.

We didn't feel we needed that, either. We felt that hiring somebody would only add more middlemen, more friction, more fees. It just wasn't necessary. We ran the process ourselves, ourselves being management and board together.

JOSH HIX, PLATED

The upshot is that the right banker can add value. They can make intros if you need that help; they can be a party to prod interested parties along as part of a bidding process; they can convince each of them that you have others ready to bid; they can help to package and present materials; and they have a depth of experience in deal-making that most entrepreneurs do not.

I think you have to have a very good reason for not engaging in an advisor when you're selling a business. For context, they were able to help us deliver an outcome that was 30 percent higher than the original unsolicited offer that we got. They also managed a lot of the workload, which allowed us to focus on the business while we were still selling the business.

GREG GERONEMUS, SMARTOURS

Every situation will be different, but it is clear that for many entrepreneurs the right banker can add value. As we touched upon when we described VCs and the deal terms for financings, your potential acquirers will most likely have more experience than you do. In that case, make sure to get the right expertise on your side as well.

...

LEVERAGE IS DESTINY

Our sector was hot. We had a public company comp-trading at a huge multiple, we had two firms interested in us, and we didn't have to do a deal. That was leverage.

JIM SHERMAN, SHERMANSTRAVEL MEDIA

In an effort to be prepared for an exit, you should do all you can to build maximum leverage, as leverage is what allows you to maximize the exit outcomes for the founding team, investors, and employees. Your company's traction, of course, will be a major contributor to leverage. But leverage also includes building an asset that others desperately want (as demonstrated by at least two companies wishing to bid for you), having industry momentum on your side, and being particularly adept at telling your story. A key to leverage is also having money and runway—and not being forced into a fire sale situation.

If you have in mind one or more companies as your ideal buyer, then you want to understand how you can fit into their growth strategy. What assets are you bringing such that it is better for them to buy you rather than build them? Are you able to convince them of the strategic fit?

With Albertsons, they were viewing us as more than a meal kit company. They viewed us as a technology company that makes meal kits. The intent is for us to make many more things over the years. And we're in early, confidential stages of doing that. The point is they were buying a technology company because obviously Amazon is a technology company. And they didn't have particularly core competency in that.

JOSH HIX, PLATED

We've seen a mix of examples from the HBS group where leverage varied. For some, leverage came from having a competitive bidding process and from having a buyer who saw strategic value. Leverage can also accrue from simply being able to say "no" and not do a deal because you don't have to.

We had seventy-seven that signed NDAs to get more information and review materials on the company. And from there down to thirty-four different potential buyers that submitted indications of interest.

We narrowed it down to twelve management meetings. Then we received eight very compelling letters of intent. From there we narrowed it down to three potential buyers that had the most exciting offers and basically said, "Who wants to win?" One group emerged with the highest and best offer.

GREG GERONEMUS, SMARTOURS

However, for some firms, leverage was not on their side. Eric of SkyMD had one potential buyer and the buyer knew that Eric was intent on closing down the business in the following two weeks. So Eric did not have the runway and time to engage in real negotiations and build a relationship with the potential buyer.

They [potential acquirers] just didn't know us well enough. And we needed to get a deal done in a very short period of time. People just couldn't move that fast because they wanted to spend some time getting to know us and maybe put a little cash into the company and watch us for a while and then decide if they wanted to jump in. I don't know if we could have done it differently. We didn't have the time.

I would have focused a little bit more on this at the conceptual stages and finding a partner that could eventually be an exit for us. I didn't do that because I was focused on building the business organically with our own team. That was one key learning.

ERIC PRICE, SKYMD

In the case of Dot & Bo, they also had run out of time and cash. Additionally there were investor conflicts on their board, and the industry overall was tainted by the experience of flash-sale home furnishing site One Kings Lane. Dot & Bo's potential buyers were very skittish.

When you're going through a sale process and people know your investor blew up because they find out during the due diligence process, they can start dictating terms and you lose all leverage in terms of trying to sell. And that's basically what happened with us.

When they know that you don't have a backstop, obviously, from the buyer's perspective, you get put in a very compromised situation.

ANTHONY SOOHOO, DOT & BO

While Dot & Bo had grown to substantial scale with sales over $100M per year, and had completed a successful Series A round, it still hit the wall and ended up with a fire sale exit. They hadn't yet achieved profitability despite their rapid sales growth. Unfortunately, when the fundraising market rapidly deteriorated in their sector, they did not have a means to quickly slash costs and get the business to break-even.

Every company goes through some point of financial stress test like we went through, just like you saw with Amazon. If they weren't able to raise their big debt round before the dot-com crash, they would not have survived. Companies go through this all the time; it just doesn't get written about. Sometimes people read about it after the fact and you don't understand vividly what happened. It is what it is. It's something I obviously signed up for as an entrepreneur. And it happened. But none of the stuff was anything I would have planned for, obviously.

ANTHONY SOOHOO, DOT & BO

Having leverage depends on many factors, including having attractive financials and runway, a growth industry, a strong management team, and a compelling strategic fit with buyers that can expand revenues and profits.

Beyond the numbers, your sheer power of persuasion can translate into leverage if you can deliver—or "sell"—a convincing story.

Just as selling a vision is what gets your startup going, you will need those same skills to steer your business one day to a successful exit.

IN CLOSING . . .

Building a startup from zero to success is quite an undertaking. While it can be less, often the journey lasts more than ten years. It requires all the things we talked about in this book, and a sheer amount of luck for events to unfold at a time and in a way that supports your success.

We hope that these stories and words of wisdom from the HBS founders will inspire you to take the jump and create your own story.

We hope that they will arm you with examples of how to do it and guide you to optimally launching, scaling, and exiting your own Smart Startup.

For us, as authors, angels, and entrepreneurs, it has been a fascinating journey that enriched our views of what it takes to become successful.

At time of publishing, Rent the Runway and Blue Apron IPO'd and are publicly traded companies. Bespoke Post, CrossBoundary, Ivy, Zumper, Sweetwell, and Yumble Kids remain independently in business. Adore Me, Dot & Bo, Gilt, Hamptons Lane, Henry the Dentist, Plated, RubiconMD, ShermansTravel Media, SkyMD, smarTours, and Werk sold to corporate buyers, and WestEnd New Media stopped operations.

Whatever the trajectory (and success), all HBS entrepreneurs were excited about what they had done. They would do it again and wanted to share their stories to help others.

I hope there is inspiration in our story. We had enormous ups and downs. These things are common to almost all startups. We were within days of bankruptcy several times. . . . Business has ups and downs and you can't lose sight of the fact that it's a grind. These are the kinds of stories that in hindsight are inspirational or fun, great to tell over a drink.

JOSH HIX, PLATED

I would have done everything differently. . . . If I have another company in me, it would not be venture backed, certainly at first.

ANNA AUERBACH, WERK

They always say first-time entrepreneurs, it's a risk because there's so much you don't know. And having been there, I agree. If I did it again, I would be so much more prepared. I'm excited to try again at some point. I had to go through this process to learn about these things.

ERIC PRICE, SKYMD

I would do it all again. Each of my ventures gave me tremendous passion and fulfillment—from Internet 1.0 to 2.0. I really loved what I was doing. Few things give me more excitement than launching something completely new that people really, really like.

JIM SHERMAN, WESTEND NEW MEDIA,
SHERMANSTRAVEL MEDIA, HAMPTONS LANE

Perhaps it's no surprise that so many of the founders we interviewed imagined how they would do things differently if they could do it all over again. What may surprise some is that most of the entrepreneurs are in fact eager to do it again, this time with the hard-won wisdom of experience to guide them.

We hope that you, too, will feel both a little wiser and also humbled by these stories of success, failure, and everything in between—and even more eager to get started. It's an exhilarating journey—the journey of entrepreneurship—and it's one of the best ways to, if not change the world, then at least leave your mark on it.

We leave you with our pearls of wisdom, one for each chapter of the book, to arm you on your adventure as you launch your own Smart Startup.

- No lemonade stand? No shame. You don't need to be born an entrepreneur.
- There is no random "lightbulb" moment. Landing a good idea often requires a deliberate, lengthy ideation process.
- A large market is not the same as a large opportunity, relevant skills matter more than industry experience, and passion drives all.
- A great idea is only as great as its business model.
- There is no one answer to the team. It's okay to go solo or team up with your spouse, best friend, or whoever is more right for you.
- To get started, you just need the cheapest, simplest version that customers want.
- Customer feedback should blow you away. Anything less means you keep refining.
- As CEO, you are the chief sales officer. You are the heartbeat of the company, its number one salesperson—and you need to tackle the first hurdles to sales.
- Scaling is a grind. Execution never comes easy, but it teaches you the essentials of your competitive advantage.
- When scaling up, keep your hands on your business's metrics and your eyes on its future.
- Few entrepreneurs excel as managers. You are likely not the best person to scale your business.
- Change your business model whenever you sense significant weakness or opportunity.
- Fundraising doesn't equal success. Wait to raise money, then wait some more. Be as capital efficient as you can be.
- Investors don't invest in an idea, they invest in you—so show them you're worth it.
- Don't shoot in all directions. The right investor may be difficult to find but easier to land.

- Don't underestimate momentum, herd mentality, and the snowball effect in fundraising. Investors can fall like dominoes.
- Uncontrollable events are unavoidable—what counts is how you manage them.
- Culture is what people do when you're not around. Hire and fire not only for skills and IQ, but especially for culture.
- If you delay defining your board until it's time to fundraise, then you're too late.
- An investor's primary concern, on day one, is your endgame.
- Whether next week or next decade, your exit can arrive at any time. Be ready to take it.

ACKNOWLEDGMENTS

We first would like to thank the HBS entrepreneurs with whom we spoke. Thank you, Alexandra Wilkis Wilson, Anna Auerbach, Anthemos Georgiades, Anthony Soohoo, Beri Meric, Carlos Reines, David Parker, Eric Price, Gil Addo, Greg Geronemus, Jake Cusack, Jenny Fleiss, Josh Hix, Justin Joffe, Matt Salzberg, Morgan Hermand-Waiche, and Steven Szaronos for sharing what you wished you had known and for being so open. Your inputs shaped this book and our own views on entrepreneurship.

We also could not have completed this journey without the suggestions of Scott Gable, Brian Harris, Brian Offutt, Ian Myers, Glenn Ramsdell, David Waage, Ryan Migge, Harry Demey, and Hiske van Dullemen. We are likewise grateful for the editorial guidance provided by those who helped us fine-tune our multiple drafts of the book. Thank you Eland Robert Mann, Keith Farrell, Kirby Sandmeyer, and Jen Schuster.

Finally, thank you, Esmond Harmsworth from Aevetis Creative literary agency and Hollis Heimbouch from HarperCollins Publishers for being our champions and guides in this journey.

AUTHORS' NOTE

FROM JIM

As a mentor to young entrepreneurs, I am occasionally asked how I ended up doing what I am doing, and how I built the businesses that I founded. Reflecting over the years, I have come to realize that there is in fact an arc that makes sense today and that I can connect the dots—but, at the time, the dots didn't seem to connect at all.

Looking far back, I always knew from a young age that I was entrepreneurial. My father was a small business owner in New Canaan, Connecticut (Mom was a part-time teacher), and I thought that maybe down the road I would pursue an entrepreneurial career. But I also liked academics. My high school years at Choate Rosemary Hall (a boarding school in upstate Connecticut) were tremendously enriching. The school not only taught me the basics and challenged me academically, but it inspired me in two important ways—one was that I launched, with a friend, a new magazine on campus, *The Spectrum*, which focused on science and science fiction. (My passion then was in the sciences.) Second, I studied the French language with our term-abroad program and lived with a French family in Paris. I didn't realize it at the time, but those two experiences—publishing and foreign travel—would come back later in life to form my future entrepreneurial journey.

After graduating from Choate, I went on to study out west at Stanford which was, up to that point, the best decision of my life. Experiencing life on "the Farm," as the campus is called, was incredibly eye-opening for an East Coaster (and a somewhat preppy one at that). While I entered college with an intent to study chemistry, I shifted to major in economics. And later, I added international relations with a specialty in Soviet studies and Eastern Europe. I loved Stanford so much that I chose to remain for a fifth year to complete my master's in international policy studies. I also figured out ways to study abroad in London, Munich, and Leningrad.

Post Stanford, I worked in consulting with Bain & Co. in San Francisco (figuring this was a good way to learn about business strategy) and later with a startup publishing company because of my feeling that I might like publishing in the long term. After four years in San Francisco, I was fortunate in having been admitted to the joint JD/MBA program at Harvard and I (reluctantly) moved back East. While I ended up not pursuing law (despite my strong passion for public policy) and completing just the MBA program in 1991, my interests led me to New York to pursue a career in media. After a marketing stint with Time Inc. and a fascinating role in corporate development (investments) in "new media" while at Pearson, I became an accidental entrepreneur.

After Pearson, I had joined, as the general manager/vice president of Online for Martha Stewart Living and was charged with building Martha's first online business. She was planning to announce her URL on TV in the fall of 1997, and she needed a website. But no one knew what that might mean. So it was my job to figure it out. Shortly after the launch (and by the way, the site crashed on its first day), I was flooded with calls from other publishers and media companies asking if I could help them craft their internet strategy. It did not take a genius to figure out that this new industry—what came to be known as Internet 1.0— was going to be big. So I left my corporate role and set off to be—what I suspected deep down I always wanted to be—an entrepreneur.

My internet strategy consulting firm, WestEnd New Media, grew quickly from just me in early 1998 to more than twenty-five high-level consultants who specialized in developing internet strategies for publishing, media, and e-commerce clients. In 2000, Omnicom's interactive division (Tribal DDB) had put forward a term sheet to buy the firm for $30 million (about $45 million in today's dollars). However, by late 2000, the internet bubble burst, Omnicom pulled the term sheet (the chairman said no to all new deals), and as fast as the projects came in, it all came to a screeching halt. Despite the lack of a company sale, though, the business had done well over the years. We had huge profit margins; the dividends were meaningful. I took a portion of funds and invested this into my second venture.

I launched ShermansTravel Media in 2002 on the belief that the nascent online advertising industry would accelerate. The business grew only after a major pivot from publishing targeted digital travel guides to instead being a curator of handpicked deals from hundreds of travel suppliers (cruise lines, airlines, hotels, etc.). Unlike West-End, for this venture I raised financing after my investment and, in 2007, sold a major portion of my equity to a PE firm. After ten years, as chairman and CEO, I stepped away in 2012, serving only on the board thereafter. However, in late 2022, I reacquired the business from the PE firm, following the pandemic.

In retrospect, those two ventures fit into an arc of experiences that had earlier included consulting, media, and foreign travel.

My third entrepreneurial venture was in e-commerce. After I left my role as CEO of ShermansTravel, I launched Hamptons Lane with a co-founder, Emily Battista, who had worked with me at ShermansTravel. This business too went through a pivot from initially being a monthly subscription to craft coffee beans to, instead, a monthly box of unique kitchen tools, recipes, and shelf stable ingredients needed to make ethnic cuisines. At the time, meal kits like Blue Apron were the rage and they targeted the person who did not know a lot about cooking. We targeted people who did know how to cook and wanted to elevate their skills.

The pivot worked and we grew the venture to a moderate size, but to scale it meaningfully, it needed to be part of a larger enterprise, and so I sold this to Try the World in 2017. The experience in e-commerce gave me the confidence to invest in several other New York startups that leveraged Facebook marketing. So I became an active angel investor by joining the HBS Alumni Angels of New York and Gaingels. My earliest deals included Bespoke Post and Plated.

Finally, as an outgrowth of my angel investing and interest in helping entrepreneurs find success, I wished to pull together the learnings of these experiences. By partnering with Catalina, I wanted us to research and write the crucial advice and wisdom that every entrepreneur should possess—and to help founders avoid the mistakes we've seen.

Looking back, I can see how all the dots connect—as a consultant, publisher, serial entrepreneur, investor, and now author. But, as I have told others, it's hard to see how events in one's life make sense until one looks back. My advice is to take advantage of what comes one's way. To reflect along the way. But not to fret if it all doesn't seem to fit logically together because one never knows how experiences may be useful in the future.

FROM CATALINA

I was not born an entrepreneur, and like many HBS entrepreneurs—I had to find the right time to jump. For me, it was after seventeen years of McKinsey & Company.

I joined McKinsey straight out of college because a friend convinced me to interview for a job as business analyst. At the time I wanted to join an advertising agency and did not know the "Firm." But, when—after more than ten interviews and a GMAT test—I got a phone call telling me that I got the job, I could not turn it down. The people I had met and the interviews I'd had were so impressive that I had to take the offer.

I was from a middle-class family. My dad had his own business in insurance brokerage but was a rather risk-averse person. My mom had not been allowed to pursue her passion in interior design and always pushed me to find and pursue my dreams and passion. When I was growing up, stability and independence were important, so a job at McKinsey sounded like a great opportunity.

The deal was that I would be an analyst for two years and then go to business school (with the possibility of coming back). I had a fantastic time, met exceptional people, and learned loads. As planned, I applied to several schools and got into Harvard—yet again an offer I could not turn down. I started at Harvard with an open mind and without the idea of rejoining McKinsey. It was the opportunity for me to try out other options and probably change course.

So, during the summer of 1990 (in between my second HBS year), I took a job as marketing intern at American Express in New York. I wanted to work for a corporation and go back to media/marketing. It turned out to be a defining experience: I had a wonderful summer but realized that corporate life was not for me—I needed a faster paced environment.

After HBS I ended up rejoining McKinsey (which works for corporations but is far from a corporation) and stayed another fifteen years. Work and colleagues were fascinating and after becoming partner, I started making good money. But in the 2000s, it became increasingly clear that there was a gap between what I wanted and who I was, and what the firm had become and could offer me.

I decided to quit with no specific plan for the next step and with the idea of taking a break. This was in 2006. Startups were on the rise in Europe but only for a happy few.

One of my mentors at McKinsey convinced me to look at a startup he had personally invested in to coinvest and become CEO. The more I did, the more I got excited and felt that—despite being an unusual move—it was the right one for me. I talked to many people, especially older than me, who could reflect on life and who knew me well, and

I realized that I had always been entrepreneurial (at least in my private life) and that it would fit my profile. I had a rich career behind me, enough money in the bank, and only my reputation to lose. So, I took the jump.

My five years as an entrepreneur have been fascinating and taught me many lessons. I thought I knew it all (after so many McKinsey years), but, boy, was I wrong! I learned on the job what it meant to get going on a shoestring, to convince and deal with investors and a board, to raise funds, and so many other things. And I learned the hard way that "money talks": when the going gets tough, it is all about who controls the money. I also saw firsthand how money brings out the worst in people. I faced uncontrollables, which ultimately made me quit. My entrepreneurial journey did not become the dream I had hoped for but I don't regret any bit of it. It gave me a wealth of knowledge and experience that I have leveraged since then.

I carefully considered my options after quitting Sweetwell and ended up deciding it was time for a break. I would only do pro bono work for a while.

I joined the board of Special Olympics Belgium and little did I know that they would ask me to take on an executive role shortly thereafter. I became CEO of the European Eurasian Games. Again an unusual move, but one of the best experiences of my life. Working with people with intellectual disabilities was so refreshing. The role allowed me to go back to my first love (media), working on media campaigns that broke the taboo around intellectual disabilities. Organizing the games was very much like doing a startup with an additional challenge: managing volunteers. That is when I really learned what leadership is about.

After this, everything happened organically as if the dots connected by themselves.

I started investing and working with startups one on one, and when my partner took a job for Nike in New York in 2015, I decided to follow. I always loved New York and the city was in the early stages of becoming one of the world's biggest startup ecosystems.

I reconnected with old HBS friends shortly after moving, including with Jim (my coauthor) and we started angel investing together. That led me to believe that European entrepreneurs should move faster to the United States, so I set up a program with ERA to help support Belgian entrepreneurs expand in the U.S. I became venture partner at ERA, where I am still active on a daily basis. In the meantime, I have also taken an active role at a Belgian/European accelerator, Birdhouse. And I continue coaching entrepreneurs, connecting them with corporations, and angel investing.

My life is entrepreneurship, from morning till evening. And I love every bit of it. I follow my passion to help (younger) entrepreneurs become successful and writing this book is the next step on my mission to do so.

INDEX

ABOUT THE AUTHORS

CATALINA DANIELS graduated from Harvard Business School in 1991 and the Free University of Brussels (B.A., M.A.). She spent the first seventeen years of her career at McKinsey & Company, where she became a partner. She left McKinsey to become an entrepreneur and eventually an angel investor. She is a venture partner at Entrepreneurs Roundtable Accelerator (ERA), the prominent New York–based tech accelerator, where she mentors U.S. entrepreneurs and helps non-U.S. entrepreneurs expand in the United States. Catalina sits on multiple boards and loves coaching young entrepreneurs. A Belgian national, she splits her time between New York, Belgium, the Netherlands, and Spain.

JAMES SHERMAN graduated from Harvard Business School in 1991 and Stanford University (B.A., M.A.). He started his career at Bain & Company as a consultant and then spent several years working in media with Time Inc. and Pearson. In 1997, he launched the internet division for *Martha Stewart Living*. He then became a serial internet entrepreneur, launching three ventures, including an internet strategy consulting firm, ShermansTravel Media, and an e-commerce firm. He also became an active angel investor in New York startups, has been a mentor to entrepreneurs, and sits on the board of HBS Alumni Angels of New York. He lives in Manhattan and Bellport, New York.